THEREFORE, BE PERFECT

**A Command of Jesus
to those who want to follow
Him faithfully.**

A Historical Novel

A Novel by Jeffrey L. Sakas

Published by:
Maudlin Pond Press, LLC
PO Box 53, Tybee Island, Georgia 31328, USA

Book Cover Design: The cover of this book is a photograph of a painting by Sandor Bodo. The painting depicts the crucifixion of Christ and other symbols of Christianity.

ISBN: 978-1-959563-34-1

Disclaimer: This book is a work of fiction and any incidental reference to any person living or dead is unintended. While the events depicted are similar to those events depicted in the Gospel account of the life and ministry, death and resurrection of Jesus Christ as written in the first four books of the New Testament of the Holy Bible this book is a fictional account of a character who is completely fictional.

*This book is dedicated to
My beloved Renae.*

PREFACE

Pastor J. Vernon McGee taught the Bible in a series of radio broadcasts that can still be heard every day on local radio stations. His daily lectures, <u>Thru the Bible,</u> is a 9-year exegesis that explained from Pastor McGee's perspective the entire Bible. From time-to-time Pastor McGee would read mail received from his listeners. On one such occasion, he read a letter from someone who asked the question, "Is the world getting better or is it getting worse?" To that question, Pastor McGee in his West Texas twang said, "The world is getting worse and better at the same time."

Pastor McGee went on to explain that anybody could pick up the newspapers or listen to the news on television and realize that the world is getting worse and worse. There are reports of mass shootings, and of unprovoked cruelty between people. The climate is changing and there are more catastrophic storms reported. From this you could surmise that the world is getting worse not to mention the divisions among politicians in the United States and the wars that are going on between Israel and Hamas in Gaza and between Russia and Ukraine now.

On the other hand, people, especially Christian people, now go out of their way to help others. There are humanitarian efforts to aid the people who have been devastated by hurricanes and tornadoes. Christian people reach out to others not only with material assistance but with love and comfort to those who are hurting. Pastor McGee concluded by saying that it is true that the world is getting worse, but the world is also getting better because of the influence of Jesus Christ on His followers.

Can we understand why the followers of Jesus Christ are ready and willing to do good in the world by reaching out to those who are suffering? Even in a world in which there is evil, and the evil seems to overpower the good that people do at times, the followers of Jesus continue to extend themselves in order to make the world better.

The purpose of this novel is to explore some of the origins of the New Testament and especially the book of Matthew which is the first Gospel found in the New Testament. Questions concerning the authorship of the gospel of Matthew have been raised over the years. Traditionally, the apostle referred to as Levi in the gospels of Mark and Luke and as both Levi and Matthew in the Gospel of Matthew were believed from early days to be the author of the first book in the New Testament. More recent historical inquiry indicates that the Gospel of Matthew was probably not written by the tax collector that Jesus called to be His apostle.

Bible scholars who have looked at the New Testament in far greater detail than the writer of this book have concluded that the Gospel of Matthew relies on the Gospel of Mark for 61% of the material that is included in the book of Matthew. Bible scholars have also concluded that the language of the Gospel of Matthew is of a high quality of Greek that would probably not have been the language used by the tax collector, Levi/ Matthew in the gospel accounts of his calling by Jesus. Whatever its origin and authorship it is obvious that the writer or writers had firsthand knowledge of the life, miracles and teachings, death and resurrection of Jesus. The writer was closely linked to the source of the text.

A reading of the book of Matthew indicates that the gospel has contained within it 5 discourses given by Jesus. The first discourse starts in the 5th Chapter of Matthew and concludes at the end of Chapter 7. This discourse is generally referred to as the Sermon on the Mount and it contains vital teachings and commands of Jesus to His disciples concerning how they are to treat others and how they are to live among themselves. The Sermon on the Mount also serves as an instruction in which Jesus Christ gives His followers a guide to live by in order to please God.

The second discourse starting in Chapter 10 centers around

Jesus's sending His disciples into the surrounding countryside. In this discourse, Jesus gave His disciples instructions on how they were to minister to the people they encountered. The disciples were given power to heal, cast out demons, and to preach the Gospel. They returned praising God for the good works that the disciples performed among the towns and villages inhabited by the Hebrew people.

The third discourse starting in Chapter 13 is an explanation of a series of parables (stories that have spiritual meanings) that the people to whom Jesus was speaking did not fully understand. It was necessary for Jesus to explain the meanings of the parables to His disciples. Jesus explains the meaning of the parables to those who have spiritual ears and spiritual understandings. It is significant that the parables could only be understood by those having a spiritual understanding. Without spiritual understanding the stories have no real meaning to those who heard and now hear the parables spoken by Jesus.

The fourth discourse found in the gospel of Matthew starts in Chapter 18 and continues through Chapter 20. It deals with responses to the disciples' questions about who would be greatest in God's kingdom and other matters related to Jesus's death and the church. In that discourse Jesus tells His disciples that He must suffer and die. His disciples did not understand the meaning of Jesus's suffering and death as a necessary part of Jesus's ministry and reconciliation of men/women to God. This vital discourse is foundational in its assertion that Jesus's death was necessary to bring salvation to those who believe that Jesus is the Son of God. Through the shedding of His blood Jesus takes on the role of a sacrificial and substitutional offering as atonement for the forgiveness of sin and salvation to those He called and who have chosen to follow Jesus.

The fifth discourse, referred to as the Olivet Discourse is Jesus's discussion of the end times and starts in Chapter 23 and continues through Chapter 25. Jesus's disciples asked Him to explain the meaning of the destruction of the Temple that Jesus told His disciples would occur. This discourse was given on the Mount of Olives and therefore it is referred to as the Olivet Discourse. In chapter 23 Jesus warns the Pharisees about their hypocrisy and pronounces 7 wows on the teachers of the law and the Pharisees. In chapter 25 Jesus tells His disciples of the great white throne judgment when all of mankind will be separated like sheep from goats and judged according to the way they treated even the least of His children.

If the words of Jesus contained in the Gospel of Matthew and especially in the 5 discourses contained in that scripture are true, (it is the belief of the writer of this novel that The Bible is be inspired word of God and that it is profitable for study and can be relied on in order to come to a full understanding of the relationship between God and man) then there must be a source for the words of Jesus on which the author of the Gospel of Matthew relied. The author or someone who heard the words of Jesus was able to provide to the writer of Matthew what was said and how it was said, so that the author could accurately report the events and the words of Jesus.

The Sermon on the Mount is of particular importance to us because in Matthew Chapter 5 verse 48 Jesus says to His disciples and followers these words, "Therefore be perfect, even as your Father in heaven is perfect". It is my intent as author of this book to explore the meaning of the words of Jesus and in particular how Jesus came to say, "Be perfect." We will also explore the meaning of those words as they impact Christians today.

As I write these pages it is clear that we are very far from perfection as a society in which there is undoubtedly division among the political parties that seek election in the United States. There is no agreement on most of the issues that politicians are called upon to enact for the welfare of our country. The media exacerbates the conflicts between conservatives and liberals and extols the virtue and the evil of the other side of their political party.

Ordinary citizens have grown weary of the constant division and vitriol between the various factions within our country. There can be honest disagreement among people of goodwill even in matters that threaten the economic well-being of the country without stooping to outright hatred of the opposing group's point of view. As Pastor McGee said in his radio broad cast it seems as if the world is getting worse as time goes by. On the other hand, those who have a personal relationship with Jesus Christ are not to give in to the political bickering and murmuring that seems to go on constantly. Christians according to the scripture are supposed to be known by their love for one another and are compelled to seek perfection, even as our heavenly Father is perfect.

So, when Jesus spoke these words of Matthew 5:48 what did He mean? When Jesus said to be perfect what was it like to be alive when Jesus spoke these words at the time and place that He said, "Therefore, be perfect"? Are we able to look back in time and come to a certain conclusion that will lead us to the answer to these questions and to other information that will assist us in becoming perfect? The answer to these questions and an explanation of the words of Jesus will be explored in this book.

CONTENTS

FOREWORD

By way of explanation regarding the organization of this book, there are actually two books contained in these pages. I have written a historical novel about the fictional characters who wrote the first two books of the New Testament, Matthew and Mark. Much of that story is based on historical facts even though the characters are fictional. The story about the writing of the book of Matthew part of this book takes place in historical Rome, Antioch, and Jerusalem from about 60 AD to around 84 AD. The village on the shores of Lake Tuz in ancient Galatia is fictional even though Lake Tuz is actually a real place that is in Turkey when it was referred to as the province of Galatia by the Romans. It is my intent to explore the basis for the writing of the Books of Mark and Matthew and come to an understanding of how Matthew 5:48 came to be included in the Bible.

In alternate chapters I have written about my experience as a Sunday school teacher at a church in Atlanta in which two men in my class (mostly fictional) who came from very different backgrounds reacted to the aging of the congregation and the financial difficulties faced by many churches today. In those chapters I have also asked the question that prompted me to write this book. What did Jesus mean when He said, "Therefore, be perfect, even as your heavenly Father is perfect"?

The personal pronouns He and Him are capitalized within these pages to denote the deity of God and Jesus.

PROLOGUE

Before creation began God in His three-persons reigned throughout all that there was. God the Father, the Son, and the Holy Spirit held council and in their infinite wisdom decided that they would share their existence with a created world surrounded by an infinite universe that would be as eternal and as infinite as they. To communicate the creation God in His three persons decided to create mankind in such a manner that God could communicate His creation and allow mankind to explore the wonders of His creation and seek fellowship with his creator.

God realized that by giving mankind the ability to explore and to seek fellowship with his Creator the creation could also reject the perfection of the world that God created. The intended fellowship could be broken because of the ability to communicate and explore. Then the Son offered a covenant with Himself and the Father and the Spirit that He, the Son, would restore the perfection of man by sacrificing Himself as an atonement for those who the Father chose and as a restoration of the perfection that God intended when He created man in His own image. God gave mankind the ability to restore man's fellowship with his Creator just as God gave mankind the ability to reject their Creator. God agreed to give mankind the ability to restore the perfection of His creation by the acceptance of the covenant and surrendering to the Son and accepting the sacrificial love of the Son. God freely gave mankind the ability to reject the Creator but offered a remedy if man would accept the love of His only begotten Son and believe in Him.

God saw that the covenant offered by the Son was pleasing to Him but asserted that He, God who knew the hearts and minds of His creation also had the right to know those who would accept the love and sacrifice of the Son. The covenant was sealed, and mankind was allowed to explore and accept or reject fellowship with his Creator and His creation.

God through His Son created the world and created mankind in His own image.

CHAPTER 1
MARK TRAVELS TO ANTIOCH

Marcus Aurelius Agustus Gaius, a Roman citizen and a relative by birth of the house of Julius Ceasar, was sent by his father to Antioch the third leading city of the Roman Empire in the spring of 64 AD. Marcus Aurelius was sent to Antioch to set up a trading venture with local merchants who bought and sold various commodities in which the family business traded. Marcus Aurelius (who for convenience's sake preferred to be addressed plainly as Mark) enjoyed getting out of Rome where he had grown up into a man of 30 years.

Mark had gone to all the best schools and had been taught by a Greek slave pedagogue the language of business and culture of the day, classic Greek. Mark grew up speaking Latin but learned the most common language of the day which happened to be Greek. Mark learned his lessons well and was able to fluently speak and write the language of business. Mark represented the family business throughout the Mediterranean/Roman Empire since he had come of age. Mark enjoyed the open road and liked to travel to new and interesting places.

Mark had never been to Antioch. He was surprised at how cosmopolitan the city of Antioch in the Province of Syria appeared to be. Antioch had a reputation, and the reputation was that of a wicked city. The population of the city of Antioch was very diverse. Antioch was in the Roman Province of Syria (the city was actually in what is now the southern part of Turkey). Antioch of Syria, located on the Orontes River about 15 miles inland from the Mediterranean Sea had a large and growing population. Business prospects were good, and Mark's family wanted to do business in Antioch.

Mark, his entourage and a large amount of luggage, arrived in Antioch by ox cart along the road that ran along the Orantes

5

River after having sailed from the Roman port of Brundisium. The Roman cargo ship on which Mark started his journey was laden with a cargo of amphorae of olive oil and wine which the galley had taken on board from a port in Provence, one of the Roman provinces (now a part of France). The galley was a medium sized vessel that traversed a regular series of ports of call. After Mark left Rome via the Appian Way to Brundisium, the ship sailed for Sicily and round the toe and heel of Italy. The galley crossed the Adriatic Sea to the Greek city of Corinth where it passed through the isthmus of Greece.

Mark had a two-day layover in Corinth, also considered to be a city filled with lust and debauchery. Corinth was full of sailors and in those day the saying was, "Men will be men, but sailors will be animals." However, within the city was also a small but growing group of people who worshiped a man called Jesus.

After crossing overland at Corinth, Mark boarded another galley that set sail for the coastal region of southern Peloponnese. A day's layover in what is now southern Greece and the galley on which Mark was a passenger sailed to Crete and then to Karpathos. All along the way the vessel constantly unloaded and loaded new cargo and passengers. After leaving Karpathos the vessel landed at Rhodes and then set sail to southern Anatolia and then to Antioch.

The voyage began in May of 64 AD the 5th year of the reign of Nero, the then current emperor of Rome. The weather was fair, and the vessel passed through calm seas on its way from the waters closest to where Mark initiated his journey. Had Mark chosen to travel by land, the journey could have taken two months. While the Roman roads were the superhighways of those days, travel was treacherous and laborious even if the traveler arranged transportation by one or several horse-drawn carts, the most elegant style of land travel of the day. In those days horse-drawn carts had no springs and the jarring of the road was absorbed by the passengers in the cart. The jarring could literally make one's teeth rattle and make the passenger's back ache for days. It was horrific.

Finally, after about two weeks of being at sea Mark arrived on the coast adjacent to the great city of Antioch. Mark's entourage included four servants who were tasked with attending to Mark's personal needs and handling his abundance of luggage. Mark carried with him letters of introduction to the governor of the Province of Syria and the local officials who oversaw the Roman Garrison stationed in Antioch. Each of the letters in Mark's possession bore the official seal of the Roman Emperor, who at the time of Mark's business trip to Antioch was Nero Claudius Caesar Augustus Germanicus, also known as Nero, Mark's uncle.

Nero was the 5th and final Roman emperor of the Julio-Claudian dynasty. Nero was extremely popular with the lower-class citizens of the Roman Empire because he treated them to bloody spectacles at the coliseum, but he was despised by the upper classes. Many felt that Nero was a debaucher and was ill-suited to govern the Roman Empire. Nero became the enemy of the Followers of the Way, as Christians were known before, they were called Christians. Followers of Jesus started to show up in Rome sometime in the early part of the decade following the crucifixion of Jesus of Nazareth.

Fire was always a threat to the structures in cities that had large populations. During the time that Nero was Emperor a fire broke out in Rome that destroyed much of the city. In those days the structures that housed the lower classes consisted of apartments made of wood and other materials that were susceptible to quickly burn. The lower classes prepared their meals on wood-burning stoves in their apartments or communal kitchens located inside the apartment buildings. If the stoves on which the people cooked their food caused any of the surrounding structures to catch on fire, large portions of the city could be destroyed.

Such a fire started on July 18, 64 AD while Nero was emperor. The Roman Senate blamed the destruction of Rome on Nero's negligence and he in turn blamed the fire on the people who belonged to The Way. As a result, there was much persecution of the followers of The Way in the aftermath of the burning of Rome.

Mark was not in Rome when the city burned. He had already left the city on his journey to Antioch and did not realize that his ancestral home and his parents were lost in the great fire. Mark did not find out about his loss until after he arrived in Antioch. The news of the fire and the loss of his parents struck Mark as if he had been hit by lightning. For a whole day Mark wandered aimlessly through the streets of Antioch and found himself in a very dangerous section of the city.

There were many people on the streets. All different sorts of nationalities, religions, ethnic cultures and men who appeared out of nowhere heavily armed and ready to do their worst. Mark found an open tavern and seated himself at a table. In order to forget the trouble that he had just become aware of, he began to order flagons of wine to drown his sorrows. Soon, the ladies of the night who saw Mark sitting by himself came to his table and offered their services to a young well-dressed Roman citizen. Mark at first welcomed their company. He found himself accompanied by two women to a room above the tavern into which he had wandered.

Several hours later, reeking of urine and gutter filth, Mark awoke with a severe headache and a swollen lip, a black eye and bruises that made him very uncomfortable, his nose was broken, and it was possible that his left leg may have also been broken. All the money that he had in his purse was gone. It was still dark when Mark found himself lying in a gutter in a deserted alley in a dangerous section of Antioch stripped mostly naked and beaten senseless.

At first, Mark had a hard time getting to his feet and remaining balanced enough to walk. Everything was spinning around as he stumbled out of the alley onto a more well-traveled street. Mark struggled to keep his balance and had to brace himself against the storefronts and apartments on the street. After taking a few steps along the street he could go no further.

The pain in his head, nose and left leg was unbearable, and he slumped against a wall.

Someone started to come by the place where Mark was lying and to his amazement a hand reached out to help him to his feet. It was a man dressed in a simple tunic who had rough strong hands that could have belonged to an ordinary laborer or more likely to a fisherman. The next thing that Mark knew he was in a small room with a younger pleasant-faced woman administering to his wounds and gently stroking his brow. When Mark was able to understand where he was and who was nursing him, he asked how he had arrived at the place where he was and who had taken him there. The young woman either did not understand the words that Mark spoke, or she was intentionally ignoring what he said. She continued to do her best to make Mark comfortable and to take care of his wounds.

Within a few moments a man entered the room in which Mark found himself and sat down beside the cot on which Mark was lying. Mark tried to sit up but found that he was too badly beaten and bruised to successfully come to a seated position. Mark's head throbbed and his leg was very painful, at his slightest movement.

The man that was sitting beside Mark said in rough and imperfect Greek, "Some people call me Peter, before I was known as Cephus until I met a man named Jesus. He told me that I would become someone who fished for men rather than the fruit of the sea. I found you early this morning on the street. It looked as if you had had some problems during the night. You are welcome to stay here until you can get back on your feet.

"The young lady that was ministering to you is also a follower of Jesus and she will take good care of you. She does not speak Greek and only speaks and understands Aramaic. If you need anything you can speak to her, and she will find me and bring me back."

Mark could not speak for a moment or two and motioned that he needed something to drink. After he had taken a few sips of water and cleared his throat in almost a whisper and speaking classical Greek said, "My name is Marcus Aurelius Agustus Gaius, I am a Roman citizen I arrived in Antioch within the last few weeks. I discovered that my ancestral home and my parents' have been lost to me in the recent fire in the imperial city of Rome. I am a man of means and will be able to pay for the kindness that you have shown me, but for now I feel badly beaten and sore, and I will take you up on your offer to allow me to rest here. Someone, however, needs to inform my servants of my whereabouts so that they can come and take care of me."

As he was saying these words, Mark fell off into a deep sleep. Peter, who had been speaking to him, said a few words to the young girl in Aramaic and departed from the room where Mark was lying. When Mark awoke again, Peter and the young girl who had been taking care of him earlier were in the room along with two of Mark's servants. Peter was talking to the servants and telling them in his rough Greek that their master was welcome to stay and be ministered to where he was now being cared for. Mark was barely aware of what was being said but had enough consciousness to tell his servants that he should stay where he was and that he would send for them later.

Mark again fell into a deep sleep and was only awakened by the fact that he had a ravenous hunger and felt better after his stay in the room to which Peter had taken him. The young girl was there, and she was attentive to Mark's needs. Mark tried speaking to her in Greek but got nowhere with his request for something to eat. He tried again in Latin but again to no avail. Finally, he pointed to his mouth and motioned that he was hungry by rubbing his stomach and the young lady immediately knew what Mark was asking. The young lady left the room and within a few minutes returned with some bread and a bowl of soup. After Mark finished eating, he looked intently at the young lady and saw that she was a most comely person and that she was eager to meet the needs that Mark required of her.

This use of motion and signals continued for another full day. Finally, on the fourth day, Peter returned and was able to communicate with Mark. Peter said, "Marcus Aurelius, you took quite a beating, and I am happy to say that you are on the mend. You have now been with us for four days and you are welcome to stay as long as you like. The young lady who has been taking care of you, her name is Rachel, and she is also a follower of Jesus. We who live under this roof are all followers of The Way. It has now been almost 30 years since Jesus surrendered Himself to the Jewish authorities and submitted Himself to be executed by the Romans in Jerusalem. That same Jesus has risen from the grave, and I saw Him ascend into heaven. It is through His commandments that we have taken you in and have ministered to your needs. We ask nothing in return, but also offer to you the hope that is in all of us that Jesus will return and that the Kingdom of God will be established in us who follow the path that He set for us."

Mark was at first confounded by what he had just heard out of the mouth of Peter, but then realized that he was in the presence of someone who believed that he had first-hand knowledge about which he was speaking.

Mark then replied, "You have just told me about matters of which I am not aware. You have said that you have firsthand knowledge of a man named Jesus who was executed by Roman authorities in the city of Jerusalem, and you have told me that after He was dead that He was raised from the dead. How can anyone believe such fantasies as you have just spoken? On the other hand, you have obviously had compassion for me and have nursed me back to health after I took a terrible beating a few days ago. I am truly grateful for what you have done for me, but do not ask me to engage in the fantasies of which you are trying to convince me."

Peter looked into Mark's eyes and the piercing eyes of Peter had a calming effect on Mark in such a manner that Mark was not as offended by what he had just been told. Mark could see in Peter's face and eyes an expression of a profound belief that what he just said was the truth and that it could be relied on by anyone who heard his words. There was not only a profound belief that what he said was true, but Peter also seemed to have such a faith that nothing could shake his understanding of what he had seen and what he had spoken concerning Jesus.

Mark was only vaguely familiar with those who followed Jesus and who began to take up residence in Rome before Mark left that city to come to Antioch. What Mark had heard concerning the followers of Jesus was not all that flattering. Mark did not take into consideration the source of his information which was mainly from those who did not know the followers of Jesus personally, but only spread rumors that Jesus's followers engaged in orgies that they referred to as "love feasts." Mark was told that Jesus's followers commemorated Jesus's death by drinking wine and referring to it as the blood of Jesus. Mark was also aware that the followers of Jesus in Rome mainly kept to themselves and did not interact with those outside their beliefs.

With all that in mind Mark was somewhat intrigued by what he had been told by Peter and before Peter left, Mark said, "While I am not inclined to believe what you have just told me, I am intrigued by why you have taken me in and did not leave me out on the street to die. I am willing to listen to you further concerning this man Jesus and to know what this Jesus has to do with how you have treated me and what He would require of me in return."

Peter replied, "You can see for yourself. This evening, we are having a gathering of Jesus followers, and you are invited to join us. We require nothing of you and my master, Jesus, does not require anything of you other than to listen politely and decide for yourself whether what I have told you about Jesus is something in which you may believe. However, if you do begin to believe what I have said and start to believe that Jesus is who He said He is, be prepared for your life to change." With that said Peter excused himself and left Mark in the hands of Rachel.

Chapter 2

The seminar about the Sermon on the Mount at Peachtree Baptist Church.

Dr. Peter Rhea Jones was invited to give a lecture series on the Sermon on the Mount at The Peachtree Baptist Church in Atlanta by Daniel Vestel the pastor of the church. Vestel was an old friend of Dr. Jones. Peter Rhea Jones had been the pastor of the First Baptist Church of Decatur, Georgia, and was currently serving as pastor emeritus of that church. He had been a professor of New Testament studies at the Southern Baptist Theological Seminary in Louisville, Kentucky. Dr. Jones was in the process of writing a new book in which he would discuss the history and influence of the Sermon on the Mount, which is found in the 5th through the 7th chapters of the book of Matthew in the New Testament.

When Dr. Jones discussed the seminar with Dr. Vestel, he did not know what kind of a reception that Jones would receive from the church members at Peachtree Baptist Church because that church had had some difficulties in the recent past. Their pastor of many years had been accused of misuse of church funds and had recently resigned. Daniel Vestel who was also a professor at McAfee Theological Seminary at Mercer University in Atlanta was acting as interim pastor of Peachtree Baptist insisted that he would make sure that there was sufficient interest in the seminar to make it worth Dr. Jones time and effort to teach the seminar on the Sermon on the Mount.

Dr. Jones decided to take the challenge of teaching a seminar at Peachtree Baptist Church starting in mid-October 2016. The seminar course would last for a total of six Sunday evenings. Because Dr. Jones was going to be writing a book regarding the Sermon on the Mount, he felt that the preparation and teaching of a seminar on the Sermon on the Mount would give him an impetus to do the research and preparation necessary to start the new book and that it would contribute to his research and writing of the new book.

The time to begin the seminar arrived and Dr. Jones was surprised that there was a group of 7 or 8 church members present in the church library ready to attend the seminar. The group was made-up of the Peachtree Baptist's current Sunday school teacher at the older men's Sunday school class, two members of that class, two younger women, and a younger couple who were in the process of planning their wedding.

The Sunday school teacher at the older men's Sunday school class was a familiar face because in the past he had been a member of the First Baptist Church of Decatur and had also taught a Sunday school class at that church. His name is Jeff and he had been a Deacon in the Baptist Church in the past. The two men from Jeff's Sunday school class were a man named James who had been an executive for a pharmaceutical company and Jim who was interested in starting a company that would take over the financial operation of not only the Peachtree Baptist Church but also other smaller Baptist churches in Atlanta.

As the seminar started, all the attendees became acutely aware that a conflict had developed between James and Jim. James was the chief financial contributor at Peachtree Baptist and had been elected as chairman of the finance committee that was in charge of all the collections from all sources that contributed to the church, and the spending of the church's money. James and Jim had a conflict because James controlled the finances of the church and Jim wanted to control the finances of the church.

After giving an introduction to the purpose and breadth of the seminar Dr. Jones ask each of the participants to introduce themselves and to state why they were interested in studying and participating in a seminar concerning the words of Jesus given in Matthew 5 through 7 also referred to as the Sermon on the Mount. During the introductions of the seminar participants, the conflict between James and Jim surfaced. It seemed as if the tension between these two men had gone on for some time and that there was a general distrust and hatred that was evident between these two men who professed to be Christians and who attended the same Sunday school class.

As a part of the seminar, Dr Jones told the participants that the Sermon on the Mount had been used by several well-known authors and political figures as a basis of their own beliefs. Dr. Jones mentioned that Leo Tolstoy, the author of <u>War and Peace</u> and other well-known novels became a devoted follower of those provisions of the Sermon on the Mount especially dealing with Jesus's admonition that we should love our enemies. Both Mahatma Gandhi and Martin Luther King, Jr, adhered to the provisions of the Sermon on the Mount for their belief in passive resistance and nonviolent action as a means of political protest.

Dr. Jones pointed out that in Matthew 5 starting at verse 43 Jesus says, "You have heard that it was said, 'Love your neighbor and hate your enemy.' but I tell you, love your enemies and pray for those who persecute you, that you may be children of your Father in heaven. He causes His sun to rise on the evil and the good and sends rain on the righteous and the unrighteous. If you love those who love you, what reward will you get? Are not even the tax collectors doing that? And if you greet only your own people, what are you doing more than others? Do not even pagans do that? Be perfect, therefore, as your heavenly Father is perfect."

Dr. Jones quoted that part of the Sermon on the Mount especially for the purpose of confronting James and Jim regarding the conflict that was obvious to all when the seminar first met in the late fall of 2016.

As the first session of the seminar came to a close that evening, Peter Rhea, as everyone referred to Dr. Jones, asked if anyone had any questions or comments regarding the study of the Sermon on the Mount. At that invitation, Jeff the Sunday school teacher, spoke up and asked, "Does Jesus really expect that His followers become perfect? What is the meaning of Matthew 5:48? How do we as Christians live up to the command to be perfect?"

Peter Rhea responded by turning the discussion over the class and said, "Would anyone like to respond to Jeff's question?"

At first nobody said anything but then one of the ladies in the group spoke up and said, "Only Jesus was perfect, and we as human beings are all imperfect. God does not expect any of us to become perfect, the standard is way too high for any of us to achieve."

Another said, "Jesus may have been referring to when Christians get to heaven, but He is certainly not demanding that Christians become perfect while we are still living."

Everyone was quiet for a minute or two then Peter Rhea spoke again, "It is true that we are very imperfect people. It is true that the standards set by Jesus in the Sermon on the Mount are very high. I do not know if it is possible for anyone to achieve the perfection that Jesus demands in this life of His followers, but it is a standard to which every Christian should strive, even while we are here and before we get to heaven."

Jeff who had asked the question in the first place then said, "If Jesus demanded perfection of Christians, then how shall we ever go about meeting that standard? Jesus said we are to become perfect just as God is perfect. How do we accomplish that high standard of our moral and spiritual conduct?"

Dr. Jones then said, "We will explore the entire subject of the words of Jesus in the text of the Sermon, but we have run out of time for this evening so an answer to the question will have to wait until we explore the words of Jesus during the next weeks."

With that the first session came to an end.

CHAPTER 3
MARK IS INTRODUCED TO JESUS CHRIST.

Peter invited Mark to attend what he called a love feast held in Antioch of Syria in 64 AD. At that time followers of Jesus were not referred to as Christians but merely referred to as followers of "The Way." The members of The Way referred to their meetings as "love feasts" because Jesus told those who believed in Him that they would be known to each other by their love for each other. They did not practice any kind of sexual perversion or orgies but merely professed their love for each other. They would often greet each other with a holy kiss and hug each other as a way of showing their affection and love for those who believed in Jesus.

Mark had heard only a little about the followers of Jesus. What he knew was that they were different from other groups that practiced the worship of the traditional deities of Rome. Mark was skeptical concerning those who believed in Jesus because he had heard rumors that the followers of Jesus drank blood and ate flesh of other members of their sect. When Peter invited Mark to attend the gathering of the members of the group that rescued him from the mean streets of the city of Antioch, he was reluctant. On the other hand, this band of men and women who put their trust in Jesus had taken Mark off the street and nursed him back to health without seeking any kind of payment or even *etch aristo* (thank you in Greek) from Mark. Because of that, Mark was curious, and he summoned enough of his curiosity in order to ask any of the group that would speak Greek to him to help him get his clothes on and take him to the meeting to which Peter had invited him.

Rachel, even though she could not speak either of the languages that Mark spoke, indicated by sign language that she would assist him and take him to the meeting about which Peter had spoken. Mark had grown fond of Rachel because she had been kind and had seen to Mark's needs while he was recovering from the beating that he had received several days before. Mark's servants did come to the place where Mark was recovering but Mark insisted that Rachel care for his needs. Besides, Rachel was also a very pretty young lady with olive colored skin and raven black hair. Rachel's eye told the true picture of her attractiveness, her eyes were dark and expressive. It was as if she could look into Mark's mind and heart and anticipate his needs and act accordingly.

Rachel accompanied Mark to an upper room in the private home of a person who was a member of the group that referred to themselves as The Way. The room was sparsely decorated and there were only benches on which those that gathered could sit. There was also a table on which the women put food and drink that would form the basis of the "love feast" at the appropriate time. There was already a gathering of 12 or 13 people, most of whom appeared to be either servants or slaves. Of all the people that were at the meeting, Mark was the most well dressed and stood out from all the others. As other people began to arrive at the meeting each one was greeted by the others with a hug and a kiss. Everyone seemed to be open and friendly with each other and willing to express their friendship and love for each other in the way they interacted. Mark had never been in such a warm and open group of people. It impressed Mark, and he sought out someone who could speak his language in order to understand why these people expressed their love in such a way.

After a few minutes Peter arrived at the meeting and with him were two men that Mark had not met before. Both of these new men came up to Mark and spoke to him in the same kind of Greek that Peter spoke. The first man introduced himself as Barnabas and he claimed that he had come to Antioch a few years before in order to escape the persecution that was being administered to members of The Way in Judea.

The other man introduced himself as Paul. Paul said that he had been brought to Antioch by Barnabas in order to assist in the teaching of the gospel to not only the Jewish population of that city and those seeking to follow Jesus, but also of the non Jewish population. Paul and Barnabas worked together and were considered to be the most passionate followers of Jesus. Peter came to Antioch after Paul and Barnabas, and he was sent from Jerusalem and the brotherhood of believers there in order to report on the progress that Paul and Barnabas were making in converting the Jews and the non-Jewish population to a belief that Jesus was sent by God to bring salvation and eternal life.

Earlier there had been a controversy between the followers of Jesus in Antioch and the believers in Jerusalem. It was the contention of some of the believers in Jerusalem, especially those who had been of the Pharisee party and who later became followers of Jesus, that in order to become a follower of Jesus the believer had to convert to Judaism and be circumcised. That controversy raged among the followers of Jesus that were still located in Jerusalem because of those who remained loyal to the Jewish traditions.

In the meantime, Peter had a dream in which he saw various forms of food delivered to him and he was told to eat the food. At first Peter protested because some of the food did not meet the standards set for Jews by their strict dietary laws. In the dream Peter was told that what God has provided cannot be unclean. Peter's dream concluded with him being told that he would be contacted by men from Joppa and asked to go there to help a Roman Centurion whose name was Corneilius. Corneilius wanted to fulfill his desire to become a follower of Jesus.

After preaching to Corneilius and his family Peter witnessed that the Centurion and his household were filled with the Holy Spirit and professed their belief in Jesus. Peter told the members of the church in Jerusalem that if God accepted non-Jewish people, then the believers in Jerusalem could not require believers to take on Judaism as a prerequisite for becoming members of "The Way."

Paul had an interesting story concerning how he came to be a follower of Jesus and how he had converted from being a

Pharisee and a persecutor of Jesus's followers to becoming a fervent believer and witness to the saving grace of Jesus Christ. After Paul's conversion he tried to interact with the believers in Jerusalem but because of his past there was much skepticism concerning whether he truly believed. As a result, Paul returned to the city of Tarsus where he was born. Tarsus was a city in the region of Syria about 200 miles northwest of Antioch.

When both Jews and non-Jews professed their faith in Jesus and it was obvious that they needed instruction in their newfound belief, Barnabas traveled to Tarsus and enlisted Paul to come to Antioch and to work with Barnabas as a teacher of the new believers who were in Antioch. It was around that time that followers of Jesus became known as Christians because they believed that Jesus was the Christ.

The word Christ comes from the Greek word "Christos" meaning "anointed one." Also, the Hebrew word for Messiah can be translated as the anointed one. Because the members of "The Way" referred to Jesus as the Christ, people in Antioch began calling those who professed to believe in Jesus "Christians" because they belonged to the Christ. Jesus then became known as Jesus Christ.

Mark did not know all the history between Peter, Paul, and Barnabas but he was happy to meet each of these men because he could communicate with them and ask relevant questions concerning their belief in Jesus.

Mark was full of questions about Jesus and about what these Christians believed. He did not understand how and why perfect strangers who he had never known and perhaps would never understand would be so generous, kind, and helpful to him. All he could see was that these people at this gathering genuinely seemed to love each other and were willing to extend themselves to each other and act upon that love. The next thing that Mark experienced at this gathering was that the women of the congregation had prepared a meal for the group to share. This meal was called a "love feast."

When Mark heard that the meal was called a "love feast" it

seemed to answer a question that he had in his mind concerning whether the followers of Jesus engaged in group sex.

After everyone had been served with the food that the women prepared and brought to the meeting, Paul stood up and prayed a blessing on the food and on those who prepared the food. Peter then related the story of the last time he and his fellow disciples that had been called by Jesus, shared a meal with each other. Peter said, "Just before Jesus submitted Himself to the Jewish authorities, He took the bread and blessed it and said, 'As often as you eat this bread do so in remembrance of me.' Likewise, Jesus took a cup of wine and told us that the wine would represent His blood that would be shed for His followers. Then Jesus said, 'As often as you take this cup in my name do so in remembrance of me.' Therefore, I tell you that we eat and drink this bread and drink this wine in remembrance of Jesus's broken body and His spilt blood. Jesus freely gave His body and His blood to fulfill the covenant between God the Father and His only begotten Son. Jesus shed blood became the blood sacrifice necessary to atone for the sins of those who were called to be a member of God's family."

When Paul and Peter had spoken, those assembled ate their food in silence and in contemplation of the sacrifice that Jesus made for His followers.

Mark observed all this and was deeply impressed with the love that those gathered in that room showed for each other. Mark was also impressed with the words that Peter and Paul spoke regarding Jesus. After the meal was finished, all the people again began to hug and comfort each other and to share what had been going on in their lives since the last time they met. After that part of the meeting ended, Peter came close to Mark and told him that he would translate the remainder of the service because Paul was going to speak in Aramaic so that the Jewish community among the followers of Jesus could better understand.

Paul again stood and started to recite stories that Jesus told not only to His disciples but also to anyone who would listen to Him while He was going about in Judea and Galilee. Peter sat close to Mark and started to relate a story about a time when Jesus was telling the story of a man who was going from Jerusalem down to Jericho when he was set upon by a band of robbers. Peter said that he was very aware of the story and that he would tell the story to Mark because Peter was there when Jesus told the story. Peter said that the story was somewhat similar to the actions regarding how Peter came upon Mark as he lay in the gutter that night in the rough sections of Antioch. Jesus told that particular story because He was confronted by a man who wanted to know how far he was to go in extending himself to his neighbors. Peter told Mark that it was a story that had a spiritual meaning because Jesus intended His followers to show compassion even to strangers when a stranger was in need.

Mark did not understand why Jesus would require His followers to look out for the needs of others and Mark asked Peter to explain why it was important for followers of Jesus to act in such a manner. Peter quickly responded that Jesus admonished His followers to love their enemies and to pray for those who would despitefully use them. Peter told Mark that Jesus had often preached in such a way so that His followers would look to the God of all men who Peter believed to be the perfect God of creation and to act in such a way as God would act towards men.

Mark was uncertain of the meaning of what he was being told by Peter and told Peter that he would have to think about these things before he could understand or even properly respond to what he had just heard. Mark did say that he would follow through with this thought and that he was very happy to have been invited to the meeting. Seeing the people and seeing what went on had changed his mind about what was being said about the followers of Jesus in Rome.

Chapter 4
Things get better at
Peachtree Baptist Church.

Peachtree Baptist Church has been in existence since before the Civil War broke out in the United States. At the time that the church was established it was in a very rural section of north Georgia. When the battle of Atlanta occurred in 1864 the location of the church was somewhat in the middle of the fighting. Both Union and Confederate soldiers were brought to the church in order for their wounds to be treated . The first church structure was a wooden frame building that sat on a parcel of land that contained approximately 30 acres. The church continued to meet in that small wooden framed building for many years after the Civil War ended and the church grew and prospered.

By the turn of the century, that is the start of the 1900s Atlanta began to grow and the property around the church started to change from primarily farmland into a community with various commercial interests. By the time that World War II started the building in which the church had been meeting became outdated and, because of the lack of space, cramped.

On December 7, 1941, Japan attacked The United States military base located at Pearl Harbor, Hawaii. When the news of the attack at Pearl Harbor finally got back to those attending the church it was early evening. The people immediately left and when they did, they forgot to put out the wood fire that was burning in the wood burning stove that heated the church. The church burned down. The congregation decided to rebuild and to build in such a way that the church would be available for a larger group when servicemen returned from the war. The building that housed the church was located at the corner of Lavista Road and Briarcliff Road NE, two main boulevards that run from the area where Emory University and the Center for Disease Control is located that was then in the northern part of the city of Atlanta. Peachtree Baptist is located just within the confines of DeKalb County and just outside of Fulton County.

By the time that World War II ended the community around Peachtree Baptist Church was undergoing a profound change. A large group of Jewish citizens began to move into the community. An orthodox synagogue purchased land not far from Peachtree Baptist on Lavista Road and on the Sabbath anyone traveling in that neighborhood could see many Jewish people, some in prayer shawls walking on Lavista to and from the synagogue. Because the congregation was made-up of orthodox Jews, when it was raining no one carried an umbrella because that would be considered as work and not permitted on the Sabbath by the orthodox faith.

Meanwhile, Peachtree Baptist continued to grow. As anticipated when servicemen who had been involved with the war effort began to return to Atlanta the area around Peachtree Baptist began to grow and when it began to grow the membership of the church also increased. In the late 50s, Peachtree Baptist added an educational wing to the campus and also refurbished the sanctuary and incorporated an array of stained-glass windows that tell the gospel story of Jesus. The stained-glass windows depict the birth, youth, baptism, teaching ministry, last supper, prayer, trial, crucifixion and resurrection of Jesus.

Atlanta also grew and property values in Atlanta increased by as much as 10% per year for many years. The property that Peachtree Baptist owned therefore became very valuable.

For a while as Atlanta prospered so did Peachtree Baptist Church. From the mid-1950s through the 1970s church attendance not only at Peachtree but also at other Baptist churches in the Atlanta area increased and as the attendance increased a need for more building projects on church campuses blossomed.

Then, starting in the late 1970's and 1980's, for many reasons, church attendance, especially in inner city churches, began to plummet. One reason for the decline in inner city churches was that there was a general tendency for families to leave the city and move to the suburbs and find local churches that met their family's needs. There was also an aging effect. Men returning from service in the military after World War II were aging and dying and there was the effect of age on the congregation. Another consequence of aging was that the children that had been brought up in the church dispersed throughout the country. James's children moved throughout the United States with one son living as far away as Oregon and another in Arizona. Jim's family initially followed him to South Carolina but then gradually moved back to the Atlanta area.

There were also scandals among the staff at Peachtree Baptist that caused the congregation to split with many of the members moving to other churches. Churches, especially out of the inner city and away from either actual or perceived scandals within the church inherited the defectors from Peachtree Baptist. Peachtree was no exception to having its own division among the congregation concerning actual or perceived infidelity of the church staff.

By the end of the 1990s, the church was struggling to meet its financial needs. The congregation had aged and many of the members were on fixed incomes. Many of the faithful contributors to the church had either moved away or passed away. The church began to explore other means of producing income in order to meet the financial burden of the property and buildings that belonged to the congregation. Because of its location, and because it had extra real estate holdings that could be used to generate income, Peachtree Baptist engaged in the lease of a cell phone tower on its property in order to generate additional and needed income.

Peachtree Baptist also leased out its facilities to commercial interests, such as a preschool program that catered to families with small children who were filling up the apartment complexes that had been built in the surrounding areas. Additionally, when some of the more will healed members passed away, they endowed the church with bequests for specific purposes. Those monies were left in trust for specific purposes and the restrictions were such that only the income from the bequests could be used by the church while the corpus of the money held in trust remained untouched.

At the end of the 1990s Peachtree Baptist found itself in a position in which it was searching for a new pastor, additional sources of income, and trying as best as it could to attract new membership. By 1998 the church found a young pastor with a young family that seemed to fill the needs of the congregation. The church also benefited from an affiliation with the McAfee Theological Seminary which is part of Mercer University. McAfee's campus is in close enough proximity to Peachtree Baptist that many of the students at McAfee began to attend Peachtree Baptist. In return Peachtree Baptist offered those seminary students' employment at the church and practical experience that was necessary in order for them to become ordained ministers. While it seemed as if Peachtree Baptist was again on an upturn soon additional problems surfaced.

CHAPTER 5
MARK IS CALLED.

Mark's wounds and body healed. News concerning the destruction of Rome by the fire of 64 AD reached Antioch and Mark had to consider what the future held. The business ventures in which Mark's family was engaged had been built over many years and the business prospects were solid. The business was based on transport of grain from Egypt by way of Provence where the fleet of galleys owned by the family took on cargoes of olive oil and wine. The galley's next port of call brought them to Sicily where they exchanged the grain for salted fish. The cargo was then transported to the ports along the western side of Italy until they came close to Rome. All along the way the ships continued to unload and reload cargo and to make money from transporting those goods. After leaving the Rome area the fleet of galleys continued on across the Aegean Sea to the port of Corinth.

In an attempt to expand the family business, Mark was attempting to gain new markets for the shipping interest that the family had developed. The Roman government had at that time cleared much of the Mediterranean from the pirates that had plagued other commercial shipping enterprises. One thing that could be said about the Roman Empire was that it insisted on law and order and anyone that interfered with the peace of Rome was subject to immediate and severe punishment. Even those that were suspected of breaching *Pax Romana* were dealt with quickly and harshly.

Mark, as a loyal Roman citizen, enjoyed the benefits of his family's position within the hierarchy of Roman society. Mark was and acted like a Roman nobleman in almost all aspects of his life. He was a man of action. He believed that Rome was destined to rule the world and that it had made great strides in conquering most of the world as was known at that time. The Roman Empire stretched across the Mediterranean, and most of North Africa was under the control of the Roman legions. The threat to Rome from Carthage had been eliminated. To the West Rome controlled the Iberian Peninsula and Roman legions had conquered all of Gaul. Julius Ceasar famously wrote concerning Gaul in his Commentaries *Veni Vidi Vici* (I came, I saw, I conquered). The empire stretched to the Horatian wall in Britannia. Roman legions controlled much of Germania and to the east Palestine and Asia minor. As a result, peace prevailed. It was a good time to be a Roman citizen and enjoy the prosperity that Roman citizenship brought.

It was Mark's belief that the benefits of Roman citizenship carried with them the responsibility of providing great wealth to his family and he hoped to accomplish that goal by advancing the family's business throughout the Roman Empire. As a man of action, Mark was very physically fit. He prided himself in keeping his body trim and active. Mark was able to defend himself appropriately and practiced daily with his sword. Mark carried defensive weapons on his body so that he could not be easily overtaken by those who would try to cause him harm. He was angry at himself because he had been overtaken on the night that he had learned that his family had perished in the fires that engulfed Rome. While he was grateful to Peter and the followers of Jesus for rescuing him and nursing him back to health, he was angry that he had been placed in such a situation by his own actions.

Mark, after being in the care of Rachel and the followers of Jesus for about two weeks, was well enough to return to the accommodations that he had taken when he first arrived in Antioch. Mark felt that it was time to get back to business and he arranged his schedule to meet with merchants and other businessmen. Because Mark carried with him introductions from the Roman emperor Nero, it did not take long for Mark to set up new business relations with several of the merchants in Antioch. Even though Antioch was a rough and wicked town, there was still plenty of prosperity among the Roman citizens.

Even though it seemed as if Mark should have been happy with the prospects of the business arrangements that he was pursuing, he often thought about the time he had spent in the company of Peter and especially Rachel. Mark had plenty of female friends when he was in Rome. Mark was a handsome young man and a part of the aristocracy and therefore he was sought after by women who also had similar backgrounds. In Rome it was not unusual for a young man such as Mark to be subject to an arranged marriage of a woman or as the case may be a young teenage girl who would add to the fortunes of the family. Mark was now 32 years old and had been successful in avoiding an arranged marriage which was quite unusual for men of his age and status.

There was something in Mark's mind that kept coming back to the time that he had spent recuperating from the beating that he had taken on the night that he had learned of his parents' death. For some strange reason Mark felt comfortable and happy while he was in the care of Rachel and the followers of Jesus. One afternoon Mark found himself meeting a group of businessmen in Antioch close to the neighborhood in which he met Peter and the others that had cared for him. After the business meeting, Mark, for no apparent reason, decided to return to the place where he had recovered from his beatings.

Mark found the street and soon found himself face to face with Rachel. Rachel was that beautiful young lady who had taken good care of Mark after his beating. Though they could not speak the same language it was apparent that they enjoyed each other's company. She had dark eyes and olive skin. She was not tall, but she was not short either. She had comely features that were appealing to Mark but more than anything she had a gentle spirit and the confidence that was unlike any other women that Mark had ever met. There was an assurance that seemed to emanate from somewhere deep in her that Mark was unable to identify. Even though Mark and Rachel could not communicate in a language that neither one of them understood, there was an immediate joy in both of them when they again met. Their joy was evident in their faces and in their countenance.

Rachel greeted Mark with the same kind of hug and kiss that he had seen the other followers of Jesus give to each other at the meetings that he attended with the followers of Jesus. Mark returned the greeting and was most happy to do so. Through sign language Mark was able to ask whether Peter or Paul was nearby so that he could at least ask either one to act as a translator.

Within a few minutes, Peter appeared and said to Mark, "We have been expecting you."

Mark, somewhat taken aback by that statement, said, "What do you mean that you have been expecting me I did not know that I was coming here until I realized that was in the neighborhood only a few blocks away. It was only then that I decided to come here and pay my respects."

Peter replied, "We believe that you have been led by the spirit to come back to us. We believe that Jesus has called you for a specific purpose and that we are here to help you understand and fulfill that purpose."

Mark again was confused by what Peter said. He thought for a moment and then shook his head as if he was trying to clear cobwebs from his mind. Mark blurted out, "Peter I am not a believer in Jesus I am a Roman citizen, I am in command of a great fortune, and I am not as you and your followers appear to be. I merely came here to pay my respects and to thank you and Rachel for the care that you provided me with when I was in need. I will hear no more of your talk about me being called for a specific purpose by your Jesus." Mark said this with somewhat of a snarl in his voice even though his facial expression was more excepting an openness than the tenor of his voice.

"We, I, can see in your face that you are somewhat confused by my words. I believe in the providential care of God. You would not have been sent into our lives unless God in His providence put you on the street that night for me to find and bring here to minister to you. God has a purpose for every meeting and every person that comes within our fellowship. You are not exempt. Our desire for you is that you will find the peace that only God can give and that you will fulfill the purpose that God has set before you. I do not know what that purpose is, only God knows at this moment, but He will put it on your heart, and you will feel the assurance of God when you submit to His will."

At first, Mark could say nothing. Slowly the words that Peter spoke to him began to sink into his mind. He looked into Peter's face. Peter's face was full of acceptance. Mark looked around the room and saw Rachel with her eyes also fixed on Mark's face. He could feel the warmth of their love for him and knew that they were very sincere in their love for each other and more so for their love of Jesus.

Mark was about to turn his back and retreat to the street from which he came. In the door however, he met Paul. Paul put his arms around Mark and said to him, "Jesus found me when I was of the Pharisee party. I was seeking to destroy anyone who believed in Jesus. I was on my way to Damascus to carry out the orders of my masters in Jerusalem. I was seeking to arrest and bring Jewish believers back to Jerusalem so that the leaders of the Jewish religion could bring an end to those that follow Jesus. As I was approaching Damascus, I was struck down on the road by a blinding white light. As I lay on the ground, I heard the voice of one who spoke directly to me. I will never forget the sound of the voice that I heard. The voice said 'Saul, Saul, why do you persecute me?' The voice was so intent yet only I heard the voice, and I immediately knew that I was being called by Jesus to go in an opposite direction. The blinding light in fact blinded me. I was led by my companions to a house in Damascus on Straight Street. For three days I sat in darkness and prayed. On the third day a man by the name of Ananias came and touched my eyes and scales fell off and I could see again. Ananias took me to a place and ministered to me and as a result I now stand before you professing my belief in the Lord Jesus Christ and asking you to hear His call and to accept Jesus into your life so that you may fulfill your destiny as a believer that Jesus is the son of God and that only He can save you."

The words of Paul penetrated Mark's heart and he fell to his knees. "I believe." It was all that Mark could say, but it was enough for everyone in that room to know that a new Christian had just accepted Jesus Christ as his savior.

When Mark said these words, Peter immediately came to him and gave him a holy kiss and hugged him. Rachel, with tears in her eyes, came over to Mark and embraced him in such a way that he knew that all those who were in the room could see into his heart and understand that he had just made a life altering decision. Mark was unable to control his emotions and began to weep. Peter, Paul, and Rachel also began to weep tears of joy. For a long time, nothing was said. Finally, Peter spoke up and said, "Mark, you are now my brother, and I am here to help you in any way that you need. Each of us who are followers of Jesus will help you to understand the decision that you have just made and what your life is going to be like as you follow Jesus."

Mark continued in the fellowship with the believers in Antioch. He continued to engage in business on behalf of his family and with other merchants, but he also continued in the fellowship of the believers. He received continual instruction from Paul and Barnabas, and he dedicated his life to understanding his calling. He listened intently to the stories that those who had seen and heard Jesus told him. Mark began to write as only he could write the stories of Jesus from the time that Jesus was baptized in the river Jordan by John the Baptist until the time of His crucifixion and resurrection from the dead. His writings were mainly based on what he was told about Jesus by Peter. Mark wrote his stories of Jesus in a manner that would be attractive to Roman citizens.

After many months of living among fellow believers in Antioch, Mark returned to Rome. By that time Paul and Barnabas had been commissioned by the followers of Jesus in Antioch to visit other believers in cities on a missionary journey for the purpose of establishing new churches and ministering to followers of Jesus who they met in Asia minor. Mark found a group of believers in Rome and joined himself to that group to continue his fellowship with Jesus and those that profess Jesus as their Lord and Savior. Mark continued to write and before long he produced a draft of writings about Jesus. The writings of Mark, after the letters that Paul wrote to the churches that he and his band of missionaries visited were words inspired by God. Mark intended to write the story of Jesus so that believers could understand that Jesus was sent by God.

CHAPTER 6
PEACHTREE BAPTIST'S ENDOWMENT.

Over the years the congregation at Peachtree Baptist changed dramatically. The neighborhood in which the church was located also changed radically. After World War II the area surrounding the church was mainly made up of single-family housing built in the 1950s. As indicated above, many Jewish families began to move into that area of Atlanta close to Emory University and the Center for Disease Control which was in the area of the church. Peachtree Baptist maintained its congregation as best it could, but the congregation aged out or moved to the suburbs of Atlanta and away from the central city as Atlanta grew from an oversized country town into a metropolitan area with a diverse and growing population. The community around the church was even more diverse. DeKalb County in which the church was located, by the late 1980s became a majority black population with many Asian, Hispanic, European, Indian and Pakistani people.

Apartment complexes sprang up in the vicinity of the church. Condos were built all along Lavista Road. Along Briarcliffe Road commercial establishments including restaurants and strip malls were being built and occupied the areas around the church. As the neighborhood underwent change so did the church.

The members of the church that had been together for many years began to age dramatically by the turn of the century. The early 2000s saw the congregation change from families with children to older couples, and then to widows and widowers. The offering plates were not as full as they had once been, and the church began to struggle to meet its regular financial obligations. Meetings were held amongst the various committees of the church to determine how the church would continue to meet its obligations and to minister to the community in which it found itself.

In order to spur growth of the congregation, the church hired a younger minister who had a young family, and it was hoped that Robert, the new pastor, and his family would attract similar families to the congregation. Everyone at the church was hopeful that Peachtree Baptist would again emerge as a place of worship and ministry in the now very urban community around Emory University.

The church undertook programs designed to attract younger families and single individuals that now made-up a larger portion of the area around the church. The church initiated an English as a second language program in which church members volunteered their time to help people who immigrated to the Atlanta area to become fluent in English. The church opened its facility to groups that prepared students to take College Board examinations and even programs that would help tutor students in an after-school program.

Programs initiated by the church in order to attract new membership had some but not great success. Some immigrants joined the church, but most did not. The church did not have much success in attracting younger families as it had hoped with its programs. The congregation at the church continued to grow older and smaller while the expenses of the building upkeep and staff of the church remained consistent.

Eventually, developers viewed the acreage around Peachtree Baptist as being a potential area for building of new condos and other commercial projects. James who as you may remember was the chairman of the Finance Committee and the single largest contributor to the church, was approached by a company wanting to install a telecommunications tower on a portion of the church's property. After a few months of negotiations, a deal was struck, and a portion of the church's property was leased to a conglomeration of companies that put their cell phone arrays on the new tower. The income from the cellphone tower was sufficient to meet the physical needs of the church as far as the heating and air conditioning bills were concerned. However, the church's finances still had many gaps.

After several years of dealing with a declining congregation and struggling to meet its financial obligations, the pastor of the church, became interested in becoming a financial planner and took graduate degree courses in order to become financially solvent and to take care of his children who were now ready for college. Some of the membership of the church took exception to the pastor's decision and a split in the congregation occurred as a result of the financial dealings that the pastor undertook. The church split right down the middle and a group of dissatisfied members left the church and formed their own congregation. That action diminished the church and the congregation to a mere handful of members attending the church on any given Sunday.

After 2010 Robert and his family decided to relocate to Columbia South Carolina where the pastor's wife obtained a faculty position at the University of South Carolina in their music department. That caused the church to look for an interim pastor to fill the pulpit on Sundays. Because of its close relationship with the McAfee School of Theology that was located just a few miles from the church, an interim pastor was found among the faculty at McAfee.

Daniel Vestel, a professor of pastoral care was persuaded to become the interim pastor of the historic Peachtree Baptist Church. Vestel was from Texas and had a long history of being the senior pastor at large Baptist churches in Texas. He had been the pastor of the First Baptist Church of Midland, Texas and came from a family of Baptist pastors.

Without telling the church that he was interested in making the congregation into an international group of believers, Vestel went about trying to bring an international group of ministers to the church. At first the older members of the congregation responded favorably to the influx of young international students from McAfee but as more and more of the old guard of the congregation realized that the church was being taken over by unfamiliar faces problems began to surface. Further, the church's finances became more precarious.

Into this mix of problems, came a windfall. One of the longtime members of the church, Howard Nash, passed away after a long illness. Howard was a good businessman and left a one-million-dollar bequest to the church. The bequest, known as the Howard Nash Trust Fund, was left in trust with the restriction that only the interest earned on the corpus of the trust could be used and that it could only be used for capital improvements to the church's infrastructure. The bequest earned about $10,000 per month in interest. The trust was administered by the Cooperative Baptist Fellowship's financial service through its Foundation. The church received payment of the trust interest in quarterly installments.

While the revenue from the Howard Nash Trust Fund relieved many of the church's financial needs it also did not fill all the holes in the budget. The pastor's salary, the janitorial services needed to keep the bathrooms cleaned and the trash picked up, the power bill and the secretarial and accounting services and the building maintenance were more expensive than the income derived from the cell tower, the Howard Nash trust and the weekly member's offerings collection that formed the total income of the church. Additionally, Pastor Vestal had campaigned to bring a new associate pastor to the staff.

Dr. Vestal had met a young couple that were living in Buford, South Carolina. The husband was the son of a Baptist Missionary who had served in Hong Kong for many years. The wife was a Chinese national who converted to Christianity. She eventually married the son of the Baptist Missionary. The husband was Paul, and the wife was Su Chen. The couple had two daughters the oldest of which was about to enter college at Mercer University in Macon, Georgia. The Capps were brought to the church with the understanding that Paul was also capable of leading the music program at the church and that he would serve as assistant pastor when Dr. Vestal was away.

The expense of adding an additional staff member would

also cause the already strapped budget to become even more strained. To help the situation James agreed, at Dr. Vestal's suggestion, to fund the hiring of Paul for a one-year period with a one-time contribution to the church in the amount of Paul's salary. James who believed that he was providing the salary for Paul not only as a favor to Dr. Vestal, but that it was in the best interests of the church for Paul Capps to take over the music ministry and to bring in younger couples to the church. Perhaps it was also in James' mind that this contribution would solidify his position as the chairman of the Finance Committee and stave off the advances of Jim to take in Jim's effort to oust James from his control of the church's finances.

Interestingly, no one took into consideration, at least on more than a superficial basis, how the Holy Spirit was leading the church and the church staff and James in the hiring of Paul Capps. It later became clear that Dr. Vestal had more of a political interest in the hiring of the Capps family because Su Chen was also being hired by the Cooperative Baptist Fellowship for a position with their foundation that tied in nicely with the Howard Nash trust that was also being administered by the foundation.

If the intrigue of the hiring of Paul and the hiring of Su Chen by the Cooperative Baptist Fellowship Foundation were not enough, James was unexpectedly contacted by a local developer for the purpose of entering into a contract for the purchase of 20 acres of the church's property. The developer was interested in the property for the purpose of erecting a condominium development adjacent to the church. It appeared as if the church's financial stress would soon be relieved by the sale of property and the proceeds from that sale would keep the church financially secure for many years.

Chapter 7
Peter comes to Rome and Mark
receives a dinner invitation from Nero.

Mark traveled to Rome after a time of fellowship with Peter in Antioch. Mark was instrumental in leading a church that met secretly in the catacombs of Rome. It was the time when Christians were still being blamed for the fire that destroyed much of Rome and which caused the death of Mark's parents in the year 64 AD. The blame was wrongfully placed, but the upper echelon of the Roman society needed to blame someone or some group and the Christians who had very little political influence were the most convenient at that time. Even though it was well known that the fire had gotten out of hand as a result of people cooking in the wooden frame structures that was the dwelling places of most of the lower classes of Romes citizens it was easy to blame the Christians because Christians were different from most Romans and they were easy targets. Christians met apart from the regular population and usually at night after their work was done. This made non-Christians weary and therefore it was easy to blame Christian for anything that went wrong in Rome.

Mark became one of the leaders of the Christian congregation because he had been with the apostle Peter after Mark was rescued by Peter in Antioch. Mark was also a friend of the missionary, Paul, who had been called to minister to non-Jews by Jesus as he was going to persecute followers of Jesus in Damascus. Mark and Paul continued to write letters to each other, filling each other in on what was happening in the places where they were ministering.

It was Paul's custom to write letters to fellow believers, admonishing them to continue in their good works for the glory of the grace that Jesus provided to those called to follow Him.

Mark wrote to Paul in order to report that the congregation in Rome needed to be instructed in the basis of the Christian belief because they were being led astray by some of the members of the congregation who insisted that the Christian believers conform to Jewish ceremonial traditions.

Paul because of the report that Mark sent to him, wrote a rather detailed account of Christian theology to the church that was located in Rome. The account of Christian theology became known as the Letter to the Romans. Mark received the letter and shared the letter with his fellow believers. The letter was intended to be a discourse concerning Paul's beliefs and it was well received by the congregation. As a result of Paul's letter, members of the Rome congregation wanted to know more and more about the life and ministry of Jesus. While Mark was still in Antioch and had accepted Jesus into his life and was baptized, he also had a hungering for more knowledge concerning the life and message of Jesus.

Mark would often sit at the feet of Peter and listen to the stories that Peter told concerning how Peter had been called by Jesus to become a "fisher of men." Mark listened to the stories that Peter told concerning how Jesus went about in the towns and villages in Galilee healing the sick, preaching good news to the poor, feeding the multitude that appeared in the wilderness to hear Jesus preach on two occasions. Mark was thrilled to hear how Jesus had calmed the seas and quieted the wind with His voice, and how Jesus loved Peter even when Peter had denied that he knew Jesus when Jesus surrendered Himself for execution by the Roman government. Mark's heart was filled with joy when he heard the words that Peter spoke about Jesus. Mark's mind hungered for an even fuller knowledge of the life of Jesus who Peter claimed to be the Messiah.

After the Roman Christian congregation received the letter from Paul many of the congregation wanted to hear the stories that Peter told to Mark and began to encourage Mark to share the stories that he had written when he was taking notes from the time Mark was listening to the stories of Jesus while he was in Antioch. The stories as Mark preserved them were read to the Christian communities that were beginning to grow throughout the Roman empire. Mark was encouraged to write a book based on his conversations with Peter.

At first, Mark was reluctant to undertake a project that he considered to be better performed by either Peter or Paul or one of the other members of the Antioch congregation or even the Jerusalem congregation who had been with Jesus while he was still ministering to the people of Galilee and Judea. Mark began to pray about what the Holy Spirit might require of him concerning writing the Gospel story of Jesus.

One day while Mark was with the congregation in the catacombs in Rome, he received word that Paul had been arrested by the Roman government and that he appealed his incarceration to the Roman emperor who at the time was Mark's uncle Nero. It would be just a matter of months before Paul would be brought to Rome to plead his case. The congregation in Rome and especially Mark was both thrilled and worried about Paul coming to Rome. Everyone wanted to meet Paul and took joy in the fact that they would soon have Paul in Rome. On the other hand, because of the persecution of Christians that was going on in Rome at the time and the fact that Nero was said to have become mad because of the way he was being treated by the Roman aristocracy, the believers felt that Paul might be sacrificed in order for Nero to gain favor with the wealthy and empowered citizens of Rome.

As the days went on before Paul was brought to Rome, suddenly and without announcement Mark's old friend and teacher, Peter, appeared in the catacombs and met with the congregation. Peter greeted Mark with a hug and a spiritual kiss as was the custom of the Christians in Antioch. Mark's heart leapt with joy when Peter appeared and greeted his brother in Christ.

Mark embraced Peter and the words tumbled out of his mouth, "My brother, how did you get here? Why are you here? If we had known you were coming, we would have made preparations!"

Peter replied, "Sometimes, my friend, it is better that no one knows where I am and where I am going. It seems that there are many people looking for me and want to know where I am these days. Even though I have been brought up as a Jewish man and have never done anything to offend my fellow Jews they all seem to want to make sure that I do not profess the majesty and glory of Jesus my Lord and Savior."

"I see your point of view; it is not even safe for this small congregation who meet in these dark and damp places under the streets of Rome. It seems as if the whole world has reacted to the gospel of good news in such a way that they want to stamp out our Lords teachings and His holiness." Mark replied with a hushed and quiet voice.

Peter put his arm around Mark's shoulder and pulled him away from the congregation for a very private conversation. "Mark my brother, you have heard by now that Paul has been arrested and he is making his way to this very city. I have come here secretly to meet with Paul. We will trust our heavenly Father to keep our meeting safe and secure. I know that you have some influence with the Roman emperor because he is your relative. I am here to seek your help on Paul's behalf and to encourage you and the congregation's faithfulness to our Lord Jesus."

"Peter, what you ask is a most dangerous and risky proposition. My uncle Nero, many say, has gone mad and he hates anyone that believes that Jesus is the Messiah. Besides, I do not believe that my uncle even knows that I am alive or remembers who I am." Mark said as the two friends spoke quietly to each other.

"Mark, we must trust God that He will protect His own, the elect of the Messiah. Jesus told the 11 of us in the upper room on the night that Judas betrayed our master that He would protect His chosen people so that we would not be afraid when we speak on His behalf. Jesus prayed for us that were with Him that night and for all those who would come after and would believe and follow Him. I wish you could have experienced the confidence that our Master provided with His words. Sometimes I look back on that night and realize that when Jesus gave those words to us that we could trust that He meant for all of His followers to act as if all that He said was a certainty in which we can absolutely have complete faith." Peter replied to Mark's fears.

"Peter, I would like to sit down with you and for you to tell me the complete story from the time that you met Jesus until the time that Jesus was crucified. Many in my congregation have asked that I write the story of Jesus so that it would be preserved for those who come after us. Because you were one of His closest disciples and you were with Him from the time that He called you to follow Him, you are in the best position to tell me what to write. I can handle the Greek language that is necessary, and I will layout the story in such a way that it will be compelling for the Romans that are here with us." Mark said with a humility that impressed Peter.

"I will sit with you and tell you my story from beginning to end as long as you agree that you will write my story in such a way that you emphasize the power and wisdom of my Master, my beloved Jesus. First, however, we must make preparations for the time that Paul will arrive in Rome, and we must set the stage for his appearance before Nero." Peter deliberately and contemplatively replied.

Mark and Peter agreed that it would be best if they were not seen together in the streets of Rome. There was already talk amongst the citizens that Peter had come from Jerusalem to Rome in anticipation of Paul's appearance before the emperor. Mark was also known to have been one of the Christians for which the pretorian guard had an interest. It was agreed that the two friends would only meet in the catacombs when it was safe, and it was certain that no one had followed them.

In the meantime, Mark was able to send a message through an old friend to his uncle the emperor Nero and to beg him for an audience. It took several weeks for Mark to receive a reply from his uncle and when Nero replied, it was not exactly what

Mark expected.

The message that the emperor Nero sent to his nephew was neither formal nor couched in language that left any uncertainty as to the emperor's intent. The letter was very personal and full of warm greetings. The message read as if the emperor truly had an affection for Mark and would very much like to entertain Mark at the palace within the next week. The message that was delivered by a member of the Pretorian Guard read as follows:

" Nero Claudius Ceasar Drusus Germanicus to his nephew Marcus Aurelius Agustus Gaius, Si vales bene est, ego valeo (If you are well that is good, I am well.) mi Marcus,

"You must not keep yourself from my company. We are family, your father was my closest relative and I relied on him for his inciteful counsel. Please come to me and let me see your father's face in you. Do not be afraid to visit your old uncle, no harm will come to you as long as I am here. I will protect you, so please come to me for dinner on next dies Martis (Tuesday)."

"Nero Claudius Ceasar Drusus Germanicus "

The letter was handed to Mark by a soldier who stood by Mark as he read the letter and waited for Mark to reply.

"Marcus Aurelius Agustus Gaius to His Excellency Nero Claudius Ceasar Drusus Germanicus, Emperor of Rome and of all the territories and provinces that are under the peace of Rome. Si Uncle Nero, thank you for your kindness and invitation to dine with you next Tuesday. I will be happy to stand next to you and renew our friendship and family ties.

"Your Nephew

"Marcus Aurelius Agustus Gaius "

As soon as the soldier left, Mark made his way to the catacombs and sent a brief message to Peter that he needed to see him as soon as possible. Within an hour, Mark and Peter were in each other's presence and Mark said to Peter, "Our prayers have been answered, look at this letter that I have received from my uncle Nero. Now what shall I say to him when I go to dinner with him next Tuesday?"

Mark, looking intently into the face of Peter, said, "My

uncle Nero may not be in touch with reality, and he is very volatile. I will need all the prayers that we can muster in order to know how to deal with my uncle and to keep myself safe from any immediate change of temperament on his part. Would it be possible for you to go with me to the palace?"

Without blinking an eye, Peter took Mark by the hand and said, "I have not thought of the possibility of standing in the presence of the emperor Nero, but now that you have brought that to my attention you and I should seek the Lord's wisdom and when the Holy Spirit moves within us, we will know exactly what we need to do."

When Peter said those words the two men immediately found the remainder of the congregation that were hidden away in the catacombs and the congregation joined hands together and knelt in prayer. They prayed for wisdom and power through the Holy Spirit to give Mark and Peter the discernment that they needed in order to act and to be safe when they met with Nero on the following Tuesday for dinner at the emperor's palace. The prayers of the congregation were specific and in earnest. They felt the movement of the Holy Spirit in their midst, and they all believed that the spirit would protect Mark and Peter when they met with the emperor.

CHAPTER 8
ANIMOSITY BUILDS BETWEEN JAMES AND JIM.

Jim returned to Peachtree Baptist because he had attended Peachtree Baptist as a young man. Jim's father joined Peachtree after he returned from World War II. Jim's father was a respected member of the church and dutifully brought his family to church services every Sunday. The older white members of the church were decidedly of the conservative point of view. They regularly voted for any Republican candidate that happened to be on the ballot in any election. Both James and Jim were staunch Republicans that never met a Democrat that they liked. They only tolerated their Sunday school teacher who regularly referred to the Pharisees as the Republicans.

It just so happened that I was called on by Robert when he was still pastor of the church to teach the older men Sunday school class of which James was a member. I dutifully prepared to teach the Sunday school class every Sunday and studied the Bible and the lesson material in order to make the topics assigned for study as lively and interesting as possible. Additionally, I always prayed that it would not be my words spoken or heard by the Sunday school class on any given Sunday but that the Holy Spirit would guide my mind and my speech to say the exact words that were necessary to be heard by the members of the Sunday school class.

By that time in my life, I had been teaching Sunday school on a regular basis for 30 or more years and I still felt inadequate at times to convey the meaning of the scripture that was the text for that Sunday, but to my great satisfaction the lessons that I taught were always well received and at times it was obvious that the Holy Spirit was moving among the members of the Sunday school class on any given Sunday.

Not long after I started teaching the older men's Sunday

school class at Peachtree Baptist it became quite evident that there was animosity between James on the one hand and Jim on the other hand. James had been attending Peachtree Baptist since he came back from Korea in the early to mid-1950s. James raised his family in the church. James' wife Betty was also a revered member of the church, having served as the director of the nursery and having taught Sunday school for elementary age children. James' 6 children were also raised in the church and participated in the programs of the church when the church was full of people and was known as a leading congregation in the Atlanta Baptist Association.

I had been teaching the Sunday school class for a couple of years when Jim started attending. James was already a fixture in the class and had been a friend of Jim's father when he was still alive. Jim left Atlanta and moved to Columbia, SC to pursue other business opportunities there. After many years in South Carolina and after Jim's father had become very sick Jim returned to Atlanta in part to attend to his older brother who had also become ill. Additionally, Jim formed a business in which he solicited the endorsement of law enforcement agents to form a security company. Either as a side business or as a second thought concerning his business, Jim also decided that because he had some background in accounting, he could also solicit business from churches to handle their financial accounting and advise churches concerning their budgetary needs.

One of the first churches that Jim had his eyes on for that purpose, i.e.. the taking over the financial administration of a church, was Peachtree Baptist Church. Jim set out to gain the favor of Dr. Vestal and to persuade him that the churches current financial situation could be vastly improved if Jim rather than James was in control of the church finances.

To achieve that end it was necessary to find a way to dislodge James as the head of the Finance Committee of the church. To accomplish that end Jim set out to sow discontent amongst the church council members and to persuade the church counsel that James had prevented the church from achieving its goals of greater attendance and use of the resources that James, in part, was instrumental in bringing to the church.

The first obstacle in Jim's path to take over the church's finances was the constitution and bylaws that had been established during the time that Robert was the pastor of the church. To say the least the constitution and bylaws of the church were not well drafted and there were many ambiguities concerning the church's governance. For many years, Peachtree Baptist like most other Southern Baptist churches was governed by a board of deacons that were elected by the congregation. During Robert's tenure as pastor Peachtree Baptist broke away from the Southern Baptist and joined the Cooperative Baptist Fellowship (Sometimes affectionately referred to as Jimmy Carter Baptist).

The main difference between the Southern Baptist denomination and the Cooperative Baptist Fellowship (CBF) was that the CBF differed with the Southern Baptist on the place of women in leadership positions in the church. For many years Peachtree Baptist had elected women as deacons and had given them authority in the governance of the church. Additionally, Peachtree also allowed women ministers to preach to the congregation without the presence of a man standing next to them on the pulpit. There was also an issue concerning the inerrancy of scripture. Southern Baptist dogma required an absolute adherence to the inerrancy of every word of the Bible. CBF congregations merely held to the position that the Bible was the inspired word of God and that it was useful for training of Christians and illuminating the life and ministry of Jesus.

While Robert was still pastor of the church, a large delegation of the members of Peachtree Baptist traveled to Savannah to attend the Georgia Baptist Convention that was closely aligned with the Southern Baptist Convention. At that meeting a vote was taken concerning the issue of inerrancy of the Bible. The vote and especially the way in which the question was presented and the way in which the votes were counted caused many churches that had been formerly Southern Baptist to split away from the Southern Baptist and join the CBF.

Mercer University had been affiliated with the Southern Baptist Convention. After the vote concerning the issues of women in the church and the inerrancy of the scripture, Mercer decided to sever its relationship with the Southern Baptist Convention and throw its support to the CBF. Mercers school of theology, McAfee Theological Seminary, has its campus in Atlanta rather than at the main campus of Mercer which is in Macon, Georgia. As I mentioned before Dr. Vestal was on the faculty of McAfee and thus had thrown in his lot with the CBF as well.

The constitution and bylaws of Peachtree Baptist gave almost complete control of the financial aspects of the church to the chairman of the Finance Committee. James was chairman of the Finance Committee, and he controlled all decisions regarding the financial stability and bill paying capacity of the church. To assist him with the accounting of the income and expenses of the church James hired his daughter, Linda. Linda was a very competent bookkeeper and had worked as a bookkeeper in an accountant's office for several years. Linda was tasked with putting all the financial data into a computer program that gave those who had access to the program continuous updates concerning the financial status of the church.

Jim took exception to the hiring of Linda to be the bookkeeper and insisted that Jim himself could do the job for no cost to the church. James awarded Linda a salary of $25,000 per year which was well below the market value of her services. Jim campaigned against James and Linda with the church council and more importantly with Dr. Vestal. Additionally, Jim campaigned to have the church's finances audited by the outside accounting firm and Jim raised the fee for the outside accounting firm from a non-member of the church.

According to Dr. Vestal when he had been the pastor of churches in Texas, he had insisted that as pastor, he would have not only input but final veto authority in the handling of the church's finances.

At a council meeting specifically called to amend the constitution and bylaws of the church and in order to strip James of the financial responsibilities that he alone held; Pastor Vestal commented that he had never been the pastor of a church in which all the financial decisions were made by a church member without the direct input of the church's pastor. Interestingly, Dr. Vestal informed James that neither James nor Linda could participate in the church council meeting because there was a perceived conflict of interest. Because James was chairman of the Finance Committee, and the purpose of the meeting was to discuss changes that affected that committee Dr. Vestel and Jim insisted that James leave the meeting until he was summoned by the church council. Also, by that time there appeared to be animosity between James and the pastor and the pastor did not want James in the meeting because he felt it would be disruptive to his agenda.

The church council met and decided to authorize an audit of the church's finances by the outside accounting firm that Jim hired. The purpose of the audit was to find discrepancies in the manner and method by which the finances of the church were handled. Jim assumed that James and his daughter Linda had misappropriated church finances and Jim intended to report to the church the findings that would prove that James and Linda had schemed to defraud the church.

Unfortunately for Jim, the audit disclosed the exact opposite of what Jim had hoped. The audit exonerated James and Linda and showed that there was no fraud, negligence, or deviation from standard accounting procedures in the collection and distribution of church finances.

Despite the report of the auditors, the church council and Dr. Vestal decided that it was time for James to retire after his many years of service to the church. A day was set aside for the celebration of James many years of service to the church. His family was brought in from all over the country and the church acknowledged that James had served the church faithfully for many years and now it was time for him to step aside from any further responsibilities. Except it was still anticipated that

James would continue to be by far the leading contributor to the income of the church.

Within a few weeks after the celebration of James contributions to the church, Dr. Vestal announced that he was also retiring and that he hoped that the church would consider the hiring of Paul Capps to be the new senior pastor. Dr. Vestal handed the reins of authority at Peachtree Baptist over to Paul Capps. Also as importantly, Jim was elected by the church as president of the church council and appointed himself to be the chief financial officer of the church.

Jim's first act as the chief financial officer was to have James' name removed from the signing authority at the church's bank account and to make himself the sole signature on the church's checking account. Even though the church's bylaws required that 2 members of the finance committee endorse all the checks on the bank account, Jim unilaterally convinced the bank that he had authority to change the check signing procedure so that only his one signature was needed. That of course was a violation of the church's bylaws and constitution.

James immediately protested the actions that had been taken by Jim because they clearly violated even the new constitution and bylaws that the church had recently adopted. Despite James protest the actions of Jim were shrugged off by the church because by then Jim had not only the ear of the pastor and the church council but he also could and did control all aspects of the church administration.

It seems that authoritarian rule is in the MEGA Republican's DNA.

Chapter 9
Mark and Peter appear before Nero.

It was in the year 67 AD when Peter came to Rome and met with Mark concerning the anticipated arrival of Paul to plead his case before Nero. In answer to the combined prayers of the Christian congregation in Rome, Mark who was Nero's nephew unexpectedly received an invitation to come to dinner at the imperial palace on Tuesday April 12. It was also arranged that Peter would attend the dinner along with Mark and pose as Mark's servant and bodyguard.

Mark and Peter took a great risk because after the great fire In Rome in AD 64, many people had blamed Nero for setting the fire just so he could see Rome burn. Instead, Nero blamed the Christians who came to Rome and who met usually in people's houses and at night after the workday was completed. Romans looked on with suspicion at any group that met privately and especially at night. They believe that those meetings were for the purpose of plotting treason against the state and thus there was a natural suspicion regarding the Christians.

Romans practiced their religions in public ceremonies including parades and festivals for all the public to see, Therefore, there was a natural suspicion against the Christians because of their private meetings. Nero took advantage of this perception by the citizens of Rome and began to persecute Christians in elaborate and public displays of torture. Christians were dressed in animal skins and set in the midst of wild animals to be torn to pieces. Christians were smeared with tar and set on fire in public displays of torture. It was even said that Nero would use Christians rolled and pitch and set on fire to light his garden when he held parties at the Imperial Palace.

Because of these activities and especially because of the volatility of Nero, Mark and Peter were aware of the dangers that they were walking into as they prepared to confront Nero concerning Paul.

When it was decided that they would go to dinner with Nero and bring up the subject of Paul's upcoming trial they and the congregation of Christians in Rome had a prayer meeting. They prayed for the protection of Mark and Peter. The entire congregation prayed that Nero would be receptive to Peter's plea to allow Paul to be set free and travel to Hispania (the Roman name for the providence of Spain.)

"Jesus promised that He would be with us and that He would protect us and even give us the words to say when we stand before Governors and Magistrates if we are brought before them for our faithful following of our Lord." Peter told Mark.

"Then we shall rely on the promises of Jesus and go boldly before Nero and plead for Paul's release" Mark replied.

The men talked into the night and began to make preparations to meet Nero within a few days. The Christian congregation avoided being seen in public and moved their meetings to the catacombs under the streets of Rome. All the while all the Christians prayed for the safety of Mark and Peter and that God would change the heart of Nero.

As they set out for their meeting with Nero, Mark and Peter wore very similar clothes with only the slightest difference so that it was obvious that Mark was a Roman citizen and Peter was his servant. Each man's tunic was made of linen and the formal outer garment or toga was draped over the knee length tunic. Mark's toga was embroidered with gold stitching and had a purple stripe at the edge of the toga. Mark's toga had a gold clasp that secured the toga at his waist. On the other hand, the toga that Peter wore was of plane woolen cloth without any embroidery or color dyed on the cloth and it was tied around Peter's waist with twine. The fact that Peter also wore a toga indicated that he was a part of Mark's household and that he was probably not a Roman citizen. Both men wore sandals though the sandals that Mark wore were more like the foot gear that Roman soldiers wore when they were not marching to battle. The sandals that Peter wore were more typical of his previous life as the Galilean fisherman. If anybody examined Peter closely, they would have been suspicious of his place as a servant from the household of the Roman emperor's nephew.

Peter met Mark at the designated spot just outside of the servants' entrance to the house that Mark was occupying with his sister in Rome. It was arranged in that manner so that it appeared that Peter was accompanying Mark as Peter embarked from the servant's quarters. This was arranged so that there would be no suspicion concerning Peters role when they approached the emperor's palace. As they walked along together, the conversation turned to the manuscript that Mark began to write after he accepted Jesus Christ and the Holy Spirit and turned his life over to Christ while he was still in Antioch.

"Peter, I have many questions concerning the life of our savior Jesus. You were with Him during His earthly ministry. There are many details that I would like to know concerning the events that you witnessed while you were with Jesus." Mark said to Peter as they walked along the main streets that led to the emperor's palace.

Peter replied, "Jesus was no ordinary man. When He talked to you there was an intensity and yet a tenderness even when He was upset with us for our lack of faith in His ministry. We all knew that Jesus loved us from the start and that He would have done anything to protect us but more importantly He wanted to teach us and to give us an example of how to live our lives and to be His faithful witnesses."

"I feel a yearning from deep within me that I must tell the story of how Jesus loved us and became obedient to the will of our heavenly Father. Is it very difficult for you to tell me the intimate details of your life with Jesus?" Mark asked.

"The answer to your question is both yes and no. I was with Jesus from the time that He was baptized in the river Jordan by John the Baptist until that fateful night when He was arrested in Jerusalem. I can tell you with great certainty the events that I witnessed, but there are certain things in my relationship with Jesus that I find hard to express.

"On the night that Jesus was arrested, me and the other disciples celebrated the Passover with Jesus. Jesus told us on more than one occasion that He was going to be arrested, abused, beaten, and crucified. I told Jesus that night that I would stand between Him and the cross. Jesus just looked into my eyes He knew exactly what was going to happen and more importantly He knew exactly what I was going to do.

"Jesus told me that I would deny Him three times before the morning rooster crowed. I told Jesus that I would go to the cross with Him that night. We left the Sader and went to the Garden of Gethsemane. It was Jesus's habit to pray and seek the will of the heavenly Father at every opportunity. He often rested in that garden and more often prayed. Jesus told me to stand by Him and keep watch, but I fell asleep. When Judas brought the crowd to arrest Jesus, I could not keep my word and I denied that I knew Him.

"So, it is with that great joy and with deep sadness inside me; even knowing that Jesus after He was raised from the dead, forgave me and put His arm around me and told me to 'feed His sheep,' that I will tell you of my experience with my Lord and my savior." Peter said to Mark in an earnest expression.

Mark heard the words of Peter and for the first time understood not only the devotion of Peter to Jesus but also the regret that Peter felt when he denied Jesus on the night that He was arrested in the Garden of Gethsemane. "Peter, I must tell you that I feel as if I am compelled to tell the story of Jesus so that believers and non-believers, will know how Jesus loved us and went to the cross to save us." Mark said as they approached the gates surrounding the emperor's palace.

As soon as they stepped out of the shadows and into the lighted area that was close to the entrance to the emperor's palace, they were confronted by a Centurion who commanded that they stop and make themselves known by presenting their credentials. Both Mark and Peter were also frisked to determine if either one of them was carrying a concealed weapon.

. The Centurion demanded that they state their business and identify themselves. Mark reached into his tunic and produced the invitation that had been sent to him a few days before by the emperor. Mark handed the invitation to the Centurion and the Centurion called for another soldier to take the invitation that Mark had just handed to the soldier into the palace for further inspection. Within a few minutes an officer of the Pretorian Guard came to the gate and he also frisked Mark and Peter a second time. "I am Marcus Aurelius Agustus Gaius nephew of the emperor and direct descendent of Julius Gaius, Ceasar." Mark spoke slowly and with an air of expectation that he would be recognized by the officer of the Pretorian Guard.

The officer looked at Mark and Peter and said, "I recognize you Marcus Aurelius Gaius, but I have no knowledge of your companion. Please identify him to us before we can open our gates."

Mark looked directly into the officer of the guard's eyes and said to him, "This is my servant and my bodyguard. I will vouch for him. You have searched him thoroughly; we carry no weapons, and we have no intent to bring harm to His Majesty. I am here simply at the invitation of the emperor, and I have brought this man with me for my own personal protection."

Evidently the officer of the guard believed what Mark told him and immediately allowed for the opening of the gate and for Mark and Peter to pass into the palace.

Upon entry into the palace the two men found themselves accompanied by several members of the Pretorian Guard. These highly armed and highly trained soldiers took up positions around both Mark and Peter. The group now consisting of Mark, Peter, and 4 soldiers from the Pretorian Guard marched into an atrium where they were greeted by the Emperor Nero Claudius Caesar Augustus Germanicus the 5th Roman emperor and final emperor of the Julio- Claudian dynasty.

Nero stood by himself. He was dressed in his royal attire, consisting of an embroidered toga that had the royal Roman emblem emblazed with gold thread. Holding the toga together was a brooch bejeweled with huge rubies embedded in gold. A golden crown was set on Nero's head that looked as if it was golden leaves thatched together. Nero stood as if in expectation of an appropriate greeting from his nephew. As Mark approached Nero held his place and acknowledged Mark's presence only by the uplifted eyebrow. Mark came forward and held his arms out to embrace his uncle. Surprisingly, this moved Nero and he immediately held his arms out in order to embrace his nephew. They kissed each other on the cheeks as was the custom before ending the embrace. Nero then became aware of the presence of Peter and said, "Nephew, who is this person that is in my presence. He is uninvited. Tell me who this person is?"

"Your majesty, this is my trusted servant who I have brought with me from when I traveled to Antioch. His name is Peter, and he is with me for my own personal protection. we walked together through the streets of Rome this evening and I felt the necessity of having Peter with me." Mark replied to Nero's inquiry.

"You are perfectly safe here. Your servant does not need to be in the room with us." Nero remarked.

Mark looked from his uncle then to Peter and said, "Your majesty if it is favorable with you I would like Peter to stay in the room with us because there is one thing that I would like to discuss with you of which Peter has first-hand knowledge and if necessary he can answer any question that may come to your mind concerning this topic."

"So, your visit to your uncle is not purely social." the emperor said as he looked squarely at Peter who was standing several yards away from Mark and Nero.

Mark thought for a moment and then replied, "Uncle, remember it was you who invited me without a hint of the purpose of your invitation. I hope that you just wanted to check up on your nephew. However, I only thought that while I was here, I would bring up a topic that might be of interest to you because you are going to be called on, in the next few weeks, to sit in judgment of a man named Paul. This man Paul is acquainted with my servant Peter. Paul was sent to you by Festus, the governor of Caesarea. This man, Paul, has been accused of causing an insurrection in Judea by Jewish zealots who stand in opposition to those who are followers of Jesus. It is Jesus who the Jewish zealots persuaded Pontious Pilate to crucify even when Pilate could find nothing against Him. It is these same Jewish zealots who incited the trouble that Paul is accused of starting."

Nero looked carefully at Mark and then suddenly took two or three steps in the direction of Peter and said with a loud voice, "I have heard of Jesus. There has been much discussion among those who advise me concerning the events that took place in Judea when my governor, Pontious Pilate, allowed a mob of radicals to crucify this man named Jesus. It seems as if there's too much discussion regarding this incident. Now you tell me that one of His followers will be here in Rome and I will be called on to sit in judgment regarding these matters?

"I am very suspicious now of your motives for bringing Peter to be with me. If you were not my nephew, I would immediately have both of you taken away and put in prison." Nero continued.

Unexpectedly, Peter spoke up, "Your majesty, as you can tell from my speech and probably from the roughness of my appearance, I am a man from Galilee of Caesarea. By trade I was a fisherman when I had an encounter with a man like no other man. Jesus came to me and called me to be His disciple. For three years I followed, listened to, ate with, and watched Him perform miracles. By His touch he healed thousands of people not only from sickness but from blindness, deafness and I even saw Him raise dead people to new life. I came to believe that He was truly the son of God and that He was sent into the world for a specific purpose and that was to save people from their sinful ways.

"Your majesty, my fellow believer in Jesus, Paul who from time to time I have not totally gotten along with, has been arrested as a result of the jealousy of my fellow Jews who believed that they can blot out what Jesus has brought into the world. Jesus has changed the world. There is no going back to life before Jesus. When Paul is brought before you, he will be accused of inciting an insurrection in Jerusalem. The only insurrection that occurred was at the hands of the Jewish zealots because they do not believe, and they want to retain their old beliefs and force those beliefs on others."

Both Nero and Mark were astonished by the words that were spoken by Peter. For many minutes no one said anything. Everyone stood silent and just gazed at each other as if they were spectators at an event in which something remarkable had just happened.

Finally, Mark spoke up again and said, "I too am a follower of Jesus. After my family was killed in the fires of which we all are aware, I wandered the streets of Antioch and was assaulted and left for dead in a gutter when Peter found me. The Christians in Antioch took care of me and restored me to my health. After being with those men and women who found such comfort and joy as followers of Jesus, I too became a believer. Uncle, it is not my intent to tell you how to judge Paul. I am just here to tell you that when Jesus comes into a man's life it changes everything. Paul is only following what he has been required to do because he is following Jesus. Paul has not committed a crime he is merely following his belief and his knowledge that Jesus seeks to save those who are lost and not to commit crimes or cause insurrections."

Nero's face became almost ashen. His temper, which was notorious among all whoever was close to him, began to show itself. Then something miraculous occurred. Instead of blurting out a crude remark or threatening Peter and Mark with a prison term or even worse, Nero said, "This Jesus that you talk about, how can I find out more about Him. What you have told me about miracles and the raising of the dead has intrigued me. How can I get such powers as those that Jesus possessed."

Peter spoke again, "The power to heal and the power to perform miracles and even to raise the dead only comes from

God. When I was with Jesus, I came to understand that Jesus was also God. If Jesus comes into you, you possess the power that God will give you. It is only through the acceptance of Jesus and a commitment to Jesus that will allow Jesus to take up residence in you."

"What if I command you to confer on me the same powers that you say Jesus possessed." Nero shouted at Peter.

"The powers that Jesus possesses are not mine to give or to take away. It is only when a person commits themselves to follow Jesus that Jesus will enter that person and the Holy Spirit will direct and lead that person as God intends." Peter said as both he and Mark started to put distance between themselves and Nero.

Nero, sensing that both Mark and Peter were not intimidated by the fact that Nero literally held their lives in his hand, calmed himself and said, "I see that you are not easily persuaded to do as I command you. It seems that this Jesus that you so boldly speak of has such a hold on you that not even I can persuade you to give me the powers that I want. However, because you are my nephew and this man that you have brought with you is in your company, I will not send you to prison or take any further actions against either of you. When the man that you have talked about is brought before me for judgment I will listen carefully. Many in Rome will want me to crucify him, but I will not. I will send him to the Extremadura where he will be free to do as he wishes as long as he stays away from Rome."

As soon as Nero said those words and with the gesture of his hand the guards returned to the room where the meeting had taken place and escorted Peter and Mark out of the palace and back into the streets of the imperial city.

When they were away from the gates of the palace, Mark grabbed Peter and said, "That could not have gone any better than it did. Our hope of intervening on behalf of Paul has been accomplished."

"Our God performs miracles in ways that we cannot comprehend. Even rulers and kings are under God's influence. Now we must talk so that I can give you the details of my experiences with Jesus. You need to listen carefully and be led by God's inspiration to write. We need to tell His story to the believers not only here in Rome but throughout the empire of Rome. The Holy Spirit has led me to believe that you are the one who will come under God's influence to write the story of how Jesus came into the world to give His life as a ransom for many." Peter said as he smiled warmly.

True to his word for the next several months Peter and those who had been with Jesus while He was teaching and preaching, healing and casting out demons, being confronted by the Pharisees and laying down His life as an atonement for the sins of believers, told their stories to Mark. Through the power of the Holy Spirit, Mark was inspired and began and to write the gospel story.

Chapter 10

A short narrative of how Baptists got to this point in history and how that impacted the confrontation between James and Jim.

The history of the Baptists varies from one historian to another. Some historians of the group that identify themselves as Baptist contend that Baptists have been in existence since the time of Jesus. They trace the origins of the Baptist Church to Jesus's baptism in the river Jordan by John the Baptist. Others contend that the Baptist Church was even founded before Christ. However, most historians look to the separatist movement in England that produced the Pilgrims in the 16th and 17th centuries as the starting point for Baptists in Europe.

The separatists reacted to the corruption of the Church of England and set up independent churches that were congregational as opposed to hierarchical. Congregational churches are governed by the local church as opposed to a hierarchy of church leaders that governs the entire denomination.

The Separatists were persecuted for their beliefs and for their refusal to submit to the Church of England. A notable group of Separatists under the leadership of John Smyth left England and formed a Separatist Baptist church in Holland in 1609. These Separatists were influenced by the Anabaptist but did not share the entirety of the Anabaptist doctrine. Eventually, the Separatists that had found religious freedom in Holland returned to England under the leadership of Thomas Helwys. Helwys authored a tract on religious freedom in which he insisted that there be a complete separation of church and state. Baptist have almost always professed that there should be a separation of church and state. For this offence Helwys was imprisoned and eventually died in prison.

While the Baptists were still in England there was an internal conflict among Baptist believers. There were the General Baptists and the Particular Baptists. The distinction between the two sects boils down to a difference between the beliefs of John Calvin on the one hand and Jacobus Arminius on the other hand. While there are many differences in the two Baptist sects the most fundamental difference is that of a belief in predestination of the elect by the Particular Baptists (in which God has preselected those who will receive salvation), and a belief in the free will of the believers (in which an individual may either accept or reject salvation as a matter of their own free will) by those who fill the ranks of the General Baptist.

Eventually, Puritans in England set out for the new world and in 1620 founded the Plymouth Bay colony in modern-day Massachusetts. Baptist soon followed the Puritans as pilgrims to Plymouth Bay colony in order to enjoy religious freedom. At first the Puritans accommodated the Baptist Separatists but eventually the Baptist were forced out of the Plymouth colony and in 1638 Roger Williams founded the First Baptist Church in America in Providence, Rhode Island. Another Baptist Church was also founded in Newport, Rhode Island almost simultaneously with the church founded by Roger Williams. Roger Williams was a Calvinist but within a short period of time the church that Roger Williams founded became more associated with the Armenian beliefs and thus became a General Baptist Church.

Baptist churches throughout the United States continued to flourish especially after the Great Awakening of the 1730s and 40s. The Great Awakening was a Protestant Christian revival that spread throughout the English colonies in America. The first Great Awakening came at a time when the idea of secular rationalism was being emphasized and passion for religion had grown stale. Throughout the English colonies revival broke out and camp meetings took place in which many were converted to Christianity and found Baptist churches as a fellowship to which they could belong.

Jonathan Edwards a Northampton Anglican minister was

one of the chief ministers of the First Great Awakening. In 1741 Edwards gave a famous and emotional sermon entitled "Sinners in the Hands of an Angry God." Edwards espoused that all men were sinners (a belief in the doctrine of original sin) and that an angry God required men to repent of their sins or face the consequences of hell. Edwards believed that salvation only came through Jesus Christ and the grace of God, both tenants of Calvinism.

The First Great Awakening came to a conclusion sometime in the mid-1740s but had a significant impact on religious life in the English Colonies that later became the United States. There was more of an emphasis on the preaching of an emotional gospel as opposed to religious rituals and ceremonies. Church members were called upon to take into consideration their individual responsibility to God and were called upon to take a personal and moral stand on behalf of Christianity.

The First Great Awakening was followed by a Second Great Awakening. It occurred in the 1770s and was instrumental in the American Revolution. Both of these Great Awakenings mainly affected Protestant denominations and spurred the growth of Baptist congregations throughout the English colonies and ultimately The United States.

Because of these revival meetings membership in Protestant denominations including the Baptist increased rapidly. Baptist differed significantly from other denominations because they insisted on "believers' baptism" (Baptist churches did not allow infant baptism but insisted that only those who were capable of making an informed decision concerning their belief in Jesus as savior, could be baptized) and also insisted upon immersion (being completely covered by water in the baptismal pool) rather than sprinkling as performed in the Methodist and Presbyterian churches.

Baptist churches in the northern part of the United States and especially New England began to associate themselves with the abolitionist movement that believed that the slaves held in the southern states should be immediately freed. Baptist churches in the South became increasingly militant with regard to the issue of slavery and eventually separated themselves from their northern Baptist counterparts. Southern Baptist eventually formed a convention of churches that continued to allow church members to own slaves.

The Southern Baptist churches especially in both North and South Carolina were more aligned with the Armenian, free will, theological perspective, while in north Georgia (where there were almost no slaves or slave owners) a more Calvinistic perspective permeated. What became known as Primitive Baptist churches (also known as Hard Shell Baptists) were and still are prominent in rural North Georgia. The form of Calvinism practiced by primitive Baptist churches in north Georgia also became radicalized to the point of a belief that members of the Baptist congregations of those churches could not determine whether they were saved merely because of their confession that Jesus died for their sins. Their belief was and is that because God's election could not be determined until the believer reached heaven that salvation could only be hoped for rather that assured by belief in Jesus.

The Southern Baptist denomination spread throughout America especially the southeastern part of the United States and incorporated more of a free will rather than a Calvinistic approach to salvation. While the Southern Baptist were much less dogmatic in their distinction between belief in predestination and the free will of the congregant, the independent churches of north Georgia (Primitive Baptist churches) clung to their belief in predestination in a rather radical sense.

Peachtree Baptist Church was formed in 1847 and soon associated itself with the Southern Baptist convention. When the Civil War came to Atlanta, the church buildings of Peachtree Baptist were used as a field hospital because much of the battle of Atlanta was fought in a close proximity to the church. After the war, the congregation struggled because life in the South in and around Atlanta was difficult. The traditions of the old South did not pass quickly or quietly. Peachtree Baptist remained a segregated and a staunchly conservative church. The church followed the predominant political atmosphere in Georgia and also remained a quiet backwater congregation because the church was located in a portion of Atlanta that had not been developed and was still considered rural.

On December the 7th 1941, when news of the bombing of Pearl Harbor reached the congregation at Peachtree Baptist the people were so upset with the news that they left a fire burning in the wooden stove that heated the sanctuary and the church buildings burned down. The church was rebuilt, and its location started to become more suburban than rural. Located at the corner of Briarcliffe Road and Lavista Road, the church was located in what would become a suburban community made up of single-family residences. As the area around the church began to develop with single family housing, the area became home to a large population of Jewish people. About four blocks to the west of Peachtree Baptist is an orthodox Jewish synagogue.

Men who had served in the military during World War II also began to settle in the neighborhoods surrounding Peachtree Baptist. By the end of the 1940s and the beginning of the 1950s membership at Peachtree Baptist grew at a rapid rate. New classroom buildings and a new sanctuary were added to the existing property. The church remained a member of the Southern Baptist Convention and became a very family oriented yet conservative church.

It was in the 1950s that the family that James started, after his service in the Marines, moved into the community near Peachtree Baptist. James and his family joined the church and James became an important contributor both financially and in terms of his commitment to the church. Likewise, Jim's mother and father also became regulars at Peachtree Baptist and Jim's father became a Deacon. James also became a Deacon and there was regular fellowship between James' family and Jim's parents.

The only difference in the two families was that James had been brought up in Cherokee County, Georgia in a Primitive

66

Baptist church while Jim's family was more closely associated with the free will part of Baptist thinking. During the years immediately following the return of men from service during World War II the distinction between free will Baptist and Primitive Baptist theology did not come into play because an emphasis was placed on missions and the missionary efforts of the church in foreign lands.

Church revivals were held on a regular basis with the preaching of so-called "fire and brimstone" messages by revival preachers. Revivals became more subdued and eventually the regularly scheduled two-week revival meetings only lasted until the mid-sixties. Revivals held at Baptist churches became more concerned with missionary efforts and the giving of offerings to support the foreign mission activities of the Southern Baptist convention. The differences in belief about the election of the saved, that may have arisen as a result of the difference in beliefs between church members was not a topic of either the preaching service or the Sunday school curriculum. After all, if the church member was willing to support the church with regular contributions it was not important to determine whether the church member believed in predestination or in free will.

Southern Baptist churches prospered in the 50s, 60s and 70s. During that time, the men who had returned from service during World War II raised their families. Children in the family were brought to church and the children participated in Sunday school, vacation Bible school, youth retreats, young people gatherings and all sorts of other church activities during those years in which Baptist churches and in particular Peachtree Baptist Church had a large enough congregation to support a growing church staff and all the infrastructure that the church had acquired.

Eventually, the men who formed the backbone of Baptist churches became older, their children moved away, new families interested in Southern Baptist missionary efforts did not move into the Toco Hills area of Atlanta and those that moved into that area did not fit in with the conservative Southern Baptist dogma that was espoused by Southern Baptist churches. It didn't help much that there were scandals within the staff of the Peachtree Baptist Church that further divided the congregation and sent other potential church members away from Peachtree Baptist to other churches in the area.

By the 1990s, the congregation of Peachtree Baptist like many other Baptist churches slowly began to diminish. Whether it was because of the age of the members who had become members of the church in the fifties, 60s, and 70s or a general demise in the number of congregants that wanted to be associated with Baptist churches, the number of people in the pews of the church on any given Sunday diminished. Men like James continued to serve in the church and to regularly attend services. Jim's family continued in the church, but Jim and his wife and children moved to South Carolina and Jim did not return to the church until around 2014.

During that time there were also scandals among evangelical television ministries that involved well known preachers. The impact of the well-publicized scandals is an unknown factor regarding church attendance, but the impact on the potential of reaching the lost was well documented. During that time there were suggestions that Peachtree drop the Baptist name from the church's name and that it simply be known as Peachtree Church. Other Baptist churches did exactly that.

When Jim and his family moved back to Atlanta and started attending Peachtree Baptist Church, Jim's father was ill and soon after he moved back to Atlanta Jim's father passed away. Jim also had a brother who lived in Atlanta and his brother also became ill. Jim and his brother owned a farm near Dublin, Georgia, and on alternate weekends Jim would travel to Dublin to attend to the farm.

Jim also decided that he wanted to form a business related to assisting churches with their finances. As mentioned above the first church that Jim thought of when it came to his new business was Peachtree Baptist Church. The only thing that stood in Jim's way from taking over the Peachtree Baptist account was the fact that James had been overseeing the finances at the church for many years.

James was a retired executive officer of a national medical products business. The medical products business was very profitable, and James received a sizable compensation package from that business. The business was run so well and was so profitable that it became the target for other businesses that wanted to buy out the business that James had made successful. James received a large amount of money in order to relinquish his shares in the business that he operated. Because James had sufficient income to live on for the rest of his life, he devoted his attention to all the daily operations of Peachtree Baptist Church.

A conflict between the business that Jim wanted to start, and James continued interest in the daily operation of Peachtree Baptist became very apparent. At times, the conflict between Jim and James was more than just apparent and it led to vocal confrontation between the two men even while they attended the same Sunday school class. James by the time all this started to occur was in his early 80s while Jim was in his early 60s.

One of the issues that became a focal point of Jim's attempt to undermine James' overseeing of the daily financial operation of the church was that James hired his daughter, Linda, as the church's bookkeeper. James, on his own initiative authorized a salary for Linda of $25,000 per year. Linda was an experienced bookkeeper who for many years was very good at organizing and maintaining the financial records of the church. Linda would make regular financial reports to the congregation at the regularly scheduled business meetings of the congregation.

Jim set out to become the president of the church council so that he could diminish the responsibilities that James had undertaken on behalf of the church. As soon as Jim became the president of the church council, he decided on his own to revamp the signing authority on the churches bank accounts by taking James's name off the authorized list at the bank and by adding his name to the authorized list as the sole signatory on the churches bank accounts.

A day or two after Jim took the initiative to remove James for signing authority on the churches' bank accounts, James was notified by the bank that he was no longer authorized to sign checks. Jim did not share that information with anybody at the church until after he had taken that action. Interestingly, Jim's actions violated the churches bylaws, but because Jim had been elected as president of the church council, he had apparent authority according to the bank to take such action.

When James found out that his name had been taken off the authorized list for signing checks, he asked for a conference with Jim, pastor Vestal and associate pastor Capps. Within a few days a meeting was held at the church and James took the position that the actions of Jim violated the bylaws and constitution of the church. Pastor Vestal took the position that the church was no longer functioning under the bylaws and constitution and that the church needed to move on from the way it had been doing business while James was acting as the chief financial officer of the church.

Pastor Vestal took the position that the pastor of the church should be intimately involved with the finances of the church and that he and not James should be the chief financial officer. In other words, it became apparent that pastor Vestal was at least acquiescing to the actions that Jim had taken in order to displace James from his long-held position as chief financial officer of the church.

CHAPTER 11
PAUL APPEARS BEFORE NERO AND MARK CONTINUES WRITING THE GOSPEL OF MARK.

Mark and Peter became very close during those days following their invitation to visit with Nero. They would sit for hours together, and Peter would pour out his heart concerning his love for his friend and his Lord Jesus. Peter explained how Jesus had called him when he was a fisherman on the sea of Galilee. He explained that Jesus guided His band of followers from Galilee to Jerusalem then back to Galilee and then back to Jerusalem.

Peter told Mark how Jesus seemed to know the thoughts of everyone around Him and that by the mere touch of His hand He could heal people of their sickness, their despair, their blindness, their deafness and even their demon possession. Peter told Mark that Jesus taught His disciples and on occasions would take them away from the crowds in order to instruct His closest followers.

On one occasion when Jesus and His disciples attempted to get away from the crowds the crowds followed them to a desolate place and Jesus had compassion on the people that had come to listen and be healed. Through a miracle Jesus took 5 barley loaves and two small fish and fed a crowd of over 5000 people. Not only did Jesus feed 5000 but He again fed another group of over 4000 with hardly any food.

On another occasion Peter, James, and John accompanied Jesus on a trip up a mountain and there to their amazement Jesus was transfigured and they all heard the voice of God telling them to listen to the words of Jesus.

Peter explained that Jesus had command not only over evil spirits but also, He could calm the water and the wind with His voice and that Peter witnessed Jesus' walking on the water and

Jesus even allowed Peter to walk on the water with Him.

Peter explained that the religious leaders in Judea were jealous of Jesus and confronted Jesus on many occasions in order to find some fault with Jesus and in order to embarrass Him in front of the people. When that didn't happen, the Pharisees plotted to kill Jesus.

Then Jesus told His disciples that He was going to suffer and die at the hands of the religious leaders of the Jews, "We did not understand." Peter told Mark that after the fact it became apparent that Jesus knew exactly what was going to happen almost as if He had planned it Himself.

Peter admitted that "I told Jesus that I would follow Him even to the point of death and that I would never abandon Him no matter what happened." With tears in his eyes Peter told Mark that on the night when Jesus was arrested in the Garden of Gethsemane that he followed Jesus to the home of Caiaphas the Chief Priest and there he denied that he even knew Jesus.

Jesus was handed over to the Roman governor, Pontious Pilate, for execution by crucifixion by the Romans.

During that time Peter admitted that he as well as the other disciples were in hiding from the Romans and also from the Jewish authorities. Only the women of the group knew exactly where Jesus had been taken after he died on the cross. Peter explained that the custom of the Jews was that because it was the evening of the Sabbath that His body could not be attended to, so the women went to the grave early on Sunday morning to do for His body as was the custom.

To their amazement Jesus was not there and they reported to us that Jesus had arisen from the dead. At first it sounded too good to believe. Me and my fellow discipled John, raced to the place where the women told us that Jesus had been buried. When we got there, Jesus was gone. In thinking back, Peter told Mark that all along Jesus had been telling His disciples that He would not remain in the grave and that He would arise and that He would appear to us and then He would ascend to His Father in heaven.

As Peter told this miraculous story, Mark wrote down every word. Mark felt led by the Holy Spirit to write as well as he could, the whole story that Peter was relaying to him concerning the life, the teachings, the miracles, the confrontation with evil spirits, and lastly the death and resurrection of his friend, and more than a friend a savior, the Messiah, the son of God, Jesus.

After several months of talking to Peter and of trying to understand the life and death of Jesus, Mark completed writing the good news about Jesus that he believed the people of Rome would understand and appreciate. Mark detailed the actions that Jesus took. Mark had no idea that Jesus had performed all the miracles that Peter witnessed. Mark began to realize that Jesus healed literally thousands of people. Mark now understood that by taking even the smallest of offerings into His hands Jesus was able to multiply the bread and the fish to feed literally thousands of people. Mark marveled at the actions of Jesus when He was confronted by the religious leaders in Judea. Mark began to realize that Jesus did not have to suffer and die but He willingly did exactly that. Jesus not only sacrificed Himself for His disciples but for all believers who would come afterwards to believe in and trust in Jesus, including Mark himself.

As he wrote, Mark felt the very presence of God instructing him and directing him. It was as if God's hand was on his hand as he wrote the words of his message to the Roman Christians. Indeed, the words that Mark wrote were the inspired words of God.

Mark read the manuscript that he had written to Peter. Peter approved the words that Mark wrote and told Mark that he should also allow the others who had been with Jesus to read the manuscript. All agreed that the work was complete and that it would be useful for all Christians and especially the Greek and Latin speaking Christians to read the story that Mark had written based on the story told to him by Peter and the others who had been with Jesus during His earthly ministry.

Mark was able to get a copy of the manuscript to Paul as he was in prison in Rome after Mark finished writing. It was not long after Paul read the manuscript that his trial before Nero took place and to everyone's amazement Paul was not put to death but was exiled to the Extremadura region of Spain where he was allowed to continue to preach at least for a short period of time.

Chapter 12
Peachtree Baptist falls asleep.

During the early 2020s there was a movement throughout the United States that extolled the virtues of becoming aware of the harm that extreme right-wing politicians were about to and were unleashing on American citizens. Journalists began to refer to this awareness as being "woke" and explained that the "woke movement" caused an awareness that something malevolent was going on especially among MAGA Republicans.

There was a backlash to the concept of "wokeness" among various Republican leaders. In Florida the cry of anti-wokeness could be heard amongst the Republican candidates for president of the United States. They believed that being aware of what Republican leaders were attempting to do to the American democracy should be met with cynicism and outright contempt. To the Republican leaders it was a matter of ridicule for a person to be labeled as woke. To the Republicans it was better for the world to stay asleep and not to understand that their message was one of self-interest because they believed that they could fool all the people all the time.

In 1 Thessalonians 5:6, Paul writes, "So then, let us not be like others, who are asleep but let us be awake and sober." In other words, Paul tells the Christians at Thessalonica not to fall asleep but to keep themselves awake. They are not to be like the others, implying non-believers (the word that Paul uses for others, implies that they are the refuse of society) who sleep their way through life and are easily led by those who do not have their best interest in mind.

The mission of an evangelistic Baptist Church like Peachtree Baptist should be to seek and to save those who are lost. In fact, Jesus just before He ascended into heaven instructed His followers to be witnesses in Judea, Samaria, and to the uttermost parts of the world and to baptize the new believers in the name of the Father the Son and the Holy Spirit. Matthew 28:18-20.

Somewhere along the line Peachtree Baptist and its membership fell asleep because they were content to sit in the pews, listen to a sermon, go home, and not engage lost people with the good news that Jesus loves them and wants them to be saved.

Even as the confrontation between James and Jim raged over the church's finances, the pastors of the church were content to allow the church to fall asleep in its mission to engage people and to even understand whether they confessed a belief in Jesus or not. Perhaps it was because the congregation had aged to a point that it was difficult for them to be out in the world. Perhaps it was the inward struggle between factions in the church that caused the congregation and the staff to fall asleep regarding the command of Jesus to go into the world and make disciples of all men. In any event the church had fallen asleep; the church was neither awake nor sober. As a result, the church continued its decline.

All around the neighborhood in which Peachtree Baptist found itself in 2015 were new apartment complexes that housed young adults and their children. There were other Baptist churches within a mile or two of Peachtree Baptist and those churches continued to baptize new believers. While the rate at which new believers were coming to mainly white Baptist churches in metropolitan Atlanta was not like in the heyday of church growth, there were plenty of other evangelical churches that continued to reach out to the lost in order to tell the gospel story and to seek professions of faith among those who were lost.

The black population of Atlanta flocked to a group of mega churches where the "Prosperity Gospel" or "Prosperity Theology" was likely to be preached.

The "Prosperity Theology" is a teaching in Protestant churches in which the Bible is said to form a contract between God and each believer so that if the believer acts in a specific way, believes in a specific doctrine, supports the church in a specific way; then they will receive the benefits of a prosperous and healthy life. Several mega churches in the Atlanta area followed this prosperity theology. Churches like World Changers, pastored by Creflo Dollar, and New Birth Missionary Baptist Church, pastured by Eddie Long, were mega churches that attracted large numbers of African American congregants in which Prosperity Theology was preached. These churches followed the Prosperity theology that had become prevalent by such other ministers as Joel Osteen and even before him by the televangelist Oral Roberts in the early 1950's.

Prosperity theology became prevalent in the United States in Protestant churches with the rise of televangelism in the mid to late 1950s. Perhaps the first televangelist of notoriety was Oral Roberts who espoused a faith healing ministry and slowly but surely Roberts morphed his theology into a "seed faith" ministry in which Roberts proclaimed that if his TV audience would continue to send in their offerings to his church that they too would be blessed by God and that they would receive a monetary blessing from God in return for their support of Oral Roberts' ministries.

The churches that followed the prosperity theology were also known to seek donations to their church by offering prayer clothes, oil for an anointment, and other religious trinkets to their television audience if they would continue to support the ministry with their cash offerings. Notorious for this kind of Televangelism was the ministry of Jim and Tammy Faye Baker at their PTL television show, who prior to the time that they were accused of operating a Ponzi scheme raked in millions of dollars from their audiences with the promise that they would receive a spiritual and financial blessing based on the amount of their offerings. It appeared that Jim and Tammy Faye, through her TV tears, were in fact receiving the blessings of a lavish lifestyle at the expense of their audience.

Those who were adherents to the Prosperity theology were generally people who were not wealthy. The typical audience of these televangelists were people who were in need either financially or from a health standpoint. Those that contributed their money to Prosperity theology ministries were seeking a financial blessing even as their ability to support the lavish lifestyles of ministers like Creflo Dollar, Eddie Long, Joel Osteen, and Oral Roberts became matters of concern for traditional Protestant denominations.

The basis for concern of the more traditional Protestant churches was that through the tenets of the Prosperity theology man elevated himself to the same level as God. There was an arm's length contract between God and man that if man met the criteria of the contract, then God was obligated to uphold His end of the bargain by making that man prosperous and healthy.

Religion became nothing more than an outgrowth of existential thought in which the individual aspirations of human beings could control the actions of God. This was a far cry from Calvinism and even invaded the thoughts of Arminius. A new religion in which man could control God's actions through buying God's grace with their offerings came into being.

While all the aspects of the Prosperity theology were swirling around metropolitan Atlanta and throughout the United States by way of television, the congregation at Peachtree Baptist Church lost their first love; to minister to the lost and dying population that was in close proximity to the church. Peachtree Baptist fell asleep to the needs of the lost and continued to slumber as it neglected the Great Commission that Jesus gave His followers when He ascended into heaven.

Soon after Jim was elected to the presidency of the church council and James had been relieved of his duties as the chief financial officer of the church, Pastor Vestal announced that he was stepping away from the church and that the duties of the senior pastor would be assumed by Paul Capps. It was not a surprising turn of events. Pastor Vestal recruited the Capps family to Peachtree Baptist, sold the congregation on the proposition that Paul Capps could and would lead the music program at the church despite the fact that he had no musical background or training in that regard.

After the controversy between James and Jim had culminated in Jim's ascendancy as the chief financial officer of the church under the direction of the pastor, Pastor Vestal resigned. Jim had waged war with James and with the aid of the pastor, James was relegated to a spectator's position with no authority to oversee or even object to whatever financial decisions Jim chose to make.

CHAPTER 13
THE GOSPEL OF MARK FINDS ITS WAY INTO THE HANDS OF LEVI.

Nero Claudius Caesar Augustus Germanicus, the 5th emperor of Rome, was well liked by the rank and file of the Praetorian Guard and the common people of Rome. He was despised by the aristocrats and those who were in control of the Senate. In June 68 AD Nero was declared an enemy of the state by the Roman Senate. He fled Rome and on June 8 of that year he committed suicide. After his death a short period of civil war broke out in the Roman Empire.

Before his death Nero had already tried the case of the apostle Paul and exiled Paul to the Roman territories in what is now the Extremadura section of Spain. Paul was admonished not to preach the gospel of Jesus Christ upon penalty of death. When Paul reached the Roman settlement in Meridia he stood in the amphitheater and preached the gospel of Jesus Christ. (A plaque on the wall of the Roman ruin of the amphitheater at Meridia states that Paul the apostle of Jesus preached at that spot). Subsequently, Paul was brought back to Rome and again imprisoned and waited to be executed for having preached the gospel.

When civil war broke out after Nero's death, Mark, the nephew of Nero again sailed to Antioch and found himself again in the presence of the Christians that he had been with when he first met Peter. Mark renewed his friendship with Rachel and by that time Mark had learned enough of the Aramaic language in order to communicate effectively with Rachel. Within a short period of time Mark and Rachel were married and within a year after their marriage, Rachel gave birth to their first child. Rachel insisted that she, Mark and the new baby, who they named Paul, travel to Jerusalem so that Rachel's family could meet the newborn baby boy and for her family to also meet Mark.

When Mark, Rachel and baby Paul arrived in Jerusalem, the Christian fellowship was led by James (James was often referred to as "old camel knees" because he spent so much time on his knees praying) who had been one of the original apostles that Jesus called during His earthly ministry. Several of the other original apostles also were in the Christian fellowship in Jerusalem. Among them was the tax collector that Jesus called to be his follower. Levi the tax collector that Jesus called as His apostle was a man who understood the Jewish law and also the history of Judaism and the scriptures of the Old Testament. He was also a man of letters and could write. Most of all, Levi who was also known as Matthew, had been with Jesus and had a profound love of Jesus and His teachings.

Mark set about to meet each of the apostles that were still alive and living in Jerusalem at that time. Eventually Mark and Levi met. Upon their meeting, Mark presented Levi with a copy of the gospel that he had written based on his discussions with Peter while they were meeting together in Rome. Mark said, "Brother Levi I wish to present to you this book that I have put together with the help of your fellow disciple, Peter. I hope that you can read it and improve the quality of the writing that I have made by the inspiration of God through the Holy Spirit."

Levi replied, "The Greek language is not the most suitable language for me. I, however, thank you for allowing me to have a copy of this book because I am profoundly interested in what you have to say and the stories about Jesus that were related to you by my brother and fellow disciple Peter. I will read your book and I think that we should meet together again and discuss the contents so that we can determine whether your book should be added to, or if another book from a more Jewish perspective should be written. We should meet again in three days' time at the same place again to discuss these matters. Three days should give me time to read your book and pray about what to do next."

After the meeting between Mark and Levi, Mark thought about the discussion that he had with Levi and came to the conclusion that it would be better for a second book telling the story of Jesus from a more Jewish standpoint to be undertaken and he believed that Levi was the exact right person to take on that project.

Three days later Mark and Levi again met at the upper room that had once served as the venue for the last supper that Jesus and His disciples observed on the night when Jesus was arrested. It was now almost 30 years since that fateful night, but the room still was used by the remaining disciples as a meeting place. By then Levi was a man approaching 70 years of age and while Mark was still a relatively young man the two of them had much in common because of their love of Jesus and their decision to set down the story of Jesus in writing.

"I have thought long and hard about your suggestion regarding the expansion of the story of Jesus that I have presented to you as a book. I think the most appropriate thing to do would be for you to write the story of Jesus from your own perspective. The book that I have written was designed to tell the story of Jesus in a way that a typical Roman citizen might want to hear. The actions that Jesus performed while He was here on earth are very appealing to us Romans. Your perspective, with your Jewish background and with your understanding of the exact words of Jesus as you heard them will be more compelling to a Jewish audience than the book that I have written." Mark said to Levi before Levi could get in a word of his own.

Levi thought for a moment and then in reply to Mark's statements, said, "I too have prayed about what we discussed the last time we met. I have read your book and agree with you that you have written a compelling account of the actions of the leader of the group that He called to follow Him. It seems almost as if it were yesterday when I heard my name called by Jesus. I followed Him for almost three years and eat the Passover Sader in this very room on the night that Jesus was arrested. Every time I am in this room, I think of that night. We were all here together. Jesus joined us after we were all here and had prepared the Passover feast. He came in and there was such sorrow on His face that we knew that something very important was going to happen and it was going to happen very soon. Without much of a greeting He stripped down to His undergarments and wrapped a towel around His waist. He took a pan of water, and He went to each of us, and He washed our feet and dried them with a towel that He was wearing. He told us that if we were to be great, we would have to become servants. We could not consider any task to be too lowly and He demonstrated that by taking on the duties of a servant and washing our dirty feet.

"When we discussed expanding your book with these stories and the memories that I have of my Lord, I thought it would be too hard of an undertaking for an old man like me. I then thought about why Jesus called me that day from the tax collectors' desk and told me to follow Him. I think He may have been calling me to take on the task of writing His story now that you have presented me with your book, I realized that I have a service to perform on behalf of my Lord and savior. I will use your book as an inspiration for me to listen carefully to the words that our heavenly Father will put in my heart to write and to use my hand to put on a scroll the words that only He is truly authorized to set before the world."

The two men standing in the upper room where Jesus had served the Last Supper and had washed His disciples' feet, embraced and agreed that whatever help Levi might need as he wrote the story of Jesus from his perspective that Mark would be close by in order to assist with the Greek language. Levi proposed to write the story in his native Aramaic and allow Mark to translate the manuscript into Greek. Mark stood in the room and marveled at the fact that Jesus had been in that very place and had spoken words to His disciples that Mark wished he, himself had head.

Within a few days, a meeting was held of all the disciples of Jesus who were still alive and living in Jerusalem. James, John, Andrew, and Levi all met again. They again used the upper room that they had used so often over the years since they had last meet together with Jesus. This time Mark was also with the group as they sat to discuss the undertaking that he and Levi had discussed a few days before.

It was decided that Levi would use the book given to him by Mark as only a reference for the book that he was going to undertake to write. It was discussed that Levi's account of the life of Jesus would be made available the other disciples for comment before it was made available to other Jewish Christians in Jerusalem and to those who had been dispersed to other places.

The men that gathered on that day determined that Levi would write a draft that would contain references to the scriptures that were available at the time so as to explain how Jesus fulfilled each of the prophecies of His birth, life, teachings, healings, confrontations, death, resurrection and assentation to heaven. The men gathered there that day discussed that the story of Jesus should be available to those who believed that Jesus was the son of God even if they had not been alive when Jesus was still on earth. The story would not be complete without a detailed reference to Jesus's arrest, trial, torture, crucifixion, burial, resurrection and assentation into heaven. Each of the men present pledged their support to Levi as he undertook the writing of the good news about Jesus.

CHAPTER 14

JESUS PRAYED THANKING HIS FATHER THAT THESE THINGS ARE HIDDEN FROM THE WISE AND THE LEARNED AND ARE REVEALED TO LITTLE CHILDREN. MATTHEW 11:25

In the Kingdom of God real knowledge of the truth is exclusively in the person and divinity of Jesus. The truth that Jesus provides to believers is very difficult for those who do not believe that Jesus is, as He claims to be the only begotten son of God, because non-believers' know their version of truth without relying on the Holy Spirit to reveal the truth that only Jesus can provide. The adage, "And the truth shall make you free" depends on which version of the truth that anyone may be relying. If you are a believer in Jesus Christ and have committed yourself to Jesus, you are aware that there are many people who think that you are a nut. There are many people who think that I am a nut.

Many people think that I am a nut because I have put my entire trust in the hands of Jesus. When I talk to people about my faith, many times I am confronted with more than skepticism and often times with contempt and even anger. I have had doors slammed in my face and even confrontations with family members who think that I am crazy. I wonder why it is so hard for some people to accept the fact that God sent His son, Jesus, into the world to draw people to God. If a person is willing to trust Jesus, Jesus will not reject him/ her but will accept him/ her and save that person from their sins.

This of course brings us to the doctrine of election. You recall we were discussing a few chapters back the difference between Particular Baptists and General Baptist. We said that Particular Baptists closely follow the teachings of John Calvin and one of the tenets of Calvin's (and many others) theology is that God has chosen or elected (also referred to in scripture as predestined) those who He has selected to be believers. On the other hand, General Baptists more closely follow the teachings of Jacobus Arminius who postulated that people were freely able to claim to be believers in Jesus and that there was no pre-destination or election of the saved by God. Additionally, there is no emphases on personal repentance because Armenian's believe that Jesus provided atonement to everybody that accepts Jesus as their savior whether that person is a part of the elect or not.

You may ask what difference does the doctrines of Calvin-ism and Arminianism make among believers today? It would be easy to say, "not much." However, the answer is much more complex than that. The difference lies in the fundamental belief in God. According to Calvin, God is sovereign and any decision that He makes concerning any subject is correct or as the Bible says righteous. Arminianism recognizes the sovereignty of God but also recognizes that men and women are capable of belief in God (or to reject God) by their own free will. Therefore, under Arminianism, men and women elevate their position to that of equality with God when it comes to God's ability to select who will (or will not) become a part of His family.

You may ask, is this not somewhat esoteric? My response is based on my observations and especially my observations of the two men, James and Jim, that we have been talking about for several chapters. As I mentioned, James was brought up in a Primitive Baptist Church in north Georgia. Congregants who attended Primitive Baptist churches had evolved their doctrine of inclusion into the family of God in a hyper-Calvinistic belief. Under hyper-Calvinism there was absolutely no free will to be-come a believer in Jesus as the Armenians believe. There is also an extreme fatalism in which no one really knows if they are saved until they reach heaven. It was my observation that from a hyper-Calvinistic point of view truth is viewed in relative terms. Primitive Baptists do not consider there to be any absolute truth concerning the commands of Jesus because either you are saved or not saved whether you want to be saved or do not want to be saved.

James grew up in rural Cherokee County, Georgia and was the son of a farmer. James had to work hard on the farm until fighting broke out on the Korean Peninsula shortly after World War II. James joined the Marines and saw combat action in Korea and was later stationed in Japan after the hostilities ceased. James came back to The United States met his wife Betty and was soon hired by a pharmaceutical company that had nationwide sales. James worked his way up through the ranks of the company and eventually became a part of the management team in the southeast region of the country. James went back to school and majored in business administration with an emphasis on accounting. James joined Peachtree Baptist Church, raised his children in the church and both he and his wife were respected members. James also became the largest contributor to the financial needs of the church.

Jim was in his late 50's or early 60's and had started attending Peachtree Baptist Church when he was a child. Jim's father had been in respected member of Peachtree Baptist Church and Jim often reminded others of the place that his father had in the church. Jim was a native of Atlanta and had gone to high school in Atlanta. After high school Jim attended college and had an associate degree from Perimeter College, (a junior College in the Atlanta area). Jim initially went to work in his father's business but later he and his wife relocated to Columbia, South Carolina. Jim became a fundraiser for various colleges and universities in South Carolina. In 2013 Jim and his family decided to move back to Atlanta and Jim and his brother after their father died decided to buy a farm near Dublin, Georgia. The brothers took turns tending to the farm on an alternate weekend basis. Jim decided that he would return to Peachtree Baptist Church in 2014. Jim's intent was that he would use his business training in order to take over church administration and parley that into the building of a business of church administration not only for

Peachtree Baptist but also for other small churches in the Atlanta metropolitan area.

James controlled the finances of Peachtree Baptist Church. Jim wanted to control the finances of Peachtree Baptist Church. A conflict between the two men was inevitable.

To make matters worse, James hired his daughter, who was a very efficient bookkeeper, to become the bookkeeper at the church. James authorized a salary for his daughter in the amount of $25,000 per year for her part time job as the church's bookkeeper. When James hired his daughter, Jim saw his opportunity to question the authority of James and to assert that James was mishandling the church's assets. Keep in mind however, that James was by then the largest financial contributor to the church and had been acting as the chairman of the Finance Committee for many years and was intimately knowledgeable of the giving patterns and expenditures of the church.

After Jim returned from South Carolina he made it a point to try to get himself elected to the church council which appointed committee chairman including the chairman of the Finance Committee. Jim engaged in church politics on a scale that reflected his determination to achieve his goal of becoming the chief financial officer of the church. A protracted battle between Jim, and James over the control of the finances of the church started very soon after Jim returned to Atlanta and renewed his membership at Peachtree Baptist.

Each of the men attended the older men Sunday school class and would often engage in arguments in front of the class concerning church finances. Jim would accuse James of mishandling the church's finances and question every financial decision that James made. James on the other hand, realized that Jim was out to displace him from the church's Finance Committee and discredit James for all of the work that James accomplished to keep the church afloat during difficult financial times.

Jim enlisted the aid of the pastor of the church, and other members of the church council in order to question the financial decisions that James made which included the hiring of James' daughter to become the church's bookkeeper. James enlisted the aid of his Sunday school teacher, who was also an attorney to render opinions concerning the churches constitution and by-laws and whether the actions of Jim in the manner in which he chose to discredit James and take over the Finance Committee were in compliance with the church's constitution and bylaws.

Jim was brought up under the General Baptist (Arminius) free will doctrine that tended to make people like Jim existentialist in their belief. As you may recall we discussed existentialism earlier. Existentialism causes people to look mainly at their own needs and how to satisfy their own needs whether in satisfying themselves they disregard the feelings or even the needs of anyone but themselves. In Jim's case, because he wanted to establish a business in which he would market his ability to handle church finances, he disregarded and even attacked James in order to discredit him and become the person to handle the Peachtree Baptist Church's finances. Additionally, the only real point that James and Jim had in common was that neither believed that there were absolute truths that had to be followed in order to fulfill the commandments of God.

On more than one occasion bickering between the two men would result in them standing nose to nose with each other. Neither man backing down from his point of view and insisting that the other man was absolutely wrong in what he was doing. I observed this behavior and was unable to resolve in my mind why either man, who should have been well respected by the other, would act in this way especially on a Sunday morning, at church, in a Sunday school class in which the gospel of Jesus Christ was taught and should have been followed by Christian men.

It was not until much later when I tried to examine the causes or the potential causes of their behaviors that it came to me that there was a difference in each man's fundamental belief and that the doctrine of election was at the center of the differences between these two men.

It was not just my observation of the differences that led to the confrontation between James and Jim. Others in the church began to observe what was going on, especially concerning how the finances of the church were being handled. While the differences between Jim and James boiled over to the point of animosity between the two men, a much more important issue was also being played out in Atlanta, Georgia, the United States, and to the uttermost parts of the world. Mankind either accepted that Jesus was the son of God or rejected that belief.

The call of Jesus on any person's life changes that person. I was a 10-year-old boy living in Hopkinsville, Kentucky when I knew that Jesus was calling me to accept Him and to turn my life over to Him. I did not know everything that I needed to know about life in general, I only knew that I was being called to become a Christian. I did not even understand that I was a totally depraved sinner who needed to repent. At that time, I felt the calling of Jesus and I knew I had to respond. I thank God that He gave me enough faith to respond positively to the distinct call of Jesus.

On the day I heard Jesus call me to accept Him as my savior, I got up from my seat and walked the aisle of the First Baptist Church of Hopkinsville, Kentucky and professed that I believed (and I still believe) that Jesus is the son of God and that I wanted it to be saved. Within a few days my parents took me to meet with the pastor of the church and in his office. The pastor explained to me what was necessary for me to believe in order to except Jesus into my life and to be baptized. All I remember about that day was that I agreed with what the pastor told me and within a short time after that I was baptized in the name of the Father the Son and the Holy Spirit and made a public confession of my belief in Jesus.

In the 11th chapter of the book of Matthew in the New Testament of the Bible, Jesus prays to our Father in heaven and thanks Him that, "I praise you, Father, Lord of heaven and earth, because you have hidden these things from the wise and the learned and revealed them to little children. Yes, Father, for this is what You were pleased to do.

"All these have been committed to me by my Father, no one knows the Son except the Father, and no one knows the Father except the Son and those to whom the Son chooses to reveal Him.

"Come to me, all you who are weary and burdened, and I will give you rest. Take my yoke upon you and learn from me, for I am gentle and humble in heart, and you will find rest for your souls. For my yoke is easy and my burden is light."

With these words Jesus is telling his followers that they have been chosen from before the beginning of time to be a part of the great congregation that Jesus has called to Himself. The scriptures are very clear that Jesus knew who His followers would be from before the time that He came to live among us. You may ask, why then is it necessary for there to be missionaries, pastors, evangelists, and teachers of the gospel if whoever was going to be a follower of Jesus was known prior to the time that they were born?

The answer can be found in the words of Jesus when he says, "I am the bread of life whoever comes to me will never go hungry, and whoever believes in me will never be thirsty. But as I told you, you have seen me and still you do not believe. All those the Father gives me will come to me, and whoever comes to me I will never drive away. For I have come down from heaven not to do my will but to do the will of Him who sent me. And this is the will of Him who sent me, that I shall lose none of those He has given me but raise them up at the last day. For my Father's will is that everyone who looks to the son and believes in Him shall have eternal life, and I will raise them up at the last day." John 6:35- 40.

By these words Jesus is telling the world that people need to repent, accept Jesus as savior, and be baptized. Therefore, even if you are a part of the elect there is still the necessity of responding to the call of Jesus and confession of sin to be saved. It is at that point that faith and repentance come together to produce a Christian. Without the convergence of repentance and faith in Jesus to save a person form their sin, mere acceptance of the fact that a person is totally incapable of saving him/herself only affirms that the person is a human. What is absolutely necessary is the remorse of sinfulness and the reliance on Jesus to remove the sinful nature of the repentant person.

Whether either or both Jim and James had reached that point in their pilgrimage is not for me to say. I can only honestly report my observations of what happened while I was their Sunday school teacher and a member of Peachtree Baptist Church. I have moved on from that responsibility and can only hope that my observations and analysis are helpful to my readers.

CHAPTER 15
THE BOOK OF MATTHEW BEGINS TO TAKE SHAPE.

Mark and Levi managed to meet on several occasions to discuss the outline of the undertaking that Levi had agreed to begin. On each occasion Levi told Mark stories concerning what Jesus said and other historical facts that Levi learned from other sources. The men determined that Mark's book would serve only as an outline for the story that Levi proposed to write. Even though it was a valuable outline, the structure and the language used by Mark in telling the story from the beginning of Jesus ministry until His death and resurrection, did not fully encompass the ministry of Jesus when He was on this earth. Mark's book did, however, provide a great framework for Levi to use.

The men determined that it was necessary for the book that Levi was writing to include much more detail concerning the teachings of Jesus. It was also determined that Levi would write the book in such a way that it was clear to Jewish believers that Jesus fulfilled each part of the Old Testament scriptures related to the Messiah who was to come into the world. Levi also met on a regular basis with the other apostles who were still in Jerusalem and others who had been with Jesus when He was among those who had seen Him perform miracles and preach.

There were many lively discussions between old friends about the exact words that Jesus had spoken. Levi did not proceed to write anything until there was a consensus of opinion as to the exact words that Jesus used. Each of those who were consulted concerning the writing gave their understanding of the words that Jesus used and then Levi would write. They all agreed that each of them would rely upon the guidance of the Holy Spirit to assist them in faithfully reporting what Jesus said and did.

On one day in particular Mark and Levi were discussing

the events that had transpired when Jesus decided that it was necessary for Jesus to teach the multitudes who were following Him. Jesus taught about how it should be among those who put their trust in Jesus. Levi told Mark that Jesus found a place on high ground. It was a place in which Jesus 's voice seemed to carry so that not only those standing near Him could hear what Jesus said but everyone that was even reasonably close could distinctly hear the words that Jesus was speaking. As was the custom of the rabbis, Jesus sat and began His sermon by saying." Blessed are the poor in spirit."

Mark had heard stories that were related to him by Peter, concerning the power of Jesus's voice when he wanted to be heard, but he had never heard the story that Levi was relating to him concerning the time that Jesus preached to the multitude when He was seated on high ground. As Levi told the story, Mark was even more grateful of the time that he was spending in Jerusalem with Levi and the others who had been with Jesus while He was still among those on earth.

Levi began to produce scrolls of his writings. He was deeply engaged in telling the life and teachings of Jesus because he had firsthand knowledge of the events and words spoken by his friend and by his Lord. Because Mark was still available it was Levi's routine to let Mark read what he had written and let him offer suggestions concerning how the translation of the Aramaic language that Levi was using could be translated into the Greek that Mark had agreed to help with. Mark gladly offered his suggestions. The two men collaborated along with the help of the other disciples that were still in life and living in Jerusalem. There were still people who were alive when Jesus walked the streets of Jerusalem that had seen and even touched Jesus. Despite the destruction of much of Jerusalem just a few years before when Vespasian the Roman commander of the legions that were sent to put down the Jews in the First Jewish-Roman War that lasted from 66 AD until 73 AD, Mark and Levi were able to meet and produce a written story of Jesus.

One passage in the book was very troubling to Mark. In the

fifth chapter (it should be noted that chapter designations were not part of the original manuscripts and verse designations, and chapter breaks were added to the manuscript in modern versions of the books of the New Testament) at verse 48, Levi quoted Jesus as saying, "Be perfect, therefore, as your heavenly Father is perfect."

Mark read this verse and said to Levi, "How can we ever measure up to the direct command of our Savior. How are we to ever be perfect? Surely, Jesus did not mean that we are to live perfect lives? I have trouble trying to go a whole day without committing one sin or another."

"Yes, Jesus said exactly those words. At the time that Jesus said to be perfect, none of us that were hearing Him speak those words knew what He meant by it either." Levi replied.

"Then what did He actually mean?" Mark continued to press the issue.

Levi said, "Jesus did not engage in idle talk. He meant every word that came out of His mouth. The day that Jesus told His disciples to be perfect there was quite a murmuring among us, and we had many questions that evening when we were alone with Him."

"Tell me what He said. What did Jesus to tell you? What did He mean when He said, 'Be perfect'," the words seemed to rush out of Mark's mouth.

"He did not tell us that night." was Levi's reply and that really stunned Mark.

"Why would He not tell you what He meant when every one of you had the same question? Why did you not get the answer so that I can know right now. Will I ever live up to the expectations of our Lord?" Mark said with desperation in his voice.

"Jesus knew that none of us were able to understand the meaning of His commandments at that time. Even though we had been with him for some months and even some going on three years we still had so much to learn, and we were not yet equipped to begin to learn what Jesus was teaching us." Levi said in a voice that was at once reassuring but also commanding a knowledge of how true wisdom is found in his reply to Marks question.

Mark was unhappy with Levi's reply and continued to question Levi while they were together in the upper room where Jesus ate His last meal on earth. Finally, Levi said to Mark, "I will tell you as best I can what the Lord meant by telling us that we would have to become perfect in order to enter into the family of God, but now is not the right time for you and me to discuss the most important command of our Lord and Savior. We need to finish the writing to which I have committed and then we shall have time to discuss why Jesus commanded His followers to be perfect. For now, it is sufficient that you put all your trust in our Lord and rely totally on Him.

Mark said, "I have committed my life to Jesus and will never doubt Him!"

Mark was happy to be in Jerusalem with Rachel and her family and to meet regularly with Levi and the other apostles even though the city was occupied by Roman soldiers, and they intimidated the Jewish population. Mark, because he was a Roman citizen, was exempt from the harassment and was able to freely deal with the city's occupation by the Roman legions. Mark was also able to keep the Christian Congregation in Jerusalem, up to date concerning the events that were going on in Rome concerning the Roman Christians who still had to meet secretly because of the fear of persecution.

After Nero's death in June of 68 AD, he was succeeded by Galba who was the preference of the Senate. Galba's reign as emperor was short lived, however. Galba was originally aided by one of his lieutenants, Otho, who marched into Rome with Galba. Otho was introduced to Nero by Nero's mistress Poppaea Sabin, who despite the fact that Poppaea remained the mistress of Nero, Otho married. Nero ordered Otho to divorce Poppaea and sent Otho to Lusitania (a province of Spain) to be governor. The next province over from where Otho was sent was under the governorship of Galba who had also been placed in that position by Nero. Galba was in power in Rome from June 8, 68 AD until January 15, 69 AD.

Evidently there was a falling out between Galba and Otho. Otho murdered Galba and became emperor on Galba's death. By that time Aulus Vitellius was the commander of the Roman legions in lower Germania and refused to swear allegiance to Otho. Otho who was effeminate though well-liked by the citizens of Rome decided that he needed to defend Rome from the rebellious Vitellius and raised an army to stop Vitellius as he and his legions approached northern Italy.

Otho's legions met the legions commanded by Vitellius at the battle of Bedriacum and despite his strategic advantage, Otho withdrew his forces from the battle and the next day Otho committed suicide thus allowing Vitellius to become the emperor. The people of Rome praised Otho for his willingness to commit suicide in order to spare the blood of his soldiers. Vitellius remained in power for eight months until the Senate proclaimed Vespasian as emperor in December of 69 AD. A short civil war broke out again in Rome and forces under the direction of Vespasian succeeded in forcing Vitellius into the open where he was murdered with brutal force by the supporters of Vespasian.

History records that these events are referred to as the time of the Four Emperors. During a period of less than a year and a half Rome was governed after Nero's death by Galba, Otho, Vitellius and then Vespasian who succeeded Vitellius.

The people of Jerusalem were well aware of Vespasian because in 66 AD Vespasian led the Roman legions into Judea when a rebellion broke out and the Jews sought to throw the Romans out of Jerusalem. The Roman legions were under the direction of Vespasian. The rebellion was suppressed and the great Temple that had been built by Herod the Great was destroyed and lay in ruins. During the time that Jesus was still with His disciples He told them that the Temple would be destroyed. Jesus told of the trouble that would occur in Jerusalem prior to His crucifixion and now that prophecy was fulfilled.

Mark and Levi continued to meet, and Mark gave his support to Levi as he produced scroll after scroll for the book that he was writing. Mark was extremely impressed with the stories and facts of Jesus life about which Levi wrote. The disciples of Jesus continued to meet, and they continued to preach that Jesus was the son of the living God and that He was and is the only way to the forgiveness of sin and eternal life. Levi produced records that confirmed that Jesus was the fulfillment of the prophecies that the Jews held to be the basis of the fulfillment of the promises of God to bring a Messiah and a new era into the world.

To the Christian believers it was evident that Jesus had come into the world at the exact right time to bring mankind into a right relationship with God.

In the Roman world however, Christians were persecuted.

Chapter 16

"See, I have refined you. though not as silver; I have tested you in the furnace of affliction." Isaiah 48:10.

God refines His chosen people. That is not to say that just because you are being placed in the furnace of affliction that you are being brought into the family of God. However, it does mean that God often seeks His elect as they are experiencing tribulation in their lives. Peachtree Baptist Church has gone through several periods of refinement. The latest time of refinement may not have come to a conclusion. There may be many more days in which the Church is faced with trials of one sort or another. On the other hand, Peachtree Baptist may have seen its last days, even though Peachtree Baptist Church has been an enduring fixture at the corner of Lavista and Briarcliff for almost a century and a half.

What does the future hold for Peachtree Baptist Church? What the future may bring, only God has the ability to see. The church has tied itself to the Cooperative Baptist Fellowship and has close ties to the McAfee Theological Seminary and Mercer University. Peachtree set itself up as a training ground for seminary students who come to Peachtree to gain experience in their chosen field of ministry before graduating from McAfee and pursuing employment in another church or organization.

The church has proven to be a valuable training ground for seminarians as they are refined by God and chosen to be ambassadors for Christ in the various ministries to which they are called. Some have gone to the foreign mission fields, some to social ministries (ministries to the poor and homeless), some have become ministers of music and programming at their local churches in their home states, some have become youth directors, and some have been called to the pulpit to preach the word

99

of God. God refines His chosen as He told Isaiah to instruct the Children of Israel before and after they were sent into bondage at the hands of the Babylonians on March 16, 597 BC.

The exile of the Jews to Babylon was a significant event in the history of Israel to say the least. Israel had been warned over and over again that the way that they were living and especially the way they were treating the poor and outcast was displeasing to God and that He would send them into exile if they continued on the course that they were traveling. When the Jews continued to pay lip service to their devotion to the one true God, He sent them into refinement in the furnaces of Babylon. Perhaps that is what is happening to Peachtree Baptist. Could it be that Peachtree Baptist because it has failed to seek and to save the lost for many years that it will be sent into the furnaces for further refinement?

God restored the Children of Israel to their promised land about 80 years after they were conquered, and the Temple in Jerusalem was restored (see the books of Ezra and Nehemiah in the Old Testament of the Bible). It was not long after their exile, relatively speaking, that the Jews fell into the same problems that they had been warned about by the Prophets that God sent to proclaim a warning. Then after all that the Jewish people had gone through by way of refinement God sent His only begotten son, Jesus into the world. Jesus came to Palestine to proclaim the Gospel of repentance to Israel.

Jesus was rejected by the religious leaders of that time and willingly offered Himself as the perfect sacrifice for the atonement of sin for those that are willing to accept Jesus as their savior. Jesus went to the cross to offer His body and blood for the forgiveness of sins and to offer a new birth to sinners such as me and you and the church. Peachtree Baptist is not an exception to the need of refinement. Every believer who confesses that Jesus is exactly who He proclaimed Himself to be, must and will go through a period of refinement.

The refinement that all believers must go through will not be the same. Some will go through trials of health, more will go through financial trials, others will lose their jobs, some will be subject to family difficulties and the loss of husbands or wives. Some believers will suffer discrimination or rejection by loved ones as a part of the refinement process. Rest assured however, that the refinement that the providence of God places on His children are meant for good and not to harm His children.

We have discussed before that Peachtree Baptist has lost its first love. Jesus came into the world to seek and to save the lost. The mission of the church that Jesus established and of every Christian church is to carry on the purpose that brought Jesus from heaven; that is to seek and to save the lost. Now however, you say if God is sovereign and has already elected and determined who shall be saved then why does the church need to perform the function that God has already accomplished? It is because God calls His elect to come to Him through confession of sin and baptism. It is plain that Jesus calls sinners to repent and be baptized. The very first words of Jesus recorded in Mark 1:15 are, "The time has come. The kingdom of God has come near. Repent and believe the good news."

Without repentance even the elect cannot be saved, evidently. Remember in the third chapter of John, Jesus tells Nicodemus that he must be born again. What does it mean that a person must be "Born Again"? It means that because we are all sinful at our physical birth, ("For all have sinned and fall short of the glory of God." Romans 3:23,) then we, each of us whether we are a part of the elect or not need to be transformed by a spiritual birth through the acceptance of salvation through Jesus Christ to become a new creation.

Paul put it like this, "Therefore if anyone is in Christ, the new creation has come. The old has gone, the new is here! All this is from God, who has reconciled us to Himself through Christ and gave us a ministry of reconciliation that God was reconciling the world to Himself in Christ, not counting people's sin against them. And He has committed to us the message of reconciliation. We are, therefore, Christ's ambassadors, as though God were making this appeal through us." 2 Corinthians

5:17 -20.

The work of the church that Jesus Christ established is not finished. Church members cannot grow weary of their duty to follow Christ in the ministry of seeking and saving the lost. Therefore, even the elect must confess that they are sinners, repent, and affirm that only Jesus has and thankfully will save them. "For the wages of sin is death but the gift of God is eternal life in Jesus Christ our Lord." Romans 6:23.

What shall we say? If I am being refined and going through affliction and I am sure that I am part of the family of God, then I must take the affliction as a sign that God is trying to get my attention and cause a change in the direction of my life. Spiritual inertia happens and can only be dynamically overcome by the acceptance of Jesus and a submission to the will of God. When we ask God to show us what needs to be changed in our lives and we allow the Holy Spirit to send us in the right direction then God will remove the affliction when we are in a right relationship with Jesus. After all Jesus said that we are to take up our own cross and follow Him.

To me it is clear that the true mission of every church including Peachtree Baptist is to seek and to save the lost sinners that includes everybody that has not confessed that Jesus is the only way to come to God.

It is also possible to grieve the Holy Spirit by not following His leadership and by continually acting against the purposes that are laid out for those that have confessed that Jesus is Lord. Could it be that the Holy Spirit abandons the church that is not following the purpose that Jesus set for His church? What happens when the Holy Spirit steps away from His leadership of any Christian? (The Holy Spirit will never completely abandon the elect of God but the actions of Christians and even churches can cause the Holy Spirit to grieve and step away from believers for a season if they continue to follow the wrong path. See Ephesians 4:30- 31, "And do not grieve the Holy Spirit with whom you were sealed for the day of redemption. Get rid of all bitterness, rage, and anger, brawling and slander along with evcry form of malice.") When the Holy Spirit steps away from any church, attendance starts to drop, the resources of the church are diminished, and the spiritual life of the church loses its sweetness. Has that happened to the church that you attend? If it has then there is the need for a revival.

Chapter 17
Hard times in Jerusalem.

While Mark and Levi continued to work on the good news of Jesus ministry before His crucifixion, and after His resurrection and ascension, the Roman occupation of Jerusalem continued to cause great hardship among the Jewish population. The hardship was again blamed on the Christians. This time it was the leaders of the religious group of Pharisees that started to cause trouble for the Christians. Christians were attacked in the streets and this in turn caused the Roman soldiers to act swiftly and harshly against both the Jewish zealots who saw the Christians as a group that were disrupting the traditions of the Jewish religion and the Christians that remained in Jerusalem.

Nothing was good for the Jews either. By 70 AD a group of Jewish rebels occupied the hilltop fortress called Masada. Another group of Pharisees took up positions in Jerusalem and temporarily drove the Romans out of the city. As a result, the Romans withdrew from the city, but then began a siege of Jerusalem. This is the time referred to as the First Jewish-Roman war that lasted from 66 AD until 70 AD.

At first the inhabitants of Jerusalem supported the Jewish zealots. As the siege continued life in the city became more and more difficult. The Pharisees burned the dwindling food supply to cause the Jewish fighters to become even more desperate and to find a way to defeat the Roman Legions that by now surrounded the city. As the siege works of the Romans progressed on a daily basis the Jewish and Christian population took to the sewers and other underground passages to escape the city.

Eventually the Romans breached the outer walls of Jerusalem and began to attack the inner parts of the city. A group of Jewish inhabitants gathered all the historical documents that told of the genealogy of the people and took them to the Temple complex even though it still laid in ruins, in order to keep these records, form the hands of the Romans who were seeking to commit genocide. The Romans attacked the Jews and anyone that they came across as they ransacked the city.

The battles around the city of Jerusalem raged and the city's defenders became more desperate. The last stand of the Jewish residents caused them to gather at the Temple mount and there to fight to the last man. The Romans were enraged, and a blood bath started. The buildings around the Temple that were mainly dwelling apartments were set on fire. The Romans killed everyone in sight and blood and gore poured down the steps of the ruins of the Temple. The fire from the adjoining buildings spread to the Temple and before long everything that could burn caught fire including the historical records that the Jews had hoped to save from the Romans.

During all of the carnage Mark took his family and escaped the blood-soaked city. Because he was a Roman citizen and could pass through the Roman siege works unquestioned by the soldiers, Mark and his family were able to escape to a village outside the walls of Jerusalem. Mark was also able to persuade Levi and some of the other Christians to escape through the old secret passages that ran under the streets of Jerusalem. Once free from the city the Christians disbursed and hid in the adjoining countryside until they could travel as far away from Jerusalem, the Romans, and the Jewish zealots as possible.

After the fall of the city of Jerusalem the Romans under General Lucius Flavius Silva laid siege to the hilltop fortress of Masada, and this temporarily diverted the attention of the Romans away from Jerusalem. The Jewish and Christian population that were able to travel began to leave Judea and disperse as far away from the harshness of the Romans as possible. The time came for Mark and Rachel to also depart and find refuge.

Even though Mark enjoyed the privilege of Roman citizenship the fact that he was married to a Jewish woman and was among his wife's family made Mark a suspect in the eyes of the Roman Governor of Judea. One day Mark was summoned to the

Governor's headquarters to have a formal meeting with Lucius Flavius Silva. The two men had been acquaintances because their families held similar rank among the elite class of Rome.

At the appointed time Mark made his way to the tent from which the Governor commanded his troops and Mark was ushered into the Governor's presence. The tent that Lucius Silva occupied was very different from the great hall where Pilate had tried the case of Jesus now almost 40 years before. Mark was greeted in the typical Roman way. Lucius Silva spoke first, "*Si vales bene est, ego valeo.* (If you are well, it is good, I am well.) The men embraced as was the Roman custom, looked each other over and subconsciously evaluated each other and how each was to respond to the other man.

Lucius Silva said to himself, "What does a Roman nobleman have to do with these Palestinian dogs that are causing me so much trouble? Why is it so important for them to form this new sect of the Jewish religion. Have we not we been tolerant of their religion long enough without them stirring up trouble among their own people."

Mark on the other hand, thought to himself, "Lucius, you have become an old man right before my eyes. If you only knew the fullness of life that Jesus who was condemned to death by your predecessor could bring to you, you would let me explain who Jesus is and what His purpose in coming to this place was all about. Maybe, I will find a way to convince Lucius that Jesus came to being peace and not the hatred that is probably the reason I have been summoned to meet here." Mark thought all of this before either man began to speak.

Finally, after several moments of silence as the men thought of what to say, Lucius Silva said in a somewhat subdued voice, "Markus Arillus, it has been reported to me that you have taken a wife from among the Jewish problem makers. Is it really worth risking your status among the civilized society of Rome to have a worthless Jew as your mistress?"

Mark looked intently into the eyes of the governor and spoke with an assurance in his voice that unnerved Lucius Silva.

"It is not any of your business to question me about my wife and family, but the woman that I have married and who is the mother of our son is, like me, a believer in the gospel of Jesus who died and rose again and who sits at the right hand of the only and true God of heaven. My wife and I are together as one and neither you nor the emperor or any power on earth can separate what God has joined."

"How dare you to talk to me in that tone." Lucius Silva shot back in his own defense.

"My family is under the protection of God. We do not need to be reminded that you and the Romans that you command hold us in contempt. To me it is obvious that you hate what you fear, and it is plain to me that you fear the people of this land because they are not like you and because they have an inner belief in the only true God that you cannot comprehend." Mark said in a calm but assuring voice.

"Do you know why I have summoned you to meet me here today, Markus Aurelius? We are going to level the city of Jerusalem and the Temple that the Jews hold in such high esteem. We are going to show them once and for all time that their religion is no match for the power of the Roman legions and that they need to quit all of this insistence that they are the chosen people of your god." The general/governor said with a demeaning tone. "It is only because of your family's position that I am telling you this so you can get away from this place before the city is destroyed and all the Jewish rebels are rounded up and crucified."

"I appreciate the warning and I will pass it along to my family members that are still in the city. I must tell you that the Jewish zealots that you are fighting do not include my family. All of my family have turned their backs on their Jewish traditions and become Christians. We are not your enemy any longer. On the contrary we Christians reach out to you to accept our ways and to believe in Jesus the Christ and be saved from your sins." Mark replied to Lucius Silva.

"It is very curious to me Markus Aurelius as to why you

offer your Jesus to me. We Romans abhor these new religions. We only have tolerated these Jewish fanatics because their religion is an ancient religion that has existed from before the time that the Greeks and now the Roman Empire has ruled the world. Romans are tolerate people as long as you do not interfere with the *Pax Romana* that we bring to all people and as long as you recognize who is in control." Lucius Silva said with the assurance of the 12,000 Roman soldiers that he commanded standing behind him.

"Why really did you want to see me, governor?" Mark asked in a manner that the governor knew that Mark was growing weary of the meeting in the tent of Lucius Silva at the foot of the Masada siege works.

The siege works were being built by slave labor. Everyday hundreds of Jewish men and boys carried loads of dirt and rock from a quarry about a mile from the Romans camp and built a ramp from the floor of the desert towards the top of the rock fortress that the Jewish fighters and their families held as their last stand against the Roman legions. Day by day the people who were under siege by the Romans realized their fate was to either starve or die fighting against an unbeatable foe. Day by day the misery of the people sheltered in the hilltop fortress at Masada understood that they would soon all perish either at the hands of the Romans or by starving to death. Eventually the Jews all committed suicide rather than being overrun or starved to death. Suicide is an abomination to the Jews, but having their wives raped, and their children slaughtered before their eyes was an even greater abomination and thus, they chose the lesser of two evils.

"It is simply my intent to warn you that Jerusalem is going to be completely destroyed and everyone caught in the city when we take this action is subject to being killed when I let my soldiers loose to do their worst. I realize that you claim to be a man of peace because of your new faith so I want you out of Jerusalem before it is too late. As to your Jewish friends their time has come to an end." Lucius Silva replied in such a matter-of-fact manner that it sent a chill up Mark's spine.

"Why must there always be such cruelty and needless slaughter of the innocents as well as those who are the actual enemies of Rome? Every time Rome is on the march poor people are slaughtered and the ground is covered with the blood of those who are no real threat to the Empire. Rome is despised by the non-Roman world all because of the cruelty that Rome seems to feast on." Mark made an agonizing reply.

"Poor people may despise Rome, but it is not love or gratitude that Rome wants. What Rome wants is to put fear into the hearts of every nation, every potential rebellious leader, and every person who stands in the way of Rome. We are the masters of the world, and we want the world to cower at our feet when we march." Lucius Silva boldly pronounced.

Mark had to reflect on what he had just heard. The words that came from the governor's lips were the exact opposite of the life and teachings of Jesus that Mark was trying to live by when he had accepted Jesus as his savior. Mark thought how Jesus willingly gave His life and blood and submitted Himself to a death on a cruel cross at the hands of the Romans. Mark thought about how Jesus taught His disciples to forgive even the most serious insults and short comings of those that came into their presence. Mark thought about how Jesus even forgave the Roman soldiers who had beaten Him, spit in His face and nailed Him to the cross on which He suffered and died. All of this was the exact opposite of the words just spoken by the Roman Governor who was now about to cause the death of innocent Jewish women and children who were helpless before their Roman masters. Rome was about to commit genocide so that the world would fear them and submit to Rome.

"Governor Silva, I have heard your words and understand that the ways of Rome are no longer compatible with the life that I now wish to live. While I am still a citizen of Rome, I can no longer abide by the cruelty that Rome causes on these helpless souls. I will not take up arms against Rome, but I will speak against Roman cruelty. Me and my family will leave this place and find a place where neither Rome nor Jewish zealots have any recognition." That was all that Mark could get out before the sorrow in his spirit overwhelmed his ability to say anything more. Mark could do nothing more that walk out of the tent in which Lucius Silva directed the siege of the hilltop fortress at Masada that would soon witness the deaths of innocent women and children.

CHAPTER 18

JESUS SAID, "A NEW COMMANDMENT I GIVE YOU. LOVE ONE ANOTHER. AS I HAVE LOVED YOU, SO YOU MUST LOVE ONE ANOTHER. BY THIS EVERYONE WILL KNOW THAT YOU ARE MY DISCIPLES, IF YOU LOVE ONE ANOTHER." JOHN 13: 34.

During the time I spent as the Sunday school teacher of the older men's class at Peachtree Baptist Church it became apparent that it was my duty to love each of the men in my class and I did. Actually, I loved and still love Peachtree Baptist and pray for the church and the men I taught on a regular basis while I was their teacher. As time has drifted away my prayers are not as frequent as they once were. I moved to my sisters after an illness and then to my daughter's home in Mississippi, and then to Texas. While living with my daughter in Tishomingo County, Mississippi, I prayed for another opportunity to serve Jesus in another capacity. My prayer was soon answered, and I again taught an older men's Sunday school class for about six months.

The men at Glendale Baptist Church in Glenn, Mississippi welcomed me into their fellowship. We had a wonderful time getting to know each other and I directed my prayers for the men in the Sunday school class in my charge as their Sunday school teacher. There did not seem to be any conflicts among the men in the class and we enjoyed a sweet spirit.

The pastor at Glendale Baptist, Jon Hames, even offered to allow me to use one of the rooms at the church as an office during the week when the church was empty. I used that office to write a book while I was in Mississippi. (Damascus Road Experience, published by Mauldin Pond Press, 2021) It was apparent that the men in the class that I taught in Mississippi loved each other, and I believe that they exhibited the Christian love that Jesus commanded of His disciples in the verse that I have quoted above.

It occurred to me, to what purpose did Jesus give "This new commandment."?

I listen to the audio sermons of Charles Spurgeon on a regular basis. Pastor Spurgeon takes the position that we are not like non-Christians and that we need to strictly follow Christs commands in our lives. The command that Christians love each other, according to Jesus, is a new commandment. How is this commandment different from any other commandments that are found in the Holy Scriptures? What makes the commandment to love one another a new commandment?

After Jesus was arrested in the Garden of Gethsemane and put on trial before the Jewish Sanhedrin and then the Roman Governor Pilate, Peter denied that he knew Jesus three times before the rooster crowed. This was just as Jesus said would happen to Peter when Peter proclaimed that he would follow Jesus even to death during the last supper that the disciples ate together on that last night during the Passover in Jerusalem.

When Jesus was crucified and arose, Jesus confronted Peter after Peter returned to his employment as a fisherman. Jesus asked Peter if Peter loved Jesus three times with a different intensity in each of the three questions. Peter responded that Jesus knew all things including what was in Peter's heart and mind. Jesus knew whether Peter indeed loved Jesus. Jesus in reply told Peter to feed His sheep.

The response of Jesus to the assertion of Peter that he did love Jesus was met by a demand of Jesus to show that love by loving God's children, the followers of Jesus. Thus, the answer most certainly to the question of why Jesus commanded His followers to love one another is because that is how Jesus wants us to show our love for Him. When we love one another, we show our love of Jesus. If we love Jesus, we must love those who are in Christ.

Until Jesus came into the world the basic instinct of mankind was self-preservation. The brutality of the Roman Empire was the standard means of ensuring the preservation of the state. Raw power and the brutality of the wielding of that power was the standard by which life was measured. Crucifixion was the cruelest form of punishment for any dissenting voice directed at the Roman Empire. The cruelty of the cross was intended to be so severe that no one in the land would willingly face the punishment that the Roman Government meted out. While also severe, the punishment of stoning by the Jews was also intended to intimidate and punish those who broke the religious standards of the Jews and especially the standards imposed on the people by the Pharisees.

When Jesus said that He was giving a new commandment it was in the context of what had gone on in the world up to that point in time. When Jesus came into the world it was a total change in the mindset of men that caused brutality to be replaced with love. At best the Roman Government and the Jewish religious leaders had no idea of what Jesus was commanding as a new view of the personality of God. The perception of God as an angry and vengeful force was replaced by a loving and caring God who was willing to forgive sin as long as Jesus was willing to give his body and blood in atonement for those who were called and accepted the invitation of Jesus to love one another.

How has the new commandment of Jesus manifested itself in the world?

Go back to the preface of this book. Remember what Pastor Vernon McGee said in response to the letter that he read on his radio program. "Is the world getting better or is it getting worse?" McGee's response still resonates in my mind. The world is getting better and worse even as I write these pages. The new commandment has made a great difference in the lives of Christians since Jesus gave this new commandment as he faced the cruelty of Roman crucifixion. On the other hand, brutality has not ceased and in even this modern world the cruelty on men is still evident throughout the so called Christian and non-Christian world.

As a Christian I must keep the commandments of Jesus because He is the focus of my life. I must always keep my mind on Jesus and His Kingdom. (Seek first the Kingdom of God and His righteousness, and all these will be given to you as well. Mathew 6:33). If I wander too far from the love of Christ I lose my focus, and I am sure to lose the ability to influence those around me to being about the love of God in my walk with my Savior.

On the other hand, failure to love our brothers and sisters in Christ acts as a great warning to the world. A failure to believe in Jesus and to follow Him leads to destruction and great sorrow. It seems that great sorrow is always close in this age. Jesus' promises that He will preserve those who are true believers in order to underscore God's faithfulness. God is faithful to save all who sincerely accept Jesus as their savior and God promises to keep them as His own. Jesus at John 17:6-25, prays for His followers including those who will become His followers after that current group of believers (His disciples) had passed from this world. In His prayer Jesus says that God will keep the faithful and bring them to heaven to manifest in the glory that God has given to Jesus from before the beginning of time.

What does the preservation of the elect mean? It means that when you have sincerely accepted Jesus as "the Way, the Truth, and the Life", you will never lose the grace of God in your life. Does it mean smooth sailing thereafter? No, it is obvious that Christians suffer from all sorts of illnesses, injuries, heartaches and persecutions. Christians have been martyred, jailed, banished and worse from the time that Jesus made His prayer until the present, but Christians have persevered and are still doing the work of Christ in this world. It means that He will never leave us or forsake us (Hebrews 13:5) and He will find a means for the elect to endure until we meet Jesus face to face in the place He has prepared for His elect.

However, it is still evident that the world has rejected the love of Christ, and it seems that those who follow Christ may have become a minority. (A feeling that many Christians' experiences. Christians should understand that the feeling of isolation is exactly what Satan wants us to think.) This has been the case ever since Jesus was present with His disciples. He reminded His followers that as He was rejected by the world that the world would also reject His elect, and it has.

A word of warning- Christians are not victims. We have been cautioned in advance by Jesus, that we will always be the cause of dissention among non-Christians. It is the life that we must submit to as followers of Christ. Those who reject Christ are at enmity with believers because they hope that Christians are wrong about God and the kingdom of heaven. Christians are seen as a reminder that the world is corrupt and will end when Christ returns to call the elect into heaven. Non-Christians cannot accept that they may be wrong and face eternal destruction. The truth about God and Christ causes many non-believers to not only reject God but also to hate those who profess to believe.

If you are a part of God's elect and profess that Jesus resides within you and that you are in Jesus, you must expect to be either overtly hated or at least looked at with skepticism by even close family relations. (I personally have firsthand experienced outright hostility because of my belief in Jesus. I consider this a badge of honor because Jesus said, "Blessed are you when people insult you, persecute you and falsely say all kinds of evil against you because of me. Rejoice and be glad because great is your reward in heaven..." Matthew 5:11-12.)

On the other hand, if you are not on the receiving end of hostility you may not be portraying the true message of the Gospel by your actions or words that is indicative of the life of a Christian. If you continually compromise your faith by your actions and express something other than the love that Jesus commanded believers to give even our enemies, then you may need to reconsider how you are living out your commitment to being a person who has taken up his/her cross to follow Christ.

One of the most fearful portions of the Sermon on the Mount is found at Matthew 7:21 where Jesus says, "Not everyone who says to me Lord, Lord will enter the kingdom of heaven, but only the one who does the will of the Father who is in heaven. Many will say on that day, 'Lord, Lord did we not prophesy in your name and in your name drive out demons and, in your name, Preform many miracles?' Then I will tell them plainly, 'I never knew you. Away from me, you evildoers.'"

To me it is without question that there are many who profess to be Christians but who do not completely follow the commandments that Jesus gave to His followers. So how then do we know if we are truly following the commandments of Jesus? It is in the way the world reacts to us as believers. If the world hates us, we may be on the right track. It does not mean that just because you are hated you are saved. You may be hated because you are a despicable person. It is only when you are hated because of your faith in Jesus that you are given the assurance that you are acting in a manner consistent with your faith. When Jesus is all sufficient in your life and your reliance on Jesus is the cause of the world's enmity, then you can rejoice in the hatred of worldly people.

As I am writing this portion of this book the war in Ukraine and the terrorist attack on Israel has taken place. There have been brutal attacks on innocent civilians both in Ukraine and Israel and now also in Gaza. Many people have been killed by senseless acts of terror. Yes, Pastor McGee, the world is getting worse.

After World War II, the world seemed to acknowledge that there should be humanitarian rules of conflict that would minimize the horror of war on innocent populations even in the countries that were and are at war with each other. It is evident that the humanitarian rules that most civilized countries (including Russia, and Israel) agreed to after the great losses of World War II (that resulted in the founding of the United Nations) and the application of these rules of war by the members of the United Nations have been disregarded. Today terror is used as a weapon directed at innocent populations for the sole purpose of causing fear and suffering. More than 1200 civilians were massacred by the Hamas terrorist. Some of the slaughtered were at an outdoor festival in the early hours of the attack on the southern sections of Israel. The mutilated bodies of dead Israelis were paraded through the streets of Gaza and cheered by the Palestinians and other Arab groups. On college campuses across the United States anti-sematic attacks on Jewish students have become widespread. All in the name of hatred.

In a small town in Ukraine, a Russian missel attack on a non-military village cafe caused the instant deaths of innocent women and children for no other purpose than to cause suffering and fear. It is feared that Israel has weaponized famine and lack of humanitarian aid to innocent people living in Gaza.

People who love God do not do the things that Russia and Hamas terrorist or even the Israeli government have carried out over these past months. Has the world reverted to the brutality that was carried on before Christ gave His commandment to love even your enemies? The answer is a resounding NO. The brutality of the world has never ceased since before Jesus told His followers that He was giving a new commandment. The answer is unquestionably that Christians have not been success-ful in spreading the message of the Gospel in such a manner that the love of Christ has penetrated the hearts and minds of even a significant portion of the world's population.

To go back to the question posed by the letter writer shared by Pastor McGee on his radio program. "Is the world getting better or worse?" I must agree with Pastor McGee. The world is still as bad as it has always been. However, Christians are not supposed to be citizens of this world but are only sojourning in the world while on their way to heaven.

Where will this all end? The brutality of the world will come to an abrupt halt upon Christ's return to this world. One day a trumpet will sound, and Christ will call His elect to Him-self in heaven. The world will self-destruct, and non-believers will be cast into a lake of burning fire to suffer for eternity. Christians will watch as this destruction occurs while safe and in the presence of Jesus.

CHAPTER 19

LEVI RELOCATES TO A LAND FAR FROM JERUSALEM AND RECEIVES A LETTER FROM PETER.

Levi received a letter that he recognized was in the handwriting of his friend Mark who had become one of the men that often accompanied his brother in Christ. "Peter an apostle of Jesus Christ, To God's elect, exiles scattered throughout the provinces of Pontius, Galatia, Cappadocia, Asia, and Bithynia, who have been chosen according to the foreknowledge of God the Father, through the sanctifying work of the Spirit, to be obedient to Jesus Christ and sprinkled with His blood: Grace and peace be yours in abundance." (1 Peter 1: 1-2.)

When the Roman legions were surrounding Jerusalem, Mark along with his family pleaded with their Christian brothers and sisters to leave Jerusalem because of the pending destruction of the city and the terrorism of the Roman soldiers. Lucious Flavious Silva the acting governor and commander of the Roman legions sent to Judea, revealed the Romans plans to Mark when Mark was summoned to the Governor's tent just before the total destruction of the Holy City. Many of the Christian escaped, including the apostles of Jesus that had remained in Jerusalem after the savior's resurrection.

After their desperate escape the Christian church of Jerusalem dispersed to lands as far away from the Romans as was possible. Levi accompanied Mark as far as Antioch. The two men and Mark's family had become very close to becoming lifelong companions except for the desire of Mark to return to Rome for the purpose of attending to Paul. Paul by 72 AD had again been arrested for preaching the gospel in the Roman province that later became known as Spain. Paul was returned to Rome and remained in prison until his death sentence was carried out after a long imprisonment.

Mark again joined Peter in Rome, but it was not long after Marks return to his hometown that the Christian church was again under constant attack by the Roman authorities. Because Mark was a Roman citizen, he could freely walk the streets while the non-Roman members of the Christian church remained in hiding and kept themselves out of the scrutiny of the authorities. Peter was also in Rome trying to see what, if anything, he could do to assist Paul before his pending execution.

Then Peter was arrested. Peter wrote to the Christian churches that are described as elect exiles, scattered throughout Asia and Bithynia (the present-day part of northern Turkey). Peter wanted to assure the followers of Christ (recall our discussion of the doctrine of the elect) that even while they were being persecuted for their commitment to Jesus that they were bound to also share in the suffering of Jesus. Peter who was also suffering at the hands of the Romans encouraged his fellow Christians to consider the suffering that they were facing as a badge of honor.

By the time that Peter was arrested by the Romans, Levi had made his way to the shores of Lake Tuz in northern Galatia (now northern Turkey) and was living with other Christians that had formed a settlement on the coast of the pink colored lake. The fellowship of Christians supported Levi as he wrote the story of Jesus that he had begun before he and the others were forced to leave Jerusalem. The community of Christians depended on each other and lived as the Christians in Jerusalem lived when the church there first started. The fellowship kept everything in common and saw to the welfare of all the members of their community. They shared meals together. They cared for the elderly as by now Levi had become, among their group and met together and prayed for the needs of the elect and for the salvation of those who had not found the peace of Christ.

Close to the Christian community were other groups who looked on the Christians with skepticism and suspicion. Sometimes outright hatred spilled out from the neighboring communities and the Christians were attacked by their non-believing neighbors. The non-believers felt that they were pleasing the Roman government or were pleasing God when they attacked the Christian community. After all the Christians did not follow the Jewish orthodoxy nor believe that the Roman emperor was a god.

For their part the Christians lived quietly and kept to themselves. They were good sheep herders and fishermen and prospered. Because the Christians were obviously blessed by God in their shepherding and fishing, that also made their non-believing neighbors jealous and caused further distrust and animosity between Christians and non-Christians.

When Levi received a copy of Peter's letter it filled his heart with joy and spurred him on to finish the book that he had started when he met Mark in Jerusalem. Levi went about his work with the assurance that he was being led by the Holy Spirit. Levi felt as if the Holy Spirit sat next to him as he carefully arranged every word that came to him as he prepared the manuscript.

When Jesus was still in His earthly ministry Levi sat at Jesus feet and listened to the words that Jesus spoke. Every word from the teachers' lips brought both wonder and questions about the meaning of the messages that Jesus preached. It was not until after Jesus promised to send the Holy Spirit to those He left in the world, that His disciples realized that the words of Jesus would be made manifest and that their understanding would be made clearly known through the inspiration of the Spirit of God. With the inspiration of the Holy Spirit, Levi was able to write the words spoken by Jesus.

Levi followed Jesus for almost 3 years and was amazed at the crowds that seemed to spring up from almost nowhere when Jesus entered a village or even when He stood beside the Sea of Galilee. Levi and the other disciples often talked among themselves and talked about what they knew of where Jesus had come from and what His life had been before they were called to become His followers. They met some of Jesus's family and often talked to His mother, Mary, and heard the story of how she was visited by an angel and by the Spirit of God before she was married to her husband Joseph. Mary claimed that God was the Father of Jesus. Mary told the story of the trip to Bethlehem and the visit of the men from the east who brought gifts to celebrate the arrival of the Massiah. Mary described how she and Joseph, and Jesus when He was still a child, escaped to Egypt when King Herod killed the male children that were the same age as Jesus in the surrounding areas of Bethlehem because of his rage that someone else would be the king of the Jews.

Levi recalled the stories and the exact words that Jesus spoke as he wrote the words that the Holy Spirit prompted. If Levi had not been with Jesus and heard His words, seen the crowds, witnessed the healing of thousands of sick and demon possessed men, women and children he thought that the story would have been unbelievable. But he was there and what he wrote was just as he witnessed it. Levi wrote only what he knew to be the truth about Jesus, and he wrote the truth so that all who read his account of the life, death, resurrection and assentation of Jesus could have faith and believe that Jesus is the son of the living God.

Levi especially wanted the message of Jesus to resonate with the Jewish people who were now scattered throughout the known world. Levi took great care to note how Jesus fulfilled the scriptures of the Old Testament prophets. He provided the genealogy of Jesus that he had gathered from the records of the Jewish people before the records were destroyed by the Romans when they completely destroyed Jerusalem in an effort to bring an end to the Jewish and Christian religions.

Levi carefully recounted the story of Jesus's mother and of her husband Joseph as they traveled to Bethlehem. Levi told how the angel of the Lord appeared to Joseph in a dream and told Joseph to accept the child and name him Jesus. Levi recalled the words of the Prophet Isaiah who prophesied that a virgin would conceive a child by the spirit of God and the child would be called Emanuel (which means God is with us). Levi told how Jesus was born in Bethlehem and how the family remained there. He recounted the story of the visit of the Magi (wise men from the east) first to King Herod in Jerusalem, and then to Bethlehem by following a star that led to the exact spot where Jesus the Messiah could be found.

Levi, who was also called Matthew in the Greek speaking world, told how the Magi brought gifts fitting for a king to Jesus and how the Magi were warned not to share the location of Jesus with King Harod through a message sent in a dream. Joseph also was warned in a dream, as Levi revealed, to take Mary and Jesus to Egypt because Harod planned to kill Jesus. Again, Levi explained how the prophesy of the Old Testament prophet Jeremiah was fulfilled when he wrote that there would be weeping and mourning in Ramah (the Palestinian name for Bethlehem) as a result of the killing of male children by Harod when he found out that Jesus had been born.

Mary told Levi and the other disciples that her husband, who had since died of an illness but had rejected Jesus's offer to heal the man who helped raise Him, had a dream in which an angel told Joseph to move to Egypt because of the danger from Harod's outrage. Mary told how the family came back to Judea but decided to travel on to Nazareth because Harod's son Archelaus had become Harod's replacement. Levi also told how the move to Nazareth fulfilled the prophesy that Jesus would be called a Nazarene.

Levi was busy putting Jesus's story on papyrus scrolls and was in contact with the Christians in Antioch on which he relied to copy the manuscript and distribute his writings to other Greek speaking Jewish Christian congregations. Unfortunately, Jewish non-Christians also began to read what Levi wrote and controversy between non-Christian and Christian Jews started to break out in the region in which the Christians and Jews dispersed after the fall of Jerusalem.

The non-Christian Jews blamed their fate on the Christians, forgetting that the Pharisee and Jewish zealots had started the fight with the Romans that led to the scattering of both the Christian and non-Christian population of Judea. Additionally, both the Christian and non-Christian Jews began to notice that non-Jewish Christians were more numerous than the Jewish Christians. This fact was also a point of grievance with the non-Christian Jews even though they did not accept Jesus as the Christ they were still angry that non-Jews were accepted into the Christian congregations.

Soon hostility became apparent between the Jewish communities and the Christian communities and Levi found himself the center of the debate between the two factions.

"Jesus followed the Jewish law, and the Christian congregations must follow Jesus's example and submit themselves to the discipline to which those who follow the law must adhere." One of the members of the community to which Levi belonged said.

Levi thought for a while before he replied, "Jesus did tell us that if we wanted to be considered great in the Kingdom of heaven that each of us must strive to fulfill even the tiniest part of the law and that our righteousness had to exceed that of the Pharisees."

"Then you agree with me that the Gentile brethren must adhere to the Jewish law and customs that we have followed all of our lives?" argued the Jewish man who was engaging Levi in this conversation.

Levi again was slow to answer. Then he thoughtfully replied, "The words of Jesus speak for themselves. It is not for me to add any meaning to what Jesus said. It is my solemn duty as a man who was with Jesus and who heard Him say the words that He said to do nothing more than to report, as accurately as God gives me the ability, the exact words that Jesus spoke. It is up to you to hear those words and to draw your own conclusion as to their meaning as the Holy Spirit gives you understanding."

The man who initiated the conversation then asked, "When Jesus spoke these words, did He not later expound on the meaning of what He said?"

"Jesus spoke and I listened to every word that He said. I can only report what I heard and nothing more. If you are asking me to tell you what I believe Jesus meant by the words that He spoke, I must tell you that I have reported what Jesus said and nothing more. The Holy Spirit called those exact words to my mind. I can say nothing further than that." Levi replied with as much gravity as he could muster.

"So do you agree with me or not that Christians should follow the law of the Hebrew people if they want to follow Jesus?" the man continued to ask.

Levi did not reply directly to that question, but instead asked several questions, "Were you there when Jesus told us that He 'had not come into the world to abolish the Law and the prophets, but He came to fulfill them?' Do you believe that Jesus accomplished exactly what He was sent into the world to do? If you believe that then believe the words that Jesus spoke and follow Him."

Chapter 20

Godliness

"Do not judge, and you will not be judged. Do not condemn, and you will not be condemned. Forgive, and you will be forgiven. Give, and it will be given to you. A good measure, pressed down, shaken together and running over, will be poured out into your lap. For with the measure you use, it will be measured to you." Luke 6: 37-38.

As Christians we are called to become godly individuals. A godly man/woman/child is a man /woman/child that takes on the attributes of God. Jesus is our model for becoming godly people. A few years ago, it became fashionable to wear bracelets with the letters "WWJD" standing for, "what would Jesus do." The bracelet was a reminder that we need to keep the ways of Jesus always on our minds as we make our ways in this earthly life.

When I became a Christian as a boy of 10 years old. My mother gave me a red-letter King James edition Bible for my birthday. It was my intent to read all the words of Jesus and to try to understand what Jesus was trying to tell me through the scriptures. Try as I might I did not learn very much about what Jesus was trying to tell me until I became older and more mature in my study of the scripture. It seems to me that the Holy Spirit reveals the scripture to Christs followers at the time that it is most appropriate for the Christian to gain understanding.

We go to church and listen to sermons and even participate in Bible study over many years and constantly find new revelation in the verses we read. As I have mentioned, I have taught a Sunday school class for many years and most times I feel that I am just starting to learn what following Jesus is all about. Last evening, I was listening to a sermon by Charles Spurgeon entitled "The Kingly Priesthood of the Saints" based on Revelations

5:10, "You have made them to our God, kings and priest, and they shall reign over the earth."

Spurgeon's premise is that when we accept Christ as our savior that we are adopted into the family of God. We are His children and thus heirs of the same royal heritage as Jesus. We have not become kings and priest fully because we have not passed from this life to the next, but we are a part of the Kingdom of God and have the right to claim our position as members of God's family. I had never considered myself as a king or a priest, but there in the scripture is that assertion that I have the heirship of Christ and that I am of the kingly and priestly family.

Jesus, in the genealogy in the first chapter of Gospel of Matthew, is presented as being of the royal blood line of King David and also presented as a priest. Jesus is able to approach God because He is the son of God and is a priest after the order of Melchizedek. See Hebrews 5:5-10. Because we have the same heirship as Jesus when we become believers, we inherit the authority of Jesus.

Where will that authority take us?

We must look at the way Jesus displayed His authority. Read again the verses that I have quoted from Luke 6:37-38. How you go about judging, condemning, forgiving and giving will be how you will be judged, condemned, forgiven and given to. Jesus did not judge anyone severely or condemn anyone even as He was dying on the cross and He was most forgiving even to those who knew not what they were really doing. Jesus gave everything to those who He loved, and He loved everybody. Therefore, if you want to be a godly person do not be judgmental, do not condemn, be forgiving and be generous in giving to others.

The point that I am trying to make is that I have read and studied the New Testament for many years and have taught Sunday school lessons too but have not considered (until now) that because of my relationship with Christ that I take on the same heirship as Christ as a member of the family of God. What an awesome blessing. However, as we know, with every blessing there is also an awesome responsibility. A king and a priest serve the congregation to which the king and priest belongs. May I fulfill my responsibilities to the glory and honor of God and His only begotten Son!

Godliness is therefore acting as closely as possible to the way that God acts towards us. Consider the way God treats us. He gave His only begotten son to suffer and die in our place. God so loved the world that He sent Jesus to become a substitute for me and to pay my debt to God for my sinful self. God listens to my prayers and responds to my prayers. God gives to me my daily bread and is my good Shepard even when I walk in the shadow of death. These are some of the attributes of God and I am sure that you can and will think of more qualities of God that if we followed, we would become godlier people.

In order to be godly people, it is important to consider who God is and how He treats His people. When we see who God is and how He deals with us we can start to become godlier. When we become godlier, then we will see more clearly who God is and become even more godly. When we finally meet God and look carefully into Jesus' face, we will become perfect because we will take on the attributes of God fully. This is how we as Christians should live our lives, constantly evaluating whether we are becoming godlier and thus becoming more perfect.

CHAPTER 21
LEVI IS CONFRONTED BY ROMANS AND JEWS.

After the fall of Jerusalem both Christians and the non-Christian Jewish people of Judea dispersed. Most of the Judeans took their belongings and their families to places as far away from the Romans as possible. Some went eastward to Babylon, some to the Mediterranean Islands of Crete, Cyprus, Malta, Sicily and others. Some of the population went to Antioch and some further in land into the provinces of Pontus, Galatia, Cappadocia, Asia and Bithynia. Levi and his family and friends formed a Christian community in the mountains that isolated them from the Roman garrisons and the Roman authorities. Levi settled in Galatia near Lake Tuz in a picturesque but somewhat isolated place where Levi could continue his writing and minister to the needs of his Christian flock.

The community in which Levi found himself was a model of Christian love and fellowship. All the members of the congregation, and there were more than a handful, were of similar mind and respected each other. They lived in harmony and followed Jesus commands to love one another. The communities that were close but not too close to the Christians were people who had dispersed from Jerusalem but were not believers in Jesus Christ and there were also non-Jewish people who considered themselves to be under the authority of Rome and adhered to the customs of the native people of that region and the various religions practiced by the Romans and the local population.

Among the native people were those who were pantheist and who worshiped the Greek gods as did the Romans. The Jewish population of the surrounding communities kept the Jewish traditions and celebrated Jewish holidays. Because many of the Christians were also of the Jewish heritage, they also continued the Jewish traditions. Into this mix of customs, religions and traditions Levi and the followers of Christ lived their lives and prospered.

Levi continued to write the story of Jesus as the Spirit of God gave him the very words that flowed from his writing instrument. Levi wrote on scrolls of sheep skin and had the scrolls delivered to the Christian community in Antioch where the scrolls were copied with great skill and intense labor onto pages of papyrus, re-copied and distributed to other Christian congregations in Egypt, Syria, Rome, Babylon and everywhere there was a known Christian community. The process of writing, shipping the written scrolls to Antioch, re-copying the scrolls onto pages, binding the pages into book form, was to say the least, labor intense, but the hand of God was evident in the process and the book of Matthew was taking the form of the Gospel story that Levi, but most importantly The Holy Spirit intended.

Levi wrote the exact words of Jesus as He taught His disciples from the hill side in Galilee. Jesus called His disciples as He sat and said,

"Blessed are the poor in spirit, for theirs is the Kingdom of heaven.

"Blessed are those who mourn, for they will be comforted.

"Blessed are the meek, for they shall inherit the earth.

"Blessed are those who hunger and thirst for righteousness, for they will be filled.

"Blessed are the merciful, for they will be shown mercy.

"Blessed are the poor in heart, for they will see God.

"Blessed are the peacemakers, for they will be called children of God.

"Blessed are those who are persecuted because of righteousness, for theirs is the Kingdom of heaven.

"Blessed are you when people insult you, persecute you and falsely say all kinds of evil against you because of me. Rejoice and be glad, because great is your reward in heaven, for in the same way they persecuted the prophets who were before you."

While Levi was not personally present at the time and place

that Jesus taught the disciples that were called before Levi was called, he personally heard Jesus say those exact words on other occasions and was told by Peter about the setting and place where Jesus first said the profound words that later became known as the "Beatitudes."

Levi wrote as the Holy Spirit directed his mind and even his hand at times.

There came a time however, that Levi was stopped from writing. Non-Christian Jews in the communities surrounding the Christian community in which Levi lived and worked on his manuscript began a time of confrontation with the Christians that included Jewish and non-Jewish settlers in the shores of Lake Tuz in Galatia.

One evening a group of non-Christian Jews visited the community where Levi lived. The leader of the group of non-Christian Jews appeared in the center of the village and in a loud and menacing voice shouted, "Jewish people of this village come to the center of this village and unite with your Jewish brothers and renounce your non-Jewish people. It has been ordained by God that the Jews of the world are God's chosen people, and we should not mingle with Gentiles."

At first there was no movement among the people of the village. Then after several minutes Levi came to the center of the village. By this time Levi had grown old and had difficulty walking without the aid of a cane and also without the assistance of a younger woman who usually accompanied Levi when he left the hut in which Levi worked, took his meals and slept. Levi was known to the people of the region as being a follower of Jesus and of having been with Jesus while He was in His earthly ministry. The leader of the Jews who had called out in the village center was well aware of who Levi was and was also aware of Levi's standing among the Christians in Galatia.

The leader of the Jews who had called out the people in Levi's village, was known as Yehuda. He scowled at Levi and spoke, "You Christians are blaspheming the one who had an unspeakable name and are condemned by the law of Moses.

You and your Christian believers according to the Law of Moses should be stoned."

"We have caused you no trouble, Yehuda. We are peaceful and respectful of the laws of this country and intend only to live our lives as God has directed us." Levi replied to the Jewish leader in the Aramaic language that all who were gathered spoke.

"We are beyond the laws of this country. We are bound by the sacred laws handed down to us by Moses and interpreted by the Scribes and Pharisees who studied the ancient Scriptures. The meaning of the law is set out for us. The true meaning of the law handed down to Moses on Mount Sinia by the Unnamed One is for the Jewish people and not for you Christians." Yehuda shouted so everyone in the village could hear his voice.

"Every one of us in this village loves and respects the law that Moses received from the Holy Father, but we also have heard the words of Jesus the only begotten son of the everlasting God. We are committed to keep the commandments of God as given to us by our savior Jesus who you persecuted and who was executed at your insistence by the Romans." Levi replied with a reverent but steadfast voice that caused Yehuda to tear his clothes and come near to Levi with his fists clinched and his face reddened in anger.

Levi stepped back as Yehuda came near and said, "We have no quarrel with the law of Moses. We are devout people and live by faith in our Lord Jesus who is the Christ and dwells at the right hand of the living God and who acts as our intercessor and protector. We have no reason to be anything but good neighbors to all the people around us. We are peaceful and kind to all because Jesus commanded us to live our lives that way."

Yehuda would have none of the reconciliation that Levi offered and instead became even more outraged. He shouted, "What you say is blasphemy and by all that is holy I call on all truly Jewish men to denounce this Jesus of yours and to bring an end to this perversion."

Yehuda picked up a rock and was ready to smash Levi's

head, but before he could act on his impulse, he was stopped by an unseen force that caused him to fall on his knees before Levi and drop the rock that was in his hand. Levi slowly walked over to Yehuda and helped him to his feet. Yehuda no longer was able to utter a word. Levi said, "Go in peace."

The people in the village who saw2 and heard all that happened on rushed to Levi and lifted him on their shoulders and carried him to his hut. One of the men in the group asked Levi, "What just happened?"

Levi calmly said, "What you just saw was a miracle and if I had not seen many other miracles while I was with Jesus, I would not have been able to tell you what just occurred. When I was with Jesus, miracles were happening every day. When Jesus spoke, people were healed. Jesus commanded Saten to release his evil hold on the lives of men, people were set free. Even when Jesus commanded the wind and the sea to be still, they obeyed. The Spirit of our Lord Jesus is more powerful than the will of men and He will protect us against the forces of evil in this world."

After the events that took place that evening in the small but growing Christian village by Lake Tuz the people of the village had courage to speak up on behalf of their belief that Jesus was the Christ and He through their good works was ready to seek and to save the lost. While there was much to be concerned about, the Christians had courage and prospered, and the non-Christian Jews kept their distance.

Then a few days later the Roman soldiers arrived. The Roman Imperial government sent emissaries to the towns and villages with an edict from Rome that all people would acknowledge that Domitian, who by then had become emperor of Rome, was a god and that all the world should acknowledge that Domitian was the deity to whom they should pay homage. Every person had to bow and recite that Domitian was god and swear allegiance to him. The penalty for refusal to swear allegiance to the Roman Emperor was at first a monetary penalty. If the person continued to refuse to swear that Domitian was god they faced prison, a beating or even death.

The year was 84 AD when the Romans arrived at the village by Lake Tuz where Levi and the Christians lived. The Romans arrived shortly after Levi and the Christian churches received the letter from Peter (now known as 1 Peter). Peter's letter offered courage to the Christians and spoke of how the Christians should live in a world that would reject their place as members of the family of God. Peter admonished the Christians to whom he was writing, to live exemplary lives so that the Roman authorities could find no moral fault in the way they conducted themselves. Peter told the Christians to obey the authorities including the emperor and the governor sent to govern them.

On the other hand, Domitian had an authoritarian agenda that required personal allegiance to his authoritarian form of governance. Domitian was well loved by the professional army and citizens who felt that they should be kept in place by a strong authority. After all Rome ruled the world and Domitian was the Emperor of Rome. The Senate despised Domitian because he further eroded the Republic and the democratic principles on which Rome had functioned.

The demand for all to pledge personal loyalty to the person of Domitian became a problem for the Christians who only worshiped Jesus.

One day Roman soldiers marched into the village where Levi and his congregation of Christians lived and shared their lives together.

The Centurian in charge of the soldiers was a large and fully muscled man who stood a head taller in height than the tallest man in his command. The Centurian also had a sense of authority surrounding him. His voice was strong and demanded attention. The Centurian spoke Aramaic and called the village to attention and sent his men throughout the village to make sure that everyone in the village was in attendance when the Centurian spoke.

"By order of the Governor and his worship the emperor

Domitian, you are commanded to swear allegiance to Domitian and declare that Domitian is the god of this land. Each person in this village shall form a line and one by one give their name to the clerk that now sits in the center of this village. Then before me and all the people here you shall swear that Domitian is God and that you will be loyal to him and to Rome." This order was given with the authority of the soldiers that now surround the village.

The people began to form a line in the street, Then Levi approached the Centurian and held out his arms and spoke. "Brothers you are welcome to our humble village. We will cause no trouble for we are peaceful and meek and only want you to see that we live exemplary lives doing good in everything and treating everyone with respect. There is one command, however, that you have made that we cannot follow. We only worship God and His son Jesus. We will always keep the peace of our community and will not disobey the commands of the Governor or the Emperor except we cannot worship Domitian because it would be against our belief in God. Our God demands that we have no other God but Jehovah."

The Centurian was not pleased with this development. In other Christian communities to which the Centurian was sent the Christian population had lined up and swore loyalty to the emperor whether they actually in their heart believed that Domitian was a deity. In fact, very few Christians from other towns or villages to which this particular Centurian had been sent refused to take a knee and acknowledge that Domitian was a god. The Centurian was perplexed and did not know exactly what to do.

Finally, the Centurian shouted with a loud and menacing voice. "We will return to this village in two days, and you will line up and one by one, kneel, and swear that Domitian is God and give your complete loyalty to him."

After that short speech the Centurian barked orders to his men in Latin, and they marched back in the direction from which they had entered the village.

When the soldiers left the village all the people gathered

134

around Levi and someone spoke up and said, "What shall we do? We are afraid. These same Romans destroyed Jerusalem and slaughtered our families and friends. We thought we had moved far enough away so that we would not be bothered by the Romans again, but maybe we have not come far enough."

Everybody looked to Levi to tell them what they should do. Levi prayed. In front of the people in the village Levi got down (with the help of some of the villagers) and asked all the people to also get on their knees. Levi then in a surprisingly strong voice for his age lifted his voice to heaven, "Dear Jesus, you have loved us before we even knew you. You have come into the world and the world has rejected you and now the world has tried to give us reason to fear. We are afraid that we will not be able to endure the suffering that you endured when you took our sins on your own perfect self and died on the cross. Some of us were there when they nailed your hands and feet to that cross. Some of us were afraid then because we had been with you and did not know what would happen when the Pharisees and Romans took you away from us. We have had to repent of our fears. You have promised to preserve those who truly believe and who truly are committed to you. We are now facing persecution because we believe in you; you said that we will be blessed when this happens to us. Dear Jesus grant us faith and courage that we also may suffer as you suffered. Let our faith in you overcome our fears and let us always be faithful to you. It is in your name that we humbly ask for courage. Amen."

The people of the village were comforted by the prayer that Levi gave. Each of the villagers returned to their huts and continued to pray for strength and courage to withstand the persecution of the Romans when they returned.

Levi went back to his writing. Levi recalled the night that he and the other disciples shared the last supper with Jesus and how Jesus told them that the bread that He gave then was a symbol of His broken body and that they should eat the bread and know that Jesus was giving His body as a ransom for the sins of those who believe in Him. Likewise, Jesus took a cup of

135

wine and said," Drink from it, all of you. This is my blood of the covenant which is poured out for many for the forgiveness of sins. I tell you I will not drink from this fruit of the vine from now until that day when I drink it new with you in my Father's Kingdom."

The night Jesus was arrested, He was betrayed by one of the twelve disciples and the disciples ran and hid because of their fear. Jesus was tried by the Jewish Sanhedrin in a patently illegal trial, sent to the Roman Governor, sent to Herod, sent back to Pilate, beaten, spit on, whipped, mocked, taken to Calvery, nailed to a cross, crucified, suffered pain, and even rejection by God because Jesus took the sins of the elect on His own self. Jesus completed His mission and died. Jesus was put in a tomb and a stone sealed the entrance to the tomb. Guards were placed to secure the body, but on the third day just as Jesus told His disciples and friends He arose from the grave and walked among His friends. Levi was there when Jesus ascended into heaven to be reunited with His father and our God!

CHAPTER 22
AUTHORITARIANISM

Why do some want to rule, and some want to follow while others have the confidence to think for themselves?

In the last chapter we considered the emperor Domitian who stayed in power in Rome from 81 AD until he was assassinated in 96 AD. Domitian was an authoritarian ruler who was loved by the common people and the military but considered a tyrant by the Roman Senate and thus the well-educated population. Domitian believed that the Roman Empire was to be governed as a divine monarchy with Domitian as both the deity, the complete ruler and censor of all moral, and religious traditions of the Roman people and the world over which Rome ruled.

Domitian had complete authority over all aspects of life in Rome and he exercised his authority by micromanaging his empire. Domitian's rule was characterized by massive building projects that benefited, among others, Domitian himself.

During Domitian's reign Christians were considered to be suspicious because their beliefs were not as ancient as the Roman and Greek gods or even as ancient as the Jewish religion. Additionally, the Christians did not participate in the Roman public celebrations and held their meetings away from public observation and mostly at night. These practices made the Christians different from the ancient Roman traditions and caused the authorities to determine that Christianity was against the common beliefs of the Roman population.

While there was no general law against being a Christian each Roman Governor was free to persecute Christians based on the common traditions from which Christians deviated. Punishment for being a Christian was at the discretion of the governor of that particular province. If the governor felt that it was suspicious to be a Christian, he was free to put a Christian on trial, find the Christian guilty of treason, and execute the Christian as the governor in his discretion decided. In most cases that meant death to the Christian unless they agreed to pay homage to the emperor.

During the time that Domitian was emperor of Rome the government was under his authoritarian rule. That meant that Domitian decided what he wanted and everyone in the government carried out Domitian's orders. Rome was still considered to be a republic because there was still a Roman Senate, but the authority of the Senate was stripped away by Domitian and the Senate became a mere ceremonial body with no power to make or even enforce its own decisions. (Does this sound like a recent presidents stated agenda if re-elected?)

The world in 2024 also has several authoritarian governments. Notably Russia is under the control of an authoritarian dictator. China is controlled by an authoritarian dictator. Hungary has become authoritarian as has Turkey and Singapore. Some countries have gone from democratic governance to authoritarian regimes in a matter of an authoritarian leader rising to power very rapidly. Other countries are on the verge of authoritarian leadership, and most notably the United States has political candidates who espouse the authoritarian form of government.

From where does authoritarianism arise?

Some time ago I was listening to a radio program on public radio (now you know that I am a public radio fan and am not your ordinary radio listener- I am also a regular public television viewer) that expressed the idea that we all start out being subject to our parent's authority because they are the only ones available to take care of our needs when we are infants. We rely on our parents for almost all of our needs (until a child reaches at least 3 he/she will die if not taken care of by a competent care giver) and we come to expect that our comfort and necessities will be met by our parents. As infants we are the product of authoritarian parents and easily conform to the authoritarian control of our parents.

Authoritarian parents naturally love their children and

therefore usually look out for their child's wellbeing. It would be unnatural for a parent of a child to consider the parent's interest above the child's best interests. Until the child reaches adolescence, he/she relies on the love and nurture of parents/ caretakers to meet the needs of the child and guide them in their lives. The love of the parent for the child is just one of many needs that the parent takes care of during the childhood of their own child. Important to the relationship between parent and child as meeting the physical needs of the child is the naturel affection between parents and child. A child's world is controlled by the authority of the parents. Parents are generally benevolent and loving despots to their children.

As humans mature and reach adolescence the normal child starts to rely on peers to make decisions. This stage of human development is generally referred to as a teenage rebellion. It seems that all humans reach a point in life when we question our parents' motives in our own development. There are many books and studies that explain this process and I will not pretend to be a child psychologist and explain why during our development we go through a teenage rebellion. For now, we will just postulate that adolescence occurs as a part of human development. Adolescence is punctuated by both a physical change in the body chemistry and brain development of normal humans. Adolescence usually occurs around the 12th or 13th year in the child's development.

During adolescence, the child begins to question every decision that affects him or her. Teenage children start to want to satisfy their personal desires in the clothes they wear, the foods they eat, and the company they keep. Sometimes this leads to conflicts between parents and their children. Thus, the concept of teenage rebellion.

Through this time of rebellion, the child's parents are often confused and ask themselves, "Where did we go wrong in our parenting of our child?" Quickly it seems that each parent has forgotten the parents own development and teenage years. Thankfully the child usually transitions from the adolescent portion of their lives to young adulthood. Teenage rebellion is a period that allows the child to transition from dependance on the authoritarian benevolence of their parents into a person capable of making independent decisions and also a person who has become self-sufficient.

A mature individual can and should be capable of independent thought and able to determine whether an authoritarian figure (usually a political party or even a religious leader) is a reasonable choice as a leader. It should also be recognized that authoritarian political leaders are most often not benevolent and generally care only for their own self-interest. Unlike the parents who love their children, an authoritarian leader only wants to exercise power for the sake of his/her ability to hold on to the power they have been able to acquire.

This is where human development can lead to a breakdown that may cause a person to revert to a time in their life in which it was more convenient to rely on the authority of others to direct their life. If the person has had a difficult time in the process of becoming a mature adult, he/she may revert to seeking an authority figure to make critical decisions in that person's life. A lack of maturity and the lack of ability to make decisions based on a well-developed brain function can and often does cause a reversion to a point of human development that will lead to reliance on an authority figure who is willing to tell the underdeveloped human how to live even when the choice is obviously wrong.

Look at what happened in Fascist Spain, Nazi Germany, Fascist Italy, Communist Russia, Communist China, and Communist North Korea. Authoritarian leaders in each of the listed countries took over the governments and attempted to remain in power in that country despite the hardships caused to the general populations of each of those countries. Neither of these authoritarian regimes is punctuated by a loving leader who kept the interests of the citizens as the foremost priority of the country. Most of these regimes resulted in a breakdown of economic and political control. The authoritarian leader merely replaced a failed regime with another failed leader.

Today, even the United States is facing a challenge to the democratic principles that are the bedrock of democracy throughout the world. Political forces are at work in the United States that would severely undermine democracy. Free and fair elections are questioned for the sake of returning a would-be dictator to a position of control that would limit who and when the population can vote. The method of turning America into an authoritarian state is a big lie. The same tactic was successfully used in Nazi Germany when Hitler accused the Jewish population of all the trouble that Germany was facing after its losses during and after WWI.

Once Japan was able to escape the authoritarian government that was in Japan before World War II and become a democracy, Japan became an economic success. The same is true of South Korea and Taiwan. Germany became the powerhouse of Europe when its right-wing tendencies were held in abeyance and West Germany embraced a pro-western democracy. When East Germany eventually was able to escape the autocratic regime that was kept in place by authoritarian Russia it too was successfully integrated first into Germany and also into the European Union.

With all the successes of western-style democracy one would think that the best economic model for all modern countries would be a no-brainer. Not so fast. How soon do we forget that authoritarian (far right) political systems are subject to failure on a much greater scale than democratic political systems? Yet people seem to be easily led down the primrose path of authoritarian rule by demigods that espouse right-wing propaganda and enormous lies.

Germany is now facing a resurgence of its right-wing authoritarian traditions. Right-wing political parties have emerged in European countries. Russia, Hungary and Turkey have fallen under authoritarian rule. Is America far behind?

Further, the authoritarian governments that are in place around the world are not benevolent guardians of the welfare

141

of their own populations. Freedom of speech, freedom of the press, freedom of religion and the right to vote in a free and fair election have been taken away in authoritarian countries. A recent article in The Atlantic and in other well written publications have sounded the alarm regarding the negative impacts on the lives of the citizens of countries living under authoritarian regimes. Additionally, it is often difficult to fully understand the impact of authoritarian governance because governments limit the amount of information that is available to journalists from countries now controlled by an authoritarian government.

Lastly, but most importantly, religion is often used as a means of invoking a right-wing authoritarian political agenda. Remember that part of the story concerning the Pharisees and the destruction of Jerusalem. The fanatical Pharisees, based on their misconceived beliefs, led a rebellion that caused the total destruction of Jerusalem and the slaughter of innocent men, women and children. Today in Israel right-wing religious settlers on the west bank of the Jordan River feel free to attack Arab inhabitants in the name of Zionism and because they believe that they are fulfilling their religious beliefs about the promised land. (The issues are much more complicated than I can hope to write about in this section of this book. I can only mention that the positions of the people affected by the settlement of the West Bank by far-right religious zealots is reminiscent of the Pharisees that I have written about in previous chapters of this novel.)

In the United States the far-right (MEGA) faction of the Republican party has affiliated itself with "Evangelical Christians" and use their opposition to women's reproductive rights as a rallying point for most of their political ambitions. The Freedom Caucus of the Republican party has used a moralistic-dogmatic agenda in order to gain and retain power in the political landscape of American society. The Republicans have entered, either openly or tacitly, into a recognition that their leader Donald J. Trump (who by the way has absolutely no religious or moral compass despite his assertion that he is a Christian) will allow them to retain and expand their power within the Republican party. The far-right's agenda includes; an opposition to LGBTQ rights, limitation of voting rights, political gerrymandering to prevent anyone but their preferred candidates from having a chance to be elected and represent the interest of their constituents, an absolute ban of abortions throughout the United States, a rollback of 1. Medicare, 2. the affordable care act, 3. social security, 4. and all other provisions of President Biden's economic recovery plan because they contend that these programs and policies must be inspired by socialism.

Republicans claim that they are carrying out an agenda that is based on their belief in the Bible. My reading of the Holy Scriptures places before me the commandment of Jesus at Matthew 7:1 "Do not judge, or you will be judged. For in the same way, you judge others, you will be judged, and with the measure you use, it will be measured to you."

Likewise, the far- right also has a religious fervor about gun ownership. It seems to me that according to the far-right, the right to possess a gun is so fundamental to them that it also takes on a religious dimension. In other words, gun ownership is an idle the breaks the second of the Ten Commandments, "You shall not make for yourself an image of anything in heaven above or on the earth beneath or in the waters below. You shall not bow down to them or worship them......" It seems that many in the United States worship at the altar of gun rights.

The AR-15 assault rifle has become the weapon of choice for those bent on mass killings. The AR-15 was developed to become the standard battle weapon used by the United States in all major combat operations (the AR-15 which is a semi-automatic weapon was renamed the M-16 which is fully automatic by the US military). The weapon can transition from simi-automatic to fully automatic settings and was designed to give American combat soldiers superior fire power when in combat. The AR-15 is widely sold in America and regularly is seen as the weapon used by those who have committed mass murder. The AR-15 is also widely available to anyone who can pass the background check required by gun sellers and who can pony up the cost of purchase. It had been reported that there are approximately 15 million AR-15s owned in the United States. The price of the AR-15 ranges from $500 to $2000. The bullet holding clip of this assault rifle holds 30 rounds of ammunition, but the magazine can be modified to hold 100 bullets. The conservative super majority of the Supreme court has just approved the sale of a bump stock feature on the AR-15. That feature makes the weapon a machine gun capable of killing quickly. Recall what happened in Los Vegas last year when 100 persons were killed and 600 were injured at a country music event when the shooter used an AR-15 equipped with a bump stock.

This brings us back to the idea of authoritarianism. Under most circumstances, authoritarian leaders seize on topics and policies that are supported by the lesser educated population. Trump when he first announced that he was running for the office of president of the United States told the public that he was going to stop the rapist, drug dealing Mexican hoards from entering the United States by building a great wall across the Mexican border with the United States and by making the Mexican government pay for the wall.

Trump played on the fears of uneducated people by making a promise to build a wall so that it would never be possible for Latin Americans to enter the United States illegally. It has become physically impossible to build a wall for the sake of keeping rapist and drug dealers out of this country. Trump was implying that all Mexicans were rapist and drug dealers when they are not. The truth regarding the immigration of Latin Americans to the United States is much more complicated than what Trump was and is implying. However, by saying that he, Trump, would prevent Mexican drug dealers and rapist from coming across the southern border, it played to the fears of those who are unwilling to understand that immigration can and does drive the US economy and has a positive effect even on the local economies were the Latin American immigrants settle.

The use of the lie about all Mexicans being rapist and drug

dealers and that Trump could get the Mexican government to pay for a wall across the entire southern boarder was designed to play to the fears of individuals who could not or would not try to understand the truth about the real problems at the US border with Mexico.

When the Trump administration was confronted with the truth about any number of subjects that were misrepresented to the voters in the United States they came up with the phrase, "fake news," or "alternate truth" and "alternate facts" as if there is another universe in which we live. A universe where truth and facts are only as determined by those who want to stay in power even when the truth and the actual facts would lead to a different reality. By claiming a different reality authoritarian leaders can lead unthinking people in a manner that will keep those who vote for them in a state of perpetual fear that their authoritarian lies will masquerade as truth.

This exact tactic was employed in Fascist Italy in the 1930's by Benito Mussolini. Mussolini proclaimed that he could save the citizens of Italy from the communist and those who would take away the freedoms enjoyed by Italian citizens. However, when Mussolini was able to become the authoritarian leader, he took away those very same freedoms. When Mussolini took control of the levers of the government and became a modern day Domitian.

If we have learned anything from the history of authoritarian leaders and their ascendancy to control of the government of a country, it is that ultimately authoritarian regimes fail and bring suffering to the people caught up in authoritarian rule. If Trump and the current Republicans in Congress regain control of the government of the United States, people will suffer and the government is most likely to fail.

CHAPTER 23
THE BOOK OF MATTHEW TAKES SHAPE.

Life in the Christian enclave in Galatia by Lake Tuz in which Levi was living in 84 AD was good and difficult at the same time. There was a sweet fellowship among the Christian brothers and sisters. The group believed that their mission in life was to follow Jesus's mission: that is, to seek and to save the lost. After all, Jesus clearly stated His mission when He asked Zacchaeus to climb down out of the sycamore-fig tree. Jesus was in Jericho and wanted to have lunch at Zacchaeus's house. The Pharisees murmured among themselves saying, "Why does He eat with tax collectors and sinners." Levi knew what was on the minds of the people because he too had been a tax collector and hated by the people.

Jesus knew exactly what He needed to say. When Jesus called Levi and then later Zacchaeus. Jesus said, "Today salvation has come to this house, because this man, too, is a son of Abraham. For the Son of Man came to seek and to save the lost." Levi remembered the words that his friend, his teacher, his master, his savior and his Lord spoke that day and realized that if he, Levi, the tax collector and sinner was to follow Jesus that he too had do the work that Jesus did while He was with His disciples: Seek and save the lost.

The fellowship among the Christians that now lived by Lake Tuz, was indeed sweet. They had everything in common. They worked together, eat together, prayed together just as Jesus had taught them. They lived in peace. On the other hand, the people of the Christian community were viewed with suspicion by the non-Christian communities that surrounded their enclave. There were constant taunts from men who happened to encounter one of the Christians as they traveled outside the village from which the Christian man or woman lived.

The Christians also worried about the return of the Roman soldiers that were camped just outside of the largest city in the region, Anyka (today Ankara the capitol of modern Turkey). The Centurian who had led a Company of soldiers to the remote village by Lake Tuz a few days before promised to return to the Christian village and make sure that the villagers paid proper respect to the emperor Domitian by kneeling in the public square of the village and pronouncing before the Centurian and all the assembled Christians that Domitian was God.

Levi told the Centurian that none of the Christians could or would do as the Centurian commanded because they believed that there was no other God than Jehovah and that Jesus was His only begotten son. The Romans promised return had the Christians worried and watchful because they knew that some of their brethren would die before they would do as the Centurian commanded them to do.

In the midst of all the worry and even the sweet fellowship among the Christians some were saying that it was better if they packed up and found another place to live even further away from their non-Christian Jewish neighbors and the Romans who demanded what they do what they believed to be the impossible; Agree that there was a god other than Jehovah. With all of this worry and sense of dread the villagers gathered at the door of Levi's hut and asked their leader for guidance.

The next eldest villager called to Levi and said, "Levi, you walked with Jesus, you heard His voice, you were with Him when He ascended into heaven, what would Jesus have told us to do?"

Levi dressed in a simple tunic and toga that covered him from head to toe appeared in the door to his hut and carefully looked at each of the men, women and children who now stood before him. For a while all was silent, but then in a clear and confident voice Levi spoke. "My children do not be afraid. Do you not remember when Yehuda from the next village came here and told us that we had to follow the Jewish law and reject our Lord, Jesus the Christ, that God protected us and preserved us. God will always be with us, and His promises will never be broken."

There was agreement from most of the villagers, but some did not seem to be as convinced by the words that Levi spoke as the majority of the Christian villagers. Levi, still looking intently but lovingly into the faces of everyone, sensed the division in their spirits. Levi spoke again, "Jesus promised to always be with us even to the end of the ages. I was there when Jesus said these words and I was there when I saw Him ascend into heaven. I will never forget that day when my Lord and Savior, who had been dead but now was alive, said that He was going to prepare a place for us in heaven. I stood there gazing at the cloudy sky when an angel suddenly appeared and said, 'Why are you standing here looking into the sky? Go back to Jerusalem and wait for the Holy Spirit to come.' We did as the angel told us to do and on the day of Pentecost the Holy Spirit did in fact come to us. I have seen mighty works, miracles, and the Holy Spirit has never left us. God always keeps His promises. Now we must rely on God's promise that He will preserve us always."

One of the men standing near to where Levi was speaking raised his arms toward heaven and shouted, "God give us faith that we will be worthy to resist the doubts and worries of this world. God give us strength to resist the evil that has come around us. God bless us with love for those who need salvation."

At that moment Levi looked into the sky and a warm smile came across his old, bearded face and he under his breath thanked God and his savior, teacher, and friend, Jesus, who had heard his prayers and had given those of this remote village by the shores of Lake Tuz in the province of Galatia, courage to face the Romans and the Jews who were at enmity with Christ and therefore with the Christians in that village far away from the life they had all left behind.

Levi continued to work on the manuscript of the life and teachings of Jesus. Levi found it productive to center his writings around the teachings of Jesus. Levi set out the first great teachings of Jesus in what Levi called the teaching of the disciples that Jesus gave from a mountainside. By time that Jesus said the words of His First Discourse, crowds of people were always around Jesus, and they were all intent to hear what Jesus was teaching.

When Jesus sat down His Disciples drew close, and Jesus spoke. It was possible to hear what Jesus said as His voice carried from the mountainside to the far reaches of the crowd. Levi was there but because he had not been called as a disciple yet, he heard those words that Jesus spoke from a distance and on other occasions, and the words were at once powerful and thrilling.

Jesus spoke of how His followers were to live in a world that was hostile to God. Jesus told His followers that they were to love those who were their enemies and that they were to even turn their other cheek when they were abused by those who hated them. Jesus commanded His followers to, "In everything, do unto others as you would have them to do to you."

Words like Jesus spoke that day were never heard from the Jewish teachers and Pharisees who wanted to be seen and heard, but the words of Jesus stuck in Levi's and the disciples' hearts and were essential to the fellowship of the true followers of Jesus. Jesus told those who were listening to Him that to be included in the Kingdom of God that they must, "Therefore be perfect, as your heavenly Father is perfect."

When the multitudes heard the words of Jesus they often remarked, "This man teaches us with an authority that neither the Pharisees nor the other teachers of the law have. There is something very different about Jesus and He speaks with authority from God."

Levi recalled the words that Jesue spoke when He selected His chosen men to go into the surrounding countryside and minister to the people. Jesus gave His disciples authority over evil spirits and over diseases and sent them to preach what they had heard Jesus preach. The disciples were to carry no money or even extra clothes with them but were to stay in the homes of the people and minister to their needs. If the disciples were rejected by the community, they were to leave and not come back.

Levi also remembered the words of Jesus as he explained the stories that He told the crowds that constantly followed Him from town to town and place to place. The stories that Jesus told had spiritual meanings that required spiritual explanations. Jesus would often say that only those who had spiritual ears could understand the meaning of the stories that He told.

Jesus spoke about things that people could readily understand, like a farmer sowing seed on the ground which was a common scene in the villages in which the people could readily understand. A worn pathway, rocky ground, ground full of weeds and thorns that would choke the seeds as they sprung up from the soil, and good fertile ground from which the harvest would be plentiful.

Jesus told stories about how a farmer sowed seeds in his field and an enemy came and filled the field with weeds, and how the kingdom of heaven was like a mustard seed. Each of the stories that Jesus told were full of spiritual truths if the listener had the right spiritual frame of reference to discern the Godly meaning in each story.

Levi also remembered the questions that he and his fellow disciples would ask Jesus about what the kingdom of God meant for each of Jesus followers. They asked who would be of the highest rank and what would be the pecking order. The disciples were truly astonished when Jesus told them that the servant of all would be the one who achieved the most.

Then Jesus told His men that He, Jesus, would suffer at the hands of the religious leaders and be put to death. Levi did not understand and neither did his Brothern because they thought that Jesus was going to overthrow the Romans and bring back the thrown to the decedents of King David. It was not until Jesus was crucified and raised from the dead that Jesus's words started to make perfect sense to even His closest friends.

It was also during that portion of His earthly ministry that Jesus confronted the Pharisees and uncharacteristically Jesus had harsh words for the religious leaders who by then were plotting to arrest and murder Jesus. Jesus called them hypocrites and a brood of vipers because they had subverted the words of God for their own purposes.

In the Olive Garden, just before Jesus suffered and died on the cross, just outside of the walls of Jerusalem, Jesus told of the end times and what the disciples could expect after He died and was raised again. Jesus told them to remain faithful because He was sending His Spirit as a guide to their understanding. Not only was He going to the heavenly Father, but He was preparing a place for them in heaven as well.

Jesus told them that there would be a judgment day when every human being who was living and who had died, would stand before the great thrown and would be judged. The people would be divided as a Shepard separates His sheep from the goats. To the sheep He will say, "Come, you who are blessed by Our Father; Take your inheritance, the Kingdom prepared for you since the creation of the world.

"For I was hungry, and you gave me something to eat. I was thirsty and you gave me something to drink. I was a stranger and you invited me in. I needed clothes and you clothed me. I was sick, and you looked after me. I was in prison, and you came and visited me.

"Then the righteous will answer Him. Lord, when did we see you hungry and feed you, or thirsty, and give you something to drink? When did we see you as a stranger and invite you in or needing clothes and clothed you? When did we see you sick or in prison and go to visit you?

"The King will reply, Truly, I tell you. Whenever you did for one of the least of these brothers and sisters of mine, you did it for me.

"Then He will say to those on the left. Depart from me, you who are cursed, into the eternal fire prepared for the devil and his angels. For I was hungry, and you gave me nothing to eat. I was thirsty, and you gave me nothing to drink. I was a stranger, and you did not invite me in. I needed clothes and you did not clothe me. I was sick and in prison and you did not look after me.

"They will also answer, Lord, when did we see you hungry or thirsty or a stranger or needing clothing or sick or in prison and did not help you?

"He will reply. Truly, I tell you, whenever you did not do for one of the least of these, you did not do for me.

"Then they will go away into eternal punishment. But the righteous to eternal life."

Levi remembered these words of Jesus and wrote the words as the Holy Spirit, who Jesus promised to send, gave Levi the remembrance and strength to tell the story of Jesus.

Days and even weeks passed, and the village was spared from further visits from Roman soldiers and the Jews from the surrounding communities. Then one night a stranger from an unknown place stumbled into the village where Levi lived. The man seemed to be half starved and injured. The man's clothes were torn, and he was dirty from head to toe. The man stumbled into the village and came to rest at the door of Levi and moaned with such a low loud voice that it immediately attracted all who were close to the entrance of Levi's hut to come running to see what was possibly was going on with the stranger that stumbled into their village.

The man could not speak coherently, and it was obvious that he was in grave distress. Levi told the men closest to him to take the man into his hut and asked some of the women to see to the stranger's immediate needs. The man could not say anything except, "Help me, help me." and even then, the words that he spoke were not in any language that anyone in the village had ever heard. The stranger then faded away into unconsciousness.

The women of the village took turns administering to the man's needs, but for a while it was uncertain if the stranger would survive because he was in such bad shape. Two days passed and on the third day the beleaguered stranger who had stumbled into the Christian enclave on the shores of Lake Tuz started to regain his ability to communicate with those who were ministering to him. The man appeared to have been a worker in one of the local salt mines that were around Lake Tuz. Because Lake Tuz was brackish it was the source of most of the salt that was used in that part of the world. Roman business men owned salt mines and employed slave labor to dig the salt from below the lake.

The man appeared to be in his mid-thirties and also appeared to be of the Celtic people who had invaded and then settled in the region around Lake Tuz. The Celtic people arrived in the region before the Greeks and Romans came to Lake Tuz. The Celtic settlers had their own language and customs apart from the Greeks and Romans.

When he finally spoke, his words were a form of Greek with heavy overtones of the Celtic language that people who had been in that district cobbled together. The language that the man spoke was not anything that the people of the village where Levi and the group of Christians with whom he had settled, understood. Prior to the conquest of Galatia and all of what is considered modern-day Turkey by the Romans, the Greeks had conquered Galatia. The Greeks under the leadership of Alexander, and before them the Persians, and before them the Celtic people arrived in Galatia and settled the region.

The man who stumbled into this particular village was a remanent of an earlier group of people who had inhabited the high plain and mountainous area that was called Galatia. Lake Tuz formed the boundary between Galatia to the north-west and Cappadocia to the east of the lake. Earlier the Apostle Paul had traveled in this region of the Roman Empire and Paul addressed a letter to the Galatians churches he visited and perhaps founded. Paul traveled through Galatia on his second missionary journey.

The man that lay on the cot in Levi's hut began to regain his strength by the fourth day after he arrived in the remote village of Christians near Lake Tuz. The man whom the villagers just called "the stranger" began to motion that he was thirsty and hungry and cold. Because the land around the village was on a high plain surrounded by mountains it was also an arid place, and the vegetation was at times sparce. Provision for food and heating were sparce.

There was an inadequate supply of wood for the purpose of heating the hut, so the villagers relied on the dried dung of the animals that they tended to supply the fuel for the fires they lit to warm their huts. The economy of the village relied on sheep herding, salt mining, and the weaving of blankets from the wool that they harvested from their herds. The pink water of Lake Tuz was a constant reminder to Levi and his congregation that they were no longer in Judea and that the Romans had displaced them form their beloved Jerusalem, their families, their property, and all that they had grown accustomed to in the life they left behind.

Now they were also confronted by "the stranger" who did not speak their language and who came from a different culture, religion, and who wanted to eat, drink and get warm from the limited supplies that this village had in store.

Because they were Christians however, they shared all that they had with the man who had stumbled into their village. After a few days everyone learned from rumors that they heard that the man's name was Pradik and that he was a slave of a large Roman trading company that mined the largest salt deposit in the region; and the Romans were looking for him. Pradik escaped from the captivity of his Roman owners by hiding in a shipment of salt and then bolting in the cover of night. Pradik wandered around avoiding his Roman enslavers for days in the cold high plateau of Galatia until he finally stumbled into this newly established village made up of a new group of migrants who were also escaping from the Romans.

There were other groups of Christians in the high plains of Galatia that the Apostle Paul had visited when he was on his second missionary trip through this region. Paul had even written to the Christians in Galatia and admonished them not to give into the Jewish settlers in Galatia who insisted that the Christians follow the Jewish traditions. Paul wrote that it was not necessary that Christian men be circumcised, and Paul admonished the Christians that he visited to be fully committed to the Holy Spirit who treated both Jew and Gentile, men and women. slave and free as if there were no differences between them. The words of Paul seemed to be very appropriate in the circumstances that the Christians in the group to which Pradik had found himself and to which Levi had found himself as the leader, belonged.

Paul wrote in his letter to the Galatians Christians that they should live in freedom from the flesh; "to avoid sexual immorality, impurity, and debauchery; discord, jealousy, fits of rage. selfish ambition, dissensions, factions and envy; drunkenness, orgies and the like. I warn you as I did before; that those who live like this will not inherit the Kingdom of God."

On the other hand, Paul told he Galatian Christians, "[That} the fruit of the Spirit is Love, Joy, Peace. Forbearance, Kindness, Goodness, Faithfulness, Gentleness and Self-control. Against such things, there is no law. Those who belong to Christ Jesus have crucified the flesh with its passions and desires, since we live by the Spirit, let us keep in step with the Spirit. Let us not become conceited, provoking and envying each other." Paul wrote these words in 49 AD, but even in 84 AD the words were still relevant.

Around 84 AD Peter wrote to the churches in Pontus, Galatia, Cappadocia, Asia and Bithynia. It seemed that the Christian congregations were facing a different threat to their existence than expressed earlier by Paul. During Paul's time the threat seemed to be from the Jewish teachers and leaders who considered those who followed Jesus to be a threat to Judaism and its tradition rather than as a separate belief about the same God that both Jews and Christians worshiped.

At the time that Peter wrote to the Christian churches it was the Romans who had become intolerant of the Christians because by then, they understood that Christianity was a totally different belief system from the more ancient Jewish religion that the Romans tolerated, taxed, but allowed even in Rome itself. The Romans thought that the Christians were a secret society that engaged in orgies because the Christian ate meals together and referred to these meetings as "love feasts."

Pradik regained most of his strength and started to leave the village, but the people thought that he should stay there until he was fully recovered and could be returned to his Roman owners. A dispute began among the Christian as to what should be done about Pradik. Some wanted Pradik to leave and never come back before the Romans knew that the Christians had harbored Pradik; while others wanted to turn Pradik over to the Romans because they as Christians were admonished to live by the law which would require the return of the Roman's property back to the Romans. A dispute between freedom and the law was something with which these Christians struggled, and it caused dissention among them and played heavily on their fellowship.

Chapter 24
Modern Day Pharisees

While Paul was returning to Jerusalem from his third missionary journey he stopped in Miletus and called for the men of Ephesus to come to him at Miletus to bid them farewell. At Acts 20: 25-35 Paul gives his last instructions to the men of Ephesus and in particular tells them at verses 26 and 27 the following, "Therefore I declare to you today that I am innocent of the blood of any of you, for I have not hesitated to proclaim to you the whole counsel of God."

What exactly did Paul have in mind when he told the Ephesians that they had heard the whole counsel of God, and what is such an admonishment's relevance to the church today?

On the occasion of the last service that Charles Spurgeon conducted at the Royal Music Hall at Surrey Garden in 1859 he preached from the text of Acts 20: 26-27 and emphasized that he had always preached the whole counsel of God to the congregation. Spurgeon stated that he called to record all the doctrines of the Bible, that is every truth no matter how great or small he though each individual truth might be. Spurgeon, the leading evangelist of his day, did not magnify one doctrine over any other truth contained within the entirety of Scripture. Spurgeon believed in the sovereignty of God and that no one truth given by God in Scripture should be emphasized more than the whole word and truth that is offered for the acceptance of Christians. Spurgeon contended that because of the personhood of Christ and the efficacy of His blood an emphasis on only a portion of the truth of Scripture is an evil ploy of Saten and does not honor God.

Spurgeon stated that a reliance on the doctrines of the Bible without also recognizing the responsibility of the Christian to practice the truth given by all of the Scripture would also result in landing in Hell. Spurgeon said that "The creation cannot question the Creator" when it comes to understanding and practicing the whole counsel of God. It is necessary to adhere to the doctrines of Scripture as well as to comply with the commandments of Jesus. In other words, a Christian should not condemn a sinner (i.e. condemn a woman who seeks an abortion) and at the same time refrain from judging the sin (i.e. lying about whether an election was stolen) because both judging the woman and lying are both sins. After all, Jesus commanded His disciples to not judge. Jesus said, "Do not judge or you will be judged. For in the same way that you judge others, you will be judged, and with the measure you use, it will be measured to you." Matthew 7:1-2. Additionally, the 9th Commandment given to Moses states, "Thou shall not give false testimony against your neighbor."

Selectively applying scripture was a particular problem of the Pharisees when Jesus admonished them at Matthew 23 because they "do not practice what they preach." "They tie up heavy cumbersome loads and put them on other people's shoulders but they themselves are not willing to lift a finger to move them." Jesus goes on to call the Pharisees hypocrites because they go out of their way to find one that will agree with them and therefore destroy that person by failing to point out that he is a sinner just like everyone else.

Take into consideration the current political situation in the United States. One group of politicians (mainly Republicans) seek to place restrictions on women and minorities. They place burdens on the shoulders of those who are affected by their restrictions while they do not walk in the shoes of those they restrict. Additionally, they turn a blind eye to a man who could care less about living a righteous life and who constantly commits crimes against the people who have supported him. Trump claims and then disdains the support of right-wing white evangelical voters. Despite the claims that these voters and the man they in cult-like fashion support they cannot be considered to be a part of the followers of Christ.

Christ does not take part in the political causes that Trump and his allies endorse. For the most part the abortion issue drove right –wing evangelicals into a coalition with far right–wing Republicans. The one issue alliance defies the admonition that Christians consider the whole counsel of God as Paul describes his plea to the Ephesians in Acts 20:26-27 and echoed by Pastor Spurgeon in his farewell sermon described above. Shall I remind you that Spurgeon calls the overemphasis of one issue from God's counsel a ploy of Saten that will ultimately lead to Hell for those caught in such practice.

If right–wing white evangelicals want to be considered as Christians, they must adhere to the whole counsel of God, including being non-judgmental, forgiving, turning from unrighteousness and refusing to turn a blind eye to someone like Trump who continually espouses revenge and victimization as the key components of his political platform. (Saying that Trump and the Republican party has a politically discernable platform is however somewhat of a stretch of the imagination.)

To be a Christian, even a white right-wing evangelical Christian, it is necessary to follow the entire counsel of God as spoken to all who will hear the whole counsel as spoken by Jesus. In the Sermon on the Mount Jesus said among many commands that His followers were to love their enemies. When Trump says that he will become a dictator on day one of his re-election and seek vengeance and retribution on his political enemies that in no way corresponds to the love your enemy's commandment of Jesus. When Jesus said to His followers that Christians were to be the salt and light of the world, He did not say that right-wing white evangelicals were exempt from that obligation while Trump was or returns to office. While Jesus did not excuse the adultery of the woman caught in the act, even though He refused to pick up a stone and bash her in the head, he told the Pharisees that "only if they had no sin" could they pick up a stone and execute the adulterous woman. (Jesus reminded the Pharisees who were going to kill the adulterous woman of their own sins and sent them and her away with the warning, "sin no more.") By refusing to reject the adulterous ravings of their cult hero right-wing white evangelicals are encouraging his behavior and that is all the encouragement that Trump needs to heighten his depravity and lead to greater sins.

The warnings that Jesus gave to the Pharisees and teachers of the Jewish law in Matthew 23, should be recognized as a warning to the Republicans that they will be held accountable before God for the hypocrisy that they are displaying in the name of evangelism because they are denying the whole counsel of God and are playing into the hands of Saten.

After Jesus gave his warnings to the Pharisees in Matthew 23 and gave them the 7 woes starting at verse 13, what action did the Pharisees take? They continued on a path of destruction. They conspired with the Romans to have Jesus executed because they disagreed with His teachings and His warnings. They persecuted the Christians and had Steven stoned to death because he was an upright man and was assisting the poor and widowed women. Then they confronted the Romans. The Pharisees succeeded in causing the Romans to siege Jerusalem and eventually the city was totally destroyed and burned to the ground as we have detailed in an earlier chapter of this book.

Why did the behavior of the Pharisees continue in the destructive path that they were warned against by Jesus in Matthew 23? The only clear conclusion that makes any sense is that they refused to give up any authority that they had gained in their place in the political and religious life of the Jewish people.

Fast forward to present day America. After WWII American prosperity reached an all-time golden era. The New Deal recovery plan after the great depression of the 1930's, brought an increased standard of living though most sectors of the American society. Taxation of the richest segments of the population and a regulated economy brought about a narrowing of the gap between the richest Americans and the middle classes and the blue-collar segment of the workforce. That prosperity continued almost unabated until 1972 when Richard Nixon became entangled in the Watergate scandal. An economic downturn occurred after the Vietnam war ended as interest rates claimed and OPEC oil prices skyrocketed.

Then after Ronald Reagan was elected the economy was shocked by the deregulation of essential safeguards that had kept the disparity of a free market economy in check for almost 4 decades. In his pertinent article in <u>The Atlantic</u> on November 25, 2023, Roge Karma, "Why America Abandoned the Greatest Economy in History"- states as follows:

"One answer is that American voters abandoned the system that worked for their grandparents from the 1940s through the 70s, sometimes called the New Deal era, U.S. law and policies were engineered to ensure strong unions, high taxes on the rich, huge public investments, and an expanding social safety net. Inequality shrank as the economy boomed. But by the end of that period, the economy was faltering, and voters turned against the post war consensus. Ronald Reagan took office promising to restore growth by pairing back government, slashing taxes on the rich and corporations, and gutting business regulations and antitrust enforcement. The idea, famously, was that a rising tide would lift all boats. Instead, inequality soared while living standards stagnated and life expectancy fell behind that of poorer countries. No other advanced economy pivoted quite as sharply to free market economics as the United States, and none experienced as sharp a reversal in income mobility, and public health trends, as America did. Today, a child born in Norway, or the United Kingdom has a far better chance of out earning their parents than one born in the US."

To further exasperate the economic problem caused by the deregulation of the economy by the Republican controlled executive branch along came the MEGA movement that further deregulated the economy under the guise of making America great again. The America that these misguided Republicans want to return to is the deregulated years preceding the great depression of the 1930's. Why do Republicans want to discard the system that caused the "Greatest Economy in History"? Because they want to continue to benefit the rich and powerful segment of the population that provides large sum of money to the Republicans to keep them in power just as the Pharisees wanted to retain authority when it resulted in the complete destruction of Jerusalem and Judea and the disbursal of the Jewish population from the holy land.

History seems to be repeating itself because the modern-day Pharisees call themselves Republicans and they are unwilling to adhere to the whole counsel of God.

CHAPTER 25

SPIRITUAL VERSES NATURAL AS TENSIONS ARISE IN THE LAKE TUZ CHRISTIAN VILLAGE.

Levi continued to work on the Gospel story that he was writing with the help of his friend Markus Aurelius Agustus Gaius who had finished the book of Mark with the help of the Apostle Peter. Mark met Peter now more than 20 years before when he was on a business trip to Antioch. Mark and Levi were introduced to each other in Jerusalem before the Romans seized all of Judea and destroyed the Jewish capitol.

Mark gave a copy of the account of the life and death of Jesus as told to him by Peter and convinced Levi to amplify the story based on Levi's personal knowledge of the events, actions and words of Jesus. Levi began to write his memories of the time he had spent with Jesus and the other disciples. When the Romans were provoked by the Pharisees to destroy Jerusalem, Levi was even reminded of the words of Jesus when He told His disciples that the Temple built by Herod the Great in Jerusalem would be destroyed. Levi and the Christian congregation that left Jerusalem and traveled with Levi first to Antioch and then to the Galatian high plain around Lake Tuz were Judeans and spoke Aramaic.

Then a stranger stumbled into the village that the group of Judean Christians had founded to meet their own needs. The stranger was a descendant of the Celtic marauders who had invaded the Galatian high plain and settled in the region before the Greeks and then the Romans became the dominant ethnic settlers and rulers of the area. Padrik, as the Christian villagers had by now learned his name, was nursed back to health and the Christian villagers shared all that they had with Padrik even though Padrik probably did not understand anything that the Christians were telling him. Padrik was happy that the Christians had taken him into their community, feed him nursed him, clothed him and visited him and treated him as an honored guest.

When Padrik was healed enough to travel a discussion between the Christian residents of the village started concerning what to do about Padrik. One group of Christians wanted to return Padrik to the Romans because Padrik had escaped from the slavery to which Padrik had been subjected to when the Romans killed his parents. Pradik was the property of the owners of the large Roman salt mine. Others argued that Padrik had obviously been mistreated, malnourished, and put into a life-threatening existence by Padrik's owners. Therefore, to send Padrik back to slavery more than likely meant that Padrik would soon die either because he had escaped from the salt mine and would be crucified by the Romans or Pradik would die by being worked to death digging salt out of the salt mine. The discussion among the Christian about what to do about Padrik was long and at times loud.

Into the mix of the discussion the villagers turned to Levi to ask, based on his close relationship with Jesus, what should the village do about Padrik?

A man to whom everyone gave deference, whose name was Ananias, spoke for the gathering that stood before Levi's door. "Levi, we, all of us here before you, want to know how we should do what is right in the eyes of God and our Lord Jesus concerning Padrik who is a stranger among us and who is the property of the Romans. The Romans insist that we follow the Roman law under which we find ourselves. Please tell us what Jesus demands of us to do in this situation that we did not create but for which we may be held responsible if we do not do the right thing."

Levi motioned the people away from the door of his hut and directed them to the center of the village and away from where Padrik was resting. When the village gathered at the center of the village, Levi spoke in a low slow voice so that only those who had gathered around him could hear his words.

Levi said, "Not long ago we received a letter from my brother in Christ, Peter, who reminded us that, 'Now that you have purified yourselves by obeying the truth so that you have sincere love for each other, Love one another deeply, from the heart. For

you have been born again, not of perishable seed, but of imperishable, through the living and enduring word of God. All people are like grass and all their glory is like the flower of the field; the grass withers and the flowers fall; but the word of the Lord endures forever.

'And this was the word that was preached to you. Therefore, come rid yourselves of all malice and all deceit, hypocrisy. envy, and slander of every kind. Like newborn babies, crave pure spiritual milk, so that by it you may grow up in your salvation now that you have tasted that the Lord is good.'

"Because we are born again to a spiritual birth, we have become spiritual people, and uniquely the children of God. Before we took on the character of Jesus, we were natural people influenced by the nature of our flesh and subject to the world. Now that we have submitted ourselves to Jesus, He has given us His Holy Spirit and we have become spiritual beings, seeing the world from a different perspective. We look at Pradik and see a man in need not only of our food and clothes but more importantly, in need of Jesus. When we have nursed Pradik back to health, we must not neglect Pradik's spiritual health so that he can make the right choice about his life. We must learn to speak Pradik's language and tell Pradik of the love of Jesus and the blessings of becoming a child of God."

When Levi finished speaking the people of the village agreed that the words of Levi were true, and that Pradik needed to stay in the village until they could tell him of the love and joy that Jesus would bring into his life. One of the Christian women of the village said that Pradik had been trying to communicate with her and that she would try to learn as much about Pradik's language as she could so that they could at least understand what Pradik wanted and needed. One of the men suggested that they build a separate hut for Pradik so that he could start to live on his own and help out with the chores of the people. All agreed that this was the best situation for Pradik, and they all got to work to accomplish what they all agreed to do.

Pradik seemed to sense that his new neighbors were trying to communicate with him and were also treating him better than he expected. Pradik joined in with the building of a new hut that Pradik expected to inhabit. Within a few weeks one of the women in the group of Christians whose name was Marium, was able to learn some of the words that Pradik used to describe that he was hungry and thirsty. Then after a few more weeks a breakthrough occurred. The woman who had been attending to Pradik learned that he could speak Latin or at least enough Latin to understand his owners' rough orders and could understand what the master's did not think he understood when they would talk freely about issues that they would have considered personal or something that they did not believe a common slave would understand.

The most common language that was spoken among the Christian villagers was Aramaic, but because they were under the authority of the Roman empire the whole world had to understand some Latin in order to survive. Pradik understood Latin more than he ever let it be known when he was a part of the slave labor camp at the Roman owned salt mining operation. Gradually, the communication level between the Christian women who saw to Pradik's needs and Pradik became good enough that they could carry on a meaningful conversation.

The woman with the most ability to communicate with Pradik was called Marium and she was a young woman who was just a girl when her parents had to flee Jerusalem. Marium had some knowledge of Latin, some ability to pick up the Celtic/Greek that Pradik cobbled together and before long Pradik and Marium were able to discuss not only Pradik's needs but also Marium was able to answer questions that Pradik had about the beliefs and culture of the Christians that he found himself depending on for his sustenance.

Pradik wanted to know why the Christians treated him as

an equal among their group even though he was an outsider to their culture, to their language and especially to their belief in a man named Jesus. When Pradik was able to ask these questions, Marium knew that it was time for the men and especially Levi to start to help Pradik learn that the group of Christian were bound together by their love for Jesus and their love for one another and that included their love for Pradik.

Finally, one cold afternoon Levi came to Pradik's hut along with Marium and they brought stools to sit on and fuel for a fire. Marium prepared a fire in the middle of the hut as there was a chimney or actually a hole in the top of the hut from which the smoke from the fire could escape. Pradik was slightly uneasy when he realized that an important discussion about his future with the community of Christians was about to take place.

Levi was not a very tall man and his age had taken a toll on his ability to stand up straight. Levi wore the traditional clothes of a man from Galilee and typical of his standing as an apostle of Jesus. Levi wore a simple knee-length, sleeveless tunic cinched at the waist with a belt, leather sandals and a mantle draped around his shoulders for extra warmth because it was cold on the high plains of Galatia. Marium was also dressed in the typical dress of a woman from Judea, a wool outer garment known as a stola which was a long-pleated dress and a vail to cover her face and neck. Pradik was clothed in the clothes with which he had been provided by the villagers because the clothes he was wearing when he stumbled into the village were in such bad repair that the women burned them because of their stench.

Levi started the conversation in the limited Latin that he was able to speak while Marium busied herself with tending to the fire and picking up objects that Pradik had left scattered on the floor of the hut. Marium was close by to help with translation if needed. Levi in a quiet voice said, "Pradik, we, the people of this village were once living in Jerusalem in Palestine. We are of Jewish ancestry and our forefathers were given the land of Palestine by Almighty God. The Jewish race was a covenant people and were given the law of God by our ancestor Moses.

As a race we could not live up to the dictates of the law as given to us by God and we broke the covenant that we as a people had made with Jehovah God. Recently, in the history of the Hebrew people, but what might seem long ago to you, God sent His son to us in human form. God's son is our Lord Jesus.

"Each of us in this village came very close to God because we have received the spirit of Jesus into our lives. Eventually, we were forced to leave out homeland because a conflict arose between the Romans and the leaders of the Jewish religion. A terrible battle was fought in our homeland and we, the people of this village and others fled Jerusalem and eventually settled in this place where we now sit.

"Before we were forced to leave Palestine and while Jesus was in our midst, I was a tax collector hired by the Romans to collect taxes from those passing through Galilee on the trade route from Egypt to Syria. Many people traveled along the trade route that passed through Galilee and through Capernaum. One day Jesus, who I had seen before, walked by my tax collection booth and told me to follow Him. Jesus called me by my name. He said 'Levi, get up from there and follow me for today I shall eat dinner at your house.' When Jesus spoke to me it was like nothing I had ever experienced. I was called by Jesus the son of the living God. I had to follow Him. I could never let go of the power of that calling and I knew instantly that my life had changed forever.

"I followed Jesus for almost three years. There was a group of twelve disciples who followed Jesus and we went from Galilee to Judea and back to Galilee three times. Everywhere that Jesus went great crowds of people gathered around Him. Jesus by His touch could heal any and all diseases that anyone who came to Him had. Merely by His spoken command evil spirits were cast out of those suffering from the evil that possess those who have been overcome by Saten. On more than one occasion when people had gathered to hear Jesus teach and to heal the suffering, Jesus fed the crowd by multiplying what little we had to feed over 5000 men and the families that were with them.

"I saw Jesus by just His command still a storm and calm the raging sea. I saw Jesus walk across the water as if it were dry ground. I heard Jesus teach the people about the true nature of God and I saw many miracles that had never been done in the history of men. There was nothing in the history of mankind anything like what I saw Jesus do. Nothing like what I saw had ever happened before. It was obvious that Jesus was and is the Son of the living God and that Jesus was and is God.

"Then one day Jesus asked us who we thought that He was, and we said some things until our fellow disciple a man named Peter said, 'You are the Christ, the son of the living God.' And we all knew that Peters words were correct, and we believed that Jesus was the Messiah promised to our race by Jehovah.

"Then out of the blue Jesus told us that He would suffer and die at the hands of the Jewish leaders and the Romans. We, His disciples, did not understand. We were too afraid to ask what Jesus meant by His pronouncement of His impending death at the hands of the Jews and Romans. Things were going very well for us as Jesus's followers. Crowds were large, we were instrumental in His ministry, and we all felt that being with Jesus should last forever. We thought that Jesus would lead a revolt against the Romans and become the king of the people that lived as the Hebrew nation.

"We went to Jerusalem to attend the Jewish festival of the Passover. We assembled in a room and Jesus told us that His time had come to offer His body and His blood as a new covenant with those that would become His people. After the Passover meal one of the twelve of His disciples met with the Jewish leaders and betrayed Jesus. We went to a nearby garden that Jesus often visited. Jesus prayed that the death that He was facing would not be necessary, but He also prayed that the will of God would be accomplished and if Jesus had to suffer, He would give His life as a ransom for His people.

"As soon as Jesus finished praying the Jewish leaders' security guard and the disciple who betrayed Jesus found us and Jesus was arrested. All of His disciples were afraid, and we all ran away from Jesus and scattered. Only John went to the Chief Priests house because he was a friend of the Chief Priest. Jesus was taken to the Jewish leader's house and the ordeal of His suffering and eventual crucifixion began. By the end of that day Jesus was tried, beaten, abused, paraded through the streets of Jerusalem and crucified.

"Throughout the entire ordeal of the trials before the Jewish authorities and their Roman counterparts, Jesus was completely in control of His body, emotions and Spirit. He did not argue with the Pharisees nor the Roman Governor. Jesus remained focused of His mission; He was in the world to offer Himself as a sacrifice for the sins of His people. Even while He was nailed to the cross, He asked the heavenly Father to forgive those who were doing this because they did not understand what they were doing. Finally, when the full price of the atonement of our sins was paid, Jesus cried with a loud triumphant voice, 'IT IS FINISHED' and He gave up His life and was dead.

"Jesus body was taken to a tomb and the tomb was sealed with a huge stone and the Romans posted a guard to make sure that no one took His body and claim that Jesus was still alive. His death occurred in the afternoon of the Friday of the Pass-over feast of the Jewish faith. I along with my fellow disciples went into hiding but we finally gathered back at the place where we had last eaten with Jesus.

"On Sunday morning after the death of Jesus some of the women got up early and went to the tomb where they had taken Jesus's body. When they arrived the stone that sealed and secured the tomb was rolled away and Jesus's body was not there. The women came rushing back with this news but we, His disciples, were skeptical. Then Jesus appeared to us and asked for food and water. He appeared again and then He appeared on the beach at lake Galilee and finally He told us that we were to continue His work and seek out sinners and to tell everyone the story that I am now telling you.

"We are to offer our Savior to you Pradik and if you ask Jesus to come into your life, we will baptize you and you will become our brother in Christ. You can ask Jesus to come into your life by saying a simple prayer. If you want Jesue to come into your life and save you from your sins just repeat after me, 'I acknowledge that I am a sinner and cannot save myself. I fully and without question acknowledge that Jesus died to save me from my sins. I repent of my sins and ask Jesus to come into my life at this very moment. In the name of Jesus, I commit myself to the care of Jesus.' If you prayed that prayer with me and believe that Jesus has saved you then you are saved and are no longer a slave to sin, but you are a born-again Christian."

When Levi stopped talking, all was silent for many minutes. Marium was silent and almost motionless. While she had been born in Palestine after Jesus was crucified and had known many who had seen and heard Jesus speak, she had not heard the story of the life of Jesus as Levi had just given it to Pradik. Her heart was instantly overcome with joy and sorrow. After more time passed Marium said in a weeping voice, "I believe that Jesus died for my sins. I repent and I before you and God, I ask for Jesus to come into my life. I want to follow Jesus and be baptized."

Both Levi and Pradik were surprised by what Marium had just confessed and for the baptism for which she asked. Then Pradik stood and walked quickly to the door of the hut and left the village.

Chapter 26
"Restore us, O God;
make your face shine on us,
that we may be saved." Psalm 80:19

In Chapter 10 of this book, I discussed the great enlightenments in the Protestant Church in America that occurred in the 1730's and the 1790's. If we had time, I would explore how the great enlightenments were a direct cause of the "Protestant Work Ethic" which historical scholars attribute to the rapid growth of the American economy in the 1800's and beyond. The topic of this chapter is to contemplate where we as Christians stand at the present and to discuss the need for a revival in the Christian church (the universal Christian Church made up of all Christians who confess that Jesus is their savior), and especially in me.

The verse from Psalm 80 above has the repeating refrain, "Restore us, O God;" as if the song master who composed these words was continually imploring God to cause a revival to break out in the congregation of the Hebrew people. Perhaps because we are the new nation of Israel (an expression of the nature of the Christian church because Christians are the chosen of God and are now a separate nation of Kings and Priest. See Revelations 1:5-6 also see 1 Peter 2:9-10), the refrain of "Restore us, O God:" is properly directed to the followers of Christ today.

We have already explored the great awakenings of the mid and late 1700's but there were also other revivals that occurred in the United States. In 1858 a revival was discussed by Charles Spurgeon in a sermon that he preached on June 20, 1858. That sermon that is entitled "The Outpouring of the Holy Spirit" was based on Acts 10:44 which states, "While Peter was still speaking these words, the Holy Spirit fell on all of them which heard the word." Spurgeon pleads for a revival to breakout in London and set aside specific times for prayer meetings to be held in order to earnestly pray for revival to break out in London.

It is imperative that a revival again break out in America. In order for a revival to break out in America the Holy Spirit must influence the hearts of people. Without the direct participation of the Holy Spirit to cause a spiritual outpouring that leads to the conversion of souls, a revival of the Christian Church will not occur.

A revival is usually characterized by a turning of men and women from their sinful pursuits to repentance and a genuine concern for the spiritual part of their lives. Revivals and revival crusades were noted in the United States during the Civil War when an estimated 300,000 soldiers equally divided between the North and South were converted to Christianity. Another spiritual awaking occurred around the end of the 1800's and beginning of the 1900's when the evangelist Billy Sunday lead revivals throughout the country. By the 1950's and through the 1970's Billy Graham lead city wide crusades that resulted in many souls being converted to Christianity.

There has not been a significant widespread revival among Christian churches in the United States for many years and it is time for a revival to again break out in America.

How do revivals usually start? The simple answer is through the power of prayer. The prayer life of Christians is the most powerful aspect of the Christians relationship with God. In Acts 9: 11-16 the Holy Spirit told Ananias to go down to Straight Street in Damascus and inquire at the house of Judas because a man named Saul of Tarsus was God's chosen instrument to proclaim the name of Jesus to the Gentiles, and to the people of Israel "for he is there praying."

That praying man, Saul of Tarsus, was Paul the Apostle and he became the instrument by which the gospel message was spread throughout western civilization and has caused the power of Christianity to be the most dynamic catalyst of change in the hearts and minds of mankind that the world has ever known. If the prayers of Paul could cause such a change in society, then the prayers of the elect of this age can effectuate a change in society in the same way. The Holy Spirit will be moved to action when Christians fervently pray for a moving of the Holy Spirit in the lives of men and women who will be converted and saved. Who will join me in such fervent and effectual prayer? Please Lord God cause a revival to start among us today.

Exactly when and how the Holy Spirit will cause the hearts and minds of Christian men and women to come to the point of revival is a mystery. After all, Jesus in the third chapter of John told Nicodemus, "Very truly I tell you, no one can enter the Kingdom of God unless they are born of water and the Spirit. Flesh gives birth to the flesh, but the spirit gives birth to the spirit. You should not be surprised at the saying you must be born again. The wind blows wherever it pleases. You hear the sound, but you cannot tell where it comes from or where it is going. So, it is with everyone born of the Spirit." John 3: 5-8.

With these words Jesus told Nicodemus, a teacher of the Jews, that the Holy Spirit works in men to bring about a new birth, a spiritual birth, that transforms men from natural men and women to spiritual men and women.

Paul puts it like this in 2 Corinthians 5:16-20, "So from now on we regard no one from a worldly point of view. Though we once regarded Christ in that way, we do so no longer. Therefore, if anyone is in Christ, the new creature has come. The old has gone, the new is here. All this is from God, who reconciled us to Himself through Christ and gave us the ministry of reconciliation. That God was reconciling the world to Himself in Christ, not judging people's sins against them. And He has committed to us the message of reconciliation. We are therefore Christ's ambassadors, as though God were making His appeal through us. We implore you on Christ's behalf be reconciled to God."

So, what does it mean to be a new creation in Christ? When we first believe and accept Jesus into our lives the Holy Spirit takes hold of our hearts and begins the process of making us new spiritual creatures. The naturel man still exists, and we are subject to the sinful passions of the world, but the new spiritual birth replaces the natural man, and a spiritual man emerges fully capable of the perfection that Jesus told His followers to be when He said, "Therefore be perfect, even as your Father in heaven is perfect." Matthew 5:48.

Where does this lead? Christ called His elect, and He turns no one away. When I was a boy of only 10 years old, I heard the specific call of Jesus to get up from my seat in church and walk the isle and profess that I would submit to Jesus's call on my life. I was baptized. I have been a follower of Jesus ever since. I have battled the natural man in me and have sinned, but Christ has washed my sinful nature away with His blood and I am a part of the family of God.

I shall ever be part of the family of God throughout eternity. My life has been full of adventure, I have felt the presence of the Holy Spirit leading me and inspiring me as I write these pages. Jesus is always with me. To Him I owe all that I have and all that I shall ever have. Jesus paid for my life with His blood and body I can never repay the price He paid for my life and my spirit.

Jesus calls all of us, everyone reading these pages to follow Him to a new spiritual birth so that the sinful man that is in me will be born anew to a spiritual birth that has the capacity to be perfect in the sight of God and therefore acceptable as a member of the eternal family of God.

Lord, please cause a revival in the United States of America. Make this your fervent prayer and the Holy Spirit will fill the hearts and minds of men/women to "Restore us O God, make your face shine on us that we may be saved." Cause a revival so that the love of Jesus will be in all of us. Amen.

CHAPTER 27
THE WANDERINGS AND QUESTIONS OF PRADIK.

Pradik left the hut where he and Marium had been listening to the words of salvation as spoken by Levi. Pradik was moved to tears by the explanation that Jesus offered Himself as a sacrifice to save Pradik. He was amazed when Marium confessed her need for a personal savior.

Pradik felt the movement of the Holy Spirit convicting him of his sinful nature, but he was not fully convinced that Jesus had specifically died on a Roman cross in Palestine for a sinner such as Pradik and the Celtic people to which he belonged. For the rest of the day after his meeting with Levi and Marium, Pradik wandered around the hills of the Galatian high lands seeking some understanding of what the words of Levi meant to him and what he should do next.

Eventually, Pradik came to the place where the village in which his parents had raised him was located. The village was no more, only a few burned-out huts and the ruins of the village. Pradik remembered how life was so simple when he was a child, how he and the other children of the village played and talked and how his parents took care of him. He remembered the love of his mother and how his father provided meat and fish for the family. Pradik loved the fresh meat and salted fish that his father would bring to their hut after he went hunting and fishing for a few days with the other men of the village.

Then Pradik remembered the Romans arriving at their village and how the Romans mercilessly killed his father and mother and burned the village to the ground. Pradik was only about 10 years old when the Romans came. He and the other children were taken away and forced to work in the salt mine that was under the control of the Romans.

Many of the other children died because the work was hard

and because of the dangerous conditions in the mine. Pradik, because he was small, was forced to crawl along the floor of the salt mine and dig the salt out of the walls of the mine shaft and put the salt in a basket that was pulled out of the mine shaft and loaded into carts and taken to the surface. As Padrik got older he became the slave that pulled the salt out of the mine and as he grew even older and survived the rigors of the work in the mine, he pushed a salt filled cart to the surface and packed the salt into bricks that were sold to other commercial interests and taken away.

Life was hard and the slaves were constantly underfed and deprived of the necessities that were needed to sustain their lives. Pradik was able to survive because he was willing to take what he needed from the other slaves even though that deprived others of a means of survival. Pradik stole food from the other slaves, he took their clothing and took water out of the hands of thirsty boys and girls to satisfy his own thirst.

Pradik thought back about how the children he had played with before the Romans came, died because Pradik had to survive. Survive he did. Survival was all that he was capable of doing.

Pradik learned how to avoid the lash of the Roman guards, he learned enough of the Romans language to anticipate the moods of the often-brutal Roman guards who enjoyed inflicting pain and misery on the slaves that they controlled and who were nothing more than the salt that was extracted from the mine. When the Roman guards got drunk, which was very often they would enjoy the sport of beating the slaves or raping the girls that were taken from the villages that they raided and exploited. Many times, after the guards were finished with their sport a slave would die and be thrown into the mine and left to be absorbed by the salt.

Pradik learned how to escape the beatings by hiding in the mine as soon as he heard the guards' drunken and foul language directed at the slaves. He would survive. At times even Pradik was beaten but somehow, he survived.

Eventually, after leaving the burned out remains of the village from which he was taken as a slave, Pradik found a cave and built a fire to keep himself warm during the night. The words of Levi were still in his brain and Pradik wondered if it was true that there was a son of God who actually cared about a man like Pradik. Pradik remembered the prayer that Levi said would allow him and Marium to accept Jesus into their lives. Pradik had never prayed before, and he did not know exactly what Levi had in mind when he asked Pradik to follow him in repeating the words that Levi was asking Pradik to repeat.

However, Pradik did understand that Levi was sincerely trying to help him to accept Jesus and that Levi absolutely and without question knew that Jesus died so that Levi and all who believed that this Jesus was sent by God to save people. Whether Pradik was one of the people that Jesus died to save was a question that Pradik needed to think about.

Pradik wondered if the people that Jesus came to save included a man who had barely survived the Romans and starvation and the hazards of the salt mine. He wondered if all that he had done to survive excluded him from being one of the people that Jesus wanted to call His own. All these thoughts kept rolling around in Pradik's mind and he could not sleep. He was cold and wished he was still in the village and among the people who he had stumbled upon when he escaped from his Roman enslavers.

Pradik hated the Romans. They killed his mother and father in front of him and laughed. The Romans made life a constant struggle and Pradik witnessed the cruelty of the Romans many times over. He saw men and children tortured, murdered and left to rot in the salt mine where he was a slave. All of this was going through Pradik's mind while he lay in a cave in the mountains of Galatia by himself on a cold night after he had heard the most amazing story about a man named Jesus. Levi said this Jesus was the son of God who wanted to make even Pradik His friend.

"Why would God care about someone such as Pradik?," he

178

asked himself. "Who is this God?," Pradik thought.

Pradik heard of the Roman gods who made war with the world and all of its people. In his village when he was a child there were other gods who saw to it that the men of the village brought back meat and fish. Pradik had seen his mother light a candle and offer a bit of the fish that they ate to one of the figures that Pradik's family kept in their hut. Pradik had never heard of a God who would send His own son into a hostile world to seek out someone like Pradik. Was it possible for this Jesus to save him from the only life that he had ever known until he stumbled into the village by Lake Tuz after he escaped from the Romans who he hated?

Before he stumbled into the village by Lake Tuz where the people took care of him without wanting anything in return, all Pradik knew was how to survive. Was Jesus looking for Pradik too? What would happen if Jesus was more like the Romans and not at all like the Christians who had taken care of him.

Pradik's mind raced when he thought of Marium who nursed him back to health and who paid attention to him when he tried to tell her what he wanted. Pradik thought of how the people of the village had built a hut for him and who had supplied him with food and clothes. Pradik realized that he would have died except for the kindness of these people who called themselves Christians.

Levi said that they did this because they also loved this man named Jesus. Pradik wondered what motivated complete strangers to be so kind and generous to him. Pradik concluded that this man they called Jesus must have been a very powerful influence on the people of the village that he stumbled into when he escaped the slavery of the Romans.

Meanwhile, Levi and Marium continued to wonder what had become of Pradik. It had now been several days since Pradik left the village. Marium was especially concerned about Pradik's wellbeing. While Levi was also concerned, he was able to turn his concern for Pradik over to the Holy Spirit because Levi knew that all things would work out for the best if Pradik was truly called by the Holy Spirit to follow Levi's friend, teacher, savior, and master, the Lord of life Jesus the Christ.

On the fifth day after Pradik had walked out of the village he walked right back in and went immediately to the hut that he had occupied and where he and Levi had last talked. Pradik was full of questions that he wanted to talk over with Levi, but he also wanted to talk to and see Marium. As soon as Pradik walked back into the village everyone in the village knew it.

Soon all the people of the village gathered at the door of Pradik's hut and waited for Levi to make his way there. Marium arrived first and immediately went inside and found Pradik sitting on the same stool that he got up from five days earlier. Marium busied herself in making a fire. She stole a view of Pradik to discover how Pradik seemed to be. On the other hand, Pradik was very much in thought about something that was troubling him.

Finally, Levi arrived, and Pradik quickly spoke up, "Tell me who God is and tell me what God wants of me?" Pradik said as best he could in the language that was available to him.

"God is the creator of all things; He is a spiritual being that is always aware of every detail of our minds, our spirits, our bodies and everything that is going on around us." Levi started and was startled that it seemed that he could speak in such a way that Pradik could understand.

"God is the very power of the heavens and earth. He created each of us in His own image. We are the sheep of His pasture; He is the perfect Shepard who makes sure that His chosen do not want." Levi went on but was still not finished.

"Our God is the only true God. The other gods that men worship or pay homage to are not really gods at all. There is only one true and everlasting God who knows all things. He is in all things and is perfect in everything He does. In order to know God people must become as perfect as God. Knowing God can only be accomplished through a personal relationship with His only begotten son, Jesus.

"I was called by Jesus while He was still with us, and I

know personally of what I speak.

"I know that what I am saying to you is a difficult thing to understand but I am willing to stay here with you and answer every question you have about who God is and what He wants from each of us and from all those who He has chosen." Levi responded and then turned to Marium and said, "Please make us some broth for us to drink to warm us so that we can talk and answer all of your and Pradik's questions. We can sit here as long as it takes for the Holy Spirit to move in the direction the He chooses."

Levi realized that it was the direction of the Holy Spirit in the life of Pradik and also Marium that would give understanding and commitment to them. The Holy Spirit would direct their minds as to what they would understand and how each would respond to the words that Levi would give as answers to their questions. Levi prayed that the Holy Spirit would give him answers to the questions that were obviously causing Pradik to come back to the village and confront Levi.

The questions that Padrik was asking happened to be the most basic questions that anyone who did not know about God would ask. Levi knew that describing God to someone who had no background in knowing who God is and who Jesus has revealed, would be a task that only divine intervention could accomplish. Levi prayed to himself that he would say the words that the Holy Spirit intended him to say, and that Pradik and Marium would hear only the words that the Holy Spirit intended them to hear and understand.

Levi looked at Pradik and Marium and asked three simple questions that would eventually have a profound impact on the lives of the three people in the room where Levi, Pradik and Marium sat.

"Is there a God? If there is a God, what is He like? If there is a God, what does He have to do with us?" Levi said in a rhetorical manner so that he could answer the questions that he knew that both Pradik and Merrium needed to ask and have answered.

Surprisingly Marium was the first to speak, "Yes there is a God. I have been brought up in the culture of the Jewish people. We worship Jehovah who is the God of our ancestors who brought us out of the land of bondage and gave us a promised land that is to be our inheritance always. Something has happened that has caused the promise of God to end and now I find myself and my relatives here in this small village far away from the promise that Jehovah gave my ancestors. Levi what happened to the God who gave us Jewish people a promised land?"

Pradik spoke, "I know nothing about your God. My people had gods that my mother offered food to. They were images of hunters and fishermen who supplied meat and fish to us when I was a boy before the Romans came and killed my parents and took me to work in the salt mine. I know nothing of the God or gods that you speak about."

Levi carefully and with compassion in his voice replied, "Yes, Marium there is a God. You have spoken of the God of the Jewish people. I am a member of that race of people and like you I grew up with the knowledge of the God of Abraham, Issac, and Jacob. The same God that delivered the Hebrew people from bondage in Egypt and sent us to the promised land of Judea. Padrik you are right to say that you do not know of the God of the Jewish people and to speak of your own bondage by the Romans.

"Marium the Jewish people rejected the very son of God that He sent to bring His people back to Him. The Jewish people had a history of following God when it suited their purposes and a history of rejecting God when they felt that they no longer needed God to take care of them.

"God wanted a relationship with his people which did not always depend on good fortune or crisis. Jesus often said that you cannot serve God and money at the same time. Unfortunately, the Jewish people wanted to serve their own interest including money instead of serving God and God alone. One of the first lessons that all people must learn is that we, all people, cannot have any other gods but the one God who rules heaven and earth. When our ancestor Moses went up Mount Sinai to receive the commandments for our people to live by, the first commandment Moses received was that 'I am the Lord your God, who brought you out of Egypt, out of the land of slavery. You shall have no other gods before Me.'

"Pradik it was the same God who brought you out of a life of slavery and who has brought you here to be with us in this village of Christians. You may not realize that the hand of God was on you and may not even know that God is near to you now, but He is. God has allowed you to survive as a slave in the salt mine, has assisted you in your escape from the Romans, and has brought you here to this particular village where we Christian people who are also under God's care, can bring about your healing, feed you, clothe you and bring the greatest gift of all, your salvation dear Pradik."

"Why does your God care about me?" asked Pradik, and Levi could only respond with these words, "Why God choose any of us to be His children is a mystery.

"God is a sovereign being; the ruler of all men and He has the right to choose those who He wants to be His children. We on the other hand, can only accept or reject God's right to choose and accept us."

Then with a face full of anxiety Pradik asked, "Why have you, everyone in this village taken me in and why have you all of you been so kind to me?"

To this Levi had an instant reply, "Our savior and Lord told His disciples of which I was one of the least, that there would come a day, 'When the Son of Man comes in His glory and all the angels with Him, He will sit on His glorious throne. All the nations will be gathered before Him, and He will separate the people from one another as a Shepherd separates the sheep from the goats. He will put the sheep on His right and the goats on His left. Then the king will say to those on the right, 'Come you who are blessed by my Father, take your inheritance of the kingdom prepared for you since the creation of the world.

'For I was hungry, and you gave me something to eat. I was

thirsty and you gave me something to drink. I was a stranger, and you invited me in. I needed clothes, and you clothed me. I was sick and you looked after me. I was in prison, and you came and visited me.

"Then the righteous will answer Him, 'Lord when did we see you hungry and feed you or thirsty and give you something to drink? When did we see you, a stranger and invite you in or needing clothes and clothes you? When did we see you sick or in prison and go to visit you?"

'The king will reply, "Truly, I tell you, whenever you did for one of the least of these brothers and sisters of mine, you did it for me."

'Then He will say to those on the left, "depart from me, you who are cursed into eternal fire prepared for the devil and his angels. For I was hungry, and you gave me nothing to eat. I was thirsty and you gave me nothing to drink. I was a stranger, and you did not invite me in. I needed clothes and you did not clothe me. I was sick and in prison and you did not look after me.'

"They also will answer, 'Lord, when did we see you hungry, or thirsty, or a stranger, or needing clothes, or sick, or in prison and did not help you?"

'He will reply, "Truly, I tell you, whenever you did not do for one of the least of these you did not do it for me."

"Then they will go away. To eternal punishment, but the righteous to eternal life."

Pradik asked, "How do you know these words?"

Levi was quick to reply, "I was there when Jesus said exactly these words and they are in my brain and in my heart forever."

"You took me in and nursed me back to health, fed me, clothed me, attended to all my needs because your Jesus told you that that is what He expected from His followers and if you did not take me in and do for me that you would be condemned to eternal fires?" Padrik asked with an expectation of an affirmative answer.

Levi looked lovingly at Pradik and Marium and said, "My Lord, Jesus, has given commands and promises that I must obey. You, Pradik came to us and Marium you have been with us, and you both know that we follow what Jesus taught us and that you are both living proof that the words of Jesus are in us and that His words are the most important words that we know."

Marium then said, "All I know is what I have seen from all of the people in the village. We share all that we have with each other, We are taken care of by each other. There is a genuine love for each other among the people of this village. When one of us is sick then all of the people here feel for that person and all pitch in to help. When one of us is fortunate to has something good happen, we all celebrate. If this is what Jesus asked His followers to be like, then it has made me truly grateful to God that I live here and that these people love me. I want Jesus to fill my heart with His presence always."

"Yes, Marium Jesus is alive in all of us who confess Him as Lord and who follow Him in baptism. Jesus will complete His work in you and will never leave you or forsake you for all eternity." Levi gladly replied.

Pradik took all of this in. He was not skeptical or even doubtful of what Levi said or what Marium said. Strangely, Pradik felt as if he was being freed from any doubt and fear of what might happen to him if he accepted Levi's offer to accept Jesus as his savoir too. Even though Pradik did not understand everything that was said and had many questions about who and what God was like, he believed that he was led to the village by Lake Tuz into which he stumbled on that eventful night for the purpose of meeting and following a man named Jesus is the Son of God.

Levi, Marium and Pradik sat in the hut by Lake Tuz in the province of Galatia. Levi silently praised God and his savior and friend Jesus for putting him and the village where it was and when it was. Levi knew that it was not by chance that all these separate incidents came together. Levi knew that the Holy Spirit was at work. Praise Be to God!!!, Levi said to himself over and over again.

CHAPTER 28
COMPELLED TO PREACH THE GOSPEL.
1 CORINTHIANS 9:16

When Paul wrote that he was compelled to preach the Gospel in his letter to the church at Corinth at 1 Corinthians 9:16 he was telling the church that he was entitled to their support in his missionary efforts to bring spiritual gifts to the lost and heathen world. Paul wrote that ministers of the Christian church are entitled to the support of the congregation for the work that the minister preforms on behalf of God. Evidently, Paul was not receiving a salary from the church at Corinth, but stated that he, Paul, was compelled to preach the gospel no matter if he was supported by the church or not. This begs the question what was it that Paul was compelled to preach? I know you will reply, Paul was compelled to preach the gospel and leave it at that. I say not so fast. What is the gospel that Paul was compelled to preach?

I am glad that you asked that question, boys and girls. Let us explore the message that Paul was compelled to preach and ask ourselves if that is the gospel message that is being preached from the pulpit of the churches that we attend. Let us compare the message that was preached at Peachtree Baptist that James and Jim heard with the massage that was preached in the Christian Church during the time that Levi was writing the Gospel of Matthew. We will make this comparison so that we can find a starting point for an evaluation of the compelling message of the Gospel that Paul was required to proclaim to the churches to which he ministered.

Simply said Paul preached Jesus. What does it mean to preach Jesus? It means that the Gospel message is the same message that Jesus preached when He started His ministry after being baptized by John the Baptist in the Jordan River when all of Jerusalem and Judea went out to the wilderness to see and hear John crying out for repentance and the forgiveness of sins. Mark 1:4-8.

Likewise, after He was baptized and tempted by Saten for 40 days in the wilderness, Jesus went to Galilee proclaiming the good news of God, "The time has come...The kingdom of God has come near. Repent and believe the good news." Mark 1:15 also see Matthew 4:17.

In the Gospel of Luke, it is written at Luke 4:16, "He went to Nazareth where he had been brought up, and on the Sabbath day, He went into the synagogue, as was His custom. He stood up to read, and the scroll of the prophet Isaiah was handed to Him. Unrolling it He found the place where it is written:

'The Spirit of the Lord is on me. Because He has anointed me to proclaim good news to the poor. He has sent me to proclaim freedom for the prisoners, and recovery of sight to the blind, to set the oppressed free, to proclaim the year of the Lord's favor.'

"Then He rolled up the scroll and gave it back to the attendant and sat down. The eyes of everyone in the synagogue were fastened on Him. He began saying to them., 'Today this scripture is fulfilled in your hearing.'"

What was Jesus proclaiming the good news of God to be? "The kingdom of God has come near." Who was in the kingdom of God? Jesus was sent from God. When Jesus was baptized heaven was torn open and the Holy Spirit descended on Him and a voice from heaven was heard to say, "You are my Son; whom I love; with you I am well pleased."

Therefore, the good news that Jesus preached was about Himself. When Jesus came among us the kingdom of God was literally nearby in the person of Jesus.

Later, Saul (who was converted to Christianity by the direct intervention of Jesus as Saul, who later changed his name to Paul, was traveling from Jerusalem to Damascus to persecute Christians), wrote at Romans 8:29-30, "For those God foreknew He also predestined to be conformed to the image of His Son that He might be the first born among many brothers and sisters. And those He predestined He also called, those He called, He also justified; those He justified, He also glorified."

According to the Gospel of Matthew Jesus preached five discourses, gave illustrations of what He preached in parables and gave specific instructions to His disciples as to how they were to live with each other and how they were to carry on His ministry. The gospel that was preached by Jesus identified Jesus and Jesus alone as being the good news that the world had been waiting for since the fall of man when Adam sinned in the Garden of Eden by specifically breaking God's commandment.

Instead of doing as God told him to do Adam did as Saten tempted our earthly father to do by eating the forbidden fruit. (Whether you believe that there was an actual man named Adam or believe that the story of Adam is allegorical is not as important as the truth that the story conveys about humanity.) That act by Adam or all of humanity caused the fall of the human race and since then we as humans have entered life as totally depraved individuals.

In other words, mankind became lost from the perfection that God intended mankind to be when sin entered into the human conscious through the sin of our ancestors. Paul puts it this way, "for all have sinned and fallen short of the glory of God..." Romans 3:23

Jesus specifically came into the world "to seek and to save the lost." Luke 19:10. Therefore, if we acknowledge that we are a totally depraved persons (a condition in which we all find ourselves) Jesus specifically came to find me/us and to save me/us and therefore I/we may enjoy the status of someone who God foreknew, and predestined to take on the image of Jesus, God's only begotten Son. This is the essence of the good news that is the Gospel message that Jesus preached, and that Paul amplified in his letters to the various churches to which he ministered.

Guess what, when we take on the image of Jesus, we begin a journey that will eventually allow each of us, who are truly Christians, to fulfill the exhortation of Jesus found at Matthew

5;48 "Therefore be perfect even as your heavenly Father is perfect."

I have not been to that many churches in my life, perhaps 30 or 40 different churches. I have already written above that the messages of the various churches have been different and I now state that the messages of the churches that I have attended do not always include the gospel as preached by Jesus in the early days of Christianity.

Messages concerning the condition of the poor and the rich are preached. How God wants you to be rich is a common theme in many churches that proclaim the so called "Prosperity Gospel." The need of the church seems to be a regular theme of many messages that I have heard in my years as a church going Christian. This morning at the church I attended a sermon that was preached about how to break bad habits. While the sermon was well preached and had many useful points to be considered, it was not a message regarding the Gospel that Paul was compelled to preach or that Jesus preached to His disciples as He traveled throughout Galilee and Judea. I would go so far as to say it was not the Gospel at all. Further it makes me think that modern churches have lost the desire to actually preach the message that Paul was compelled to preach and for which Jesus came into the world.

I can only wonder what the gospel message, as proclaimed by Jesus, if preached to James and Jim would have produced in their separate lives. If Jim and James were attentive to the message that Jesus gave and as it is recorded in the first four books of the New Testament and the other scriptures that proclaim the message that Jesus called the "Good News" would they have had a brotherly love for each other? What if both Jim and James were taught that they were to be conformed to the image and likeness of Jesus? Would the animosity between the two members of Peachtree Baptist Church have developed in the same manner as it developed and caused a division in the church? What would have been the outcome of the development of the churched resources if the church had followed Jesus in seeking

189

and saving the lost? We can only speculate because none of that happened, but we can assure ourselves that the outcome would have been exactly as the Holy Spirit would have directed.

It is my observation that Christian churches these days are full of members who are hearers of the word only. Read James 1:22. That is; church members are content to come to church to be bench warmers and not active participants in the Gospel of Jesus in which the lost are sought out and the plan of salvation is presented. There is no warning that repentance is necessary in many churches today, nor are there many sermons in which the teacher or preacher warns that sin is prevalent in the lives of all mankind. There is very little or no part of the message that tells the lost that they face God's judgment if they continue to live a life of sin without the atonement offered by the acceptance of Jesus into their life. There is no emphasis on the belief that Jesus and only Jesus can bring reconciliation between the wrath of God and the perfection that God demands. Psalms 7:12.

Christian churches are not very likely to admit that there is a sovereign God who not only has the right to choose the members of His heavenly kingdom but who in fact does choose His elect based on His choice that was made before the world began. It would seem that the modern Christian church offers a combination of good works and good behavior as the plan of salvation rather than the grace of God.

There is no discussion in church that the blood of Jesus was shed for His elect or how one could determine if he/she is part of the elect. Even though Jesus Himself told His followers that, "I am the Bread of Life whoever comes to me will never go hungry, and whoever believes in me will never be thirsty. However, as I told you, you have seen me, and still, you do not believe. All those who the Father gives Me will come to Me, and whoever comes to Me, I will never drive away. For I have come down from heaven not to do My will, but to do the will of Him who has sent Me. And this is the will of Him who has sent Me, that I shall lose none of all those He has given Me but raise them up at the last day. For my Father's will is that everyone who looks to the Son and believes in Him shall have eternal life, and I will raise them up at the last day." John 6:35-40.

Therefore, if you believe that Jesus is the Son of God and that He can and will forgive your sins, you shall be saved. If you have become saved then you should follow Jesus's example, be baptized and share your faith by becoming a witness to all those who God causes to come before you who are lost. If on the other hand, you do not believe that Jesus will save the lost of which you are member, you are condemned and will suffer eternal damnation.

If you are a part of God's elect, you will be brought to salvation by the influence of the Holy Spirit and you are powerless to resist the calling of the Holy Spirit. Paul puts it like this, "What then shall we say? Is God unjust? Not at all! For he says to Moses. 'I will have mercy on whom I have mercy. And I will have compassion on whom I have compassion.'

"It does not, therefore, depend on human desire or effort, but on God's mercy. For scripture says to Pharaoh; I raised you up for this very purpose. That I might display my power in you, and that my name might be proclaimed in all the earth. Therefore, God has mercy on whom He wants to have mercy, and He hardens whom He wants to harden." Romans 9:15-18.

Again, God is totally sovereign, and He alone determines who He will call and make a part of His elect.

This doctrine is not in vogue in the modern church, and where election is preached (especially in Primitive Baptist churches) the doctrine has become hyper-Calvinistic and is taught so that the congregant cannot know whether he/she is saved but must go through life guessing whether God has called that person to salvation.

I once asked a pastor what predestination means and whether it is a doctrine that is adhered to by the Baptist church. As I recall I received no direct answer to my question but was admonished to figure out for myself how I felt about that part of the Calvinistic belief in the sovereignty of God and the election of the saints. Part of the reason that I am writing this book is to answer that question for myself and to determine if the admonition of Jesus to be prefect is possible.

Lastly, the doctrine of the preservation of the saints teaches that a believer once saved is always saved. If a Christian is called by God and is a part of the elect, he/she will remain a Christian and cannot fall from grace. This does not mean that a Christian cannot backslide (a term that was very much in vogue when I was a young man starting out on my lifelong adventure as a Christian) and come under the chastisement of God. It does, however, mean that once you are saved the love of Jesus and His blood will finally and completely save you for all eternity.

Jesus says, "I did tell you, but you do not believe. The works that I do in my Father's name testify about Me, but you do not believe because you are not My sheep. My sheep listen to My voice; I know them, and they follow Me. I give them eternal life and they shall never perish; No one will snatch them out of My hands. My Father who has given them to Me is greater than all: No one can snatch them out of my Father's hand. I and the Father are one." John 10:25-30.

Is it possible to be perfect as our heavenly Father is perfect? The answer is an emphatic **YES** because if you are going to heaven and will stand before God you must be perfect just as Jesus is perfect.

Jesus is perfect in body, mind and spirit. When we admit that we are sinners, repent, ask for Jesus to enter our lives, and accept that the blood of Jesus has saved us, then the perfection process begins in the life of each born-again Christian. Ultimately, a born-again Christian will stand before God and stand there as if we were the perfection that God intended when He created man in His own image. That perfection is only possible because Jesus came into the world and shed His precious blood on my behalf. Thanks be to God!!

CHAPTER 29

LEVI COMPLETES WRITING THE GOSPEL THAT WAS GIVEN TO HIM BY JESUS AND THE HOLY SPIRIT.

Both Pradik and Marium repented of their sins and confessed that Jesus was the Son of God and that He and only He could reconcile their lives to God. They followed Jesus's example and were baptized, and the Holy Spirit sealed them for service to God.

Levi continued to watch over the village by Lake Tuz. Levi continued to write the words and acts of Jesus as the Holy Spirit gave him the ability to remember clearly what had happened while he and the other disciples of Jesus followed Him around Galilee and Judea. Levi wrote about how each of them witnessed the miracles, the healings and the casting out of evil spirits from the thousands that came from far and near to see and hear Jesus.

Levi continued to send the drafts of his writings to Antioch where Mark and Rachel now spent most of their time. Mark anxiously received each dispatch from Levi and edited the draft and put it into the Greek language that Mark used in his Gospel and in the society to which he belonged. After Mark put into the Greek language the Aramaic words used in the draft of the story as written by Levi, he sent it on to the group of scribes hired by Mark. The scribes copied the draft onto papyrus pages. The pages were then complied to form a book that could be carried to other congregations of Christians. Other Christian congregations were continuing to spring up in Asia Minor and in Europe mainly thanks to the missionary efforts that had started when Paul and Silas were called to come over to Macedonia. Acts 16:9-10.

As soon as any part of the Gospel of Matthew, as the book written by Levi was called by the scribes of Antioch, the pages were sent to a preselected group of churches who in turn shared the Gospel with other churches. Also traveling evangelist often carried a copy of the available pages of the Gospel of Matthew with them as they roamed throughout the Christian churches in Asia Minor, Greece, Spain and even to Rome itself when the Imperial Roman government was not looking. Some of these traveling evangelists also carried the Gospel as written by Mark. Generally, the Gospel of Mark was more suited to be read to the Roman, non-Jewish Christians while the Gospel written by Levi was read to the Jewish Christians as the traveling evangelist encountered the different churches that they visited.

As the traveling evangelist took the words of the writers of Matthew and Mark with them, they spread the Gospel of the birth, life, teachings, healings, casting out of demons, confrontation with the Pharisees, promises of Jesus, trial, death and resurrection of Jesus to the distant parts of the Roman and even non-Roman world as it existed in 85 AD. When Levi started to write the Gospel that became known as the Book of Matthew, he set out to amplify the good news that his friend and collaborator Mark had written when he was told the story of Jesus as related to Mark by Peter. Because both Peter and Levi had been disciples of Jesus they had seen and experienced all of the events, teachings and circumstances of the ministry of Jesus when He said to each of them "Follow Me."

While Mark had not been with Jesus as had Levi and Peter, Mark had a different prospective on the meaning of the life of Jesus than either Peter or Levi. Mark instead was a man who had very little prospective regarding the background of the Jewish law and traditions of the Jewish people and how that manifested in the people who Jesus encountered while he conducted His earthly ministry. Mark was a man who heard the good news and even though he was a Roman citizen, was moved by the Holy Spirit to accept the words of Peter and the other Apostles and commit his life to the belief that Jesus is the Son of God and that he, Mark, was also called to be a witness to the love and sacrifice of Jesus the Christ.

On the other hand, Levi was a Jew. Levi grew up in the

Jewish tradition. Levi's life was infused with the Jewish religion that demanded loyalty to the law and a commitment to the traditions of the Jewish people. The Jews saw themselves as the chosen people of God. The Jews thought that God had promised the Jewish nation to be superior to the gentiles who were only fit to serve as fuel for the fires of hell.

Unlike Mark, who could tell the story of Jesus without the baggage of Judaism, Levi was so emersed in Judaism that he had to untangle the story of Jesus from the traditions and history of the Jewish people. Levi's task was to convey the Gospel in such a way that the people that he was writing to came to believe that Jesus was exactly who He claimed to be, and that Jesus fulfilled the prophesy concerning the Messiah that the Jews were expecting to come and set matters straight. Prior to the advent of Jesus, the Jews believed that the Messiah would restore the Jewish people to their rightful place in the world order and especially get rid of the gentiles that kept showing up in Palestine and causing problems for the Hebrew people.

To accomplish the task of convincing the Jews that Jesus is the true Messiah, Levi undertook to use the Old Testament Scriptures to assert that Jesus met all of the prophesies of the Old Testament. Not only the prophesies, but also all of the traditions that the Jews of his day believed about the Messiah, would need to be confronted. The notion that God would send the Messiah to re-establish Israel to the place that it desired and thought it should hold in the world had to be dispelled. Jesus, Levi had to explain, was sent to seek and to save the lost and not to win a war with Rome.

Levi was fortunate that when he met Mark in Jerusalem that there still existed public records keep by the Jewish officials that Levi could research to verify the lineage of Jesus. Levi because he was a tax collector and had knowledge of both the Jewish law and traditions, and he also had access to the Roman taxation records, was able to find the lineage of Jesus and copy it before the Romans destroyed all of the public records when they totally destroyed Jerusalem in 70 AD.

The linage of Jesus was necessary to confirm that Jesus was of the ancestry of the prominent people in Jewish history. Jesus earthly father and mother was from the lineage of King David. As a direct descendant of King David Jesus's authority to rule the Jewish people was established. That fact was very important to the Jews who put their trust in Jewish traditions.

To allow the Jewish people to find a basis for belief that Jesus derived His authority from God. Levi spent time and effort to establish that the genealogy of Jesus was in fact a part of the Jewish ruling class. Levi characterized the genealogy as an important fact in establishing the basis of the claim the Jesus was the promised Messiah.

It is unknown concerning the source of Levi's knowledge of the visit of the angel to Joseph, Jesus's earthly father. Perhaps the source of that part of Jesus's birth was provided by Mary, Jesus's mother. We really do not know the origine of that part of the story of the birth of Jesus, but considering the lengths that Levi went to in order to confirm the genealogy of Jesus, it would be very unlikely that Levi left the detail of the angel's visit in a dream when Joseph discovered that Mary his betrothed was pregnant, to someone outside of Jesus's immediate family. Levi undoubtedly reported the facts surrounding Jesus's birth accurately and confirmed the story with firsthand sources.

Next Levi was aware of the story of the visit of the Magi and again probably confirmed the story with firsthand accounting of the words that he wrote. Jesus was most likely the source of the visit of the Magi because by then He would have been a child of around 2 years old and capable of telling the time and place of the Magi's visit to Bethlehem. The story was also important to the Jewish, class conscious seekers of evidence of the status of Jesus, because it shows that embassies of other peoples recognized the royalty and divinity of Jesus from the earliest days of Jesus's life on this earth.

As Levi continued to write the story of the birth of Jesus, he would often pause and pray that God through the Holy Spirit would give him clarity of mind and purpose to accomplish the will of God. Levi prayed that the words that he used would be the words that God wanted and that those who read the words would hear what God wanted to be heard. Levi also prayed that the pages he was writing would find their place in the hands of those who would distribute those pages to the people who would most benefit from the words and the story he was telling. Levi prayed that God would consecrate his efforts and convert Levi's talents to the benefit of God and his savior and friend, Jesus.

The story of King Herod's attempt to kill Jesus and the escape to Egypt was told to Levi by Mary. Levi included that part of the story as another confirmation that the life of Jesus fulfilled the prophesy of the Old Testament writers that Jesus was the Messiah. Again, the Jewish readers needed this confirmation that Jesus fit completely all that had been foretold in Scripture.

When John the Baptist appeared on the scene and all of Judea and Jerusalem went out to hear him preach, Levi went too. Levi was in the crowd when Jesus was baptized and heard the voice from heaven proclaim that this very same Jesus was His beloved son. Levi saw the dove like spirit descend on Jesus and was mystified by the significance of those events. It was not until Jesus saw Levi collecting taxes in Galilee that Jesus called Levi to follow Him. When Jesus called, Levi then understood the meaning of Jesus relationship with God.

Levi continued to pray, think, and feel the leadership of the Holy Spirit, and write. He kept himself busy and lived a good life on the shore of Lake Tuz. The Christians that he lived with recognized that Levi was responding to the call of God even as an old man in a place very far away from where he was first called and very far away from the trouble that had caused the death of his friend and teacher Jesus, the Messiah.

Then one day when it was least expected, Roman soldiers dressed ready for combat arrived on the edge of the village and fear struck the Christian community. As you will recall some time ago Roman soldiers had visited the village and demanded that each of the Christians swear allegiance to the emperor Domitian. The Romans insisted that these Christians declare that

Domitian was god and had complete authority over the religious beliefs of all the subjects of the Roman Provinces. That included Galatia, and the village near Lake Tuz in which Levi lived.

The village was a Christian community that believed that there was only one God and Domitian was not the god that they worshiped. In other Christian communities the Christians, at times, give into the Roman demands and would take a knee to Domitian. No doubt those Christians would secretly deny their loyalty to the emperor and confess Jesus as Lord. However, in the village where Levi lived, the Christians only would acknowledge Jesus as the true Lord of their lives. This of course created an immediate problem.

To make matters worse, Pradik remained in the village, and he was an escaped slave of a Roman citizen and there was a price on his head that gave an incentive to the Roman soldiers to find Pradik and get the reward for bringing him back to his Roman masters. The Roman soldiers believed that Pradik was in this particular Christian village and that the Christians had aided Pradik to avoid being returned to his owners. Informers had seen Pradik and reported to the Romans that Pradik was in the village where Levi lived.

For an hour the Roman soldiers rested at the edge of the village and the village population was frozen with anxiety about what might happen next. Finally, after an hour of waiting the Romans marched into the middle of the village, and the Centurian shouted in the Aramaic language for all to hear, "Everyone in this village come to the center of the village and form a line."

Slowly, everyone in the village, including Pradik and Levi, made their way to the village center and formed a line as the Centurian had demanded. The Centurian walked down the line of people and grabbed Pradik by his neck and threw him to the ground and two of the soldiers grabbed Pradik and tied his hands behind his back and kicked his head until he was unconscious.

The Centurian then came to Levi and also pulled him from the line and separated him from the remainder in the villagers.

The Centurian took Levi into a hut and removed his helmet and sat down on the only chair that was in the hut. Levi stood in the hut wondering what was to occur next.

The Centurian said nothing for a minute or two then he said, "My father was a Centurian and served in Galilee. I learned the Aramaic language as a child when we lived in Galilee. My father's servant was very sick and was suffering. My farther heard that your Jesus was in Capernaum which was a day and a half journey away from where we lived. The servant was a close and trusted servant and was loved by everyone in our family. My father traveled the distance to beg Jesus to heal our beloved servant. My father believed that your Jesus could and would heal our servant because my father was a man with great authority, and everyone did as my father demanded.

"When Jesus said that He would come to our home to do as my father asked, my father said, 'I do not deserve that you come under my roof. But just say the word and my servant will be healed. For I am man under authority, with soldiers under me. I say to this one "Go" and he goes; and to this one "Come" and he comes. I say to my servant "do this" and he does it.'

"Your Jesus said that it would be done as my father had asked and at that very moment our servant was healed. Do you know anything about what I just said to you?"

Levi replied, "I was with Jesus that day. I recall your father coming to Jesus. I remember how a crowd of people were always following Jesus and us because Jesus drew people to Him. Everyone wanted to see and hear Jesus and they all wanted to press close to Him because Jesus loved all the people. It was late in the morning when the Centurian, evidently, your father, approached us. We were walking from the home of Peter's mother's home headed to another town near Capernaum. The day before Jesus preached on the other side of the lake and had healed a man with leprosy. As we were in the boat crossing the lake a fierce storm came up. Jesus was asleep in the stern of the boat. The winds blew and the waves came crashing oner the sides of the little boat that we were rowing from one side of the lake to the other. The storm was so fierce that even the seasoned fishermen, who were used to the lake and the storms that came up suddenly at times, started to become anxious about our chances of getting through the storm without some of us drowning.

"The storm was so bad that we had no choice but to wake Jesus and tell Him that we were about to sink and some of us would surely drown. Jesus looked at us with those loving eyes of His. He said in a voice of command that I can still remember as if He were here with us today, 'Peace, be still' and the waves and the wind immediately obeyed, and it was calm.

"The Centurian was not the only one to want Jesus to heal the sick. Multitudes of people came to Jesus and He never turned them away. Yes, I remember that day and I remember the Centurian, and I believe that he must have been your father."

The Centurian that now rose from the seat in the hut came slowly towards Levi. When he was directly in front of Levi he spoke in a low and malevolent voice, I am under orders to make an example of you and your village. We are here to burn the village down, kill the men and take the women and children into slavery. That poor creature who was a slave that my men just kicked around will be crucified by tomorrow. We were ordered to kill you this afternoon. However, my father owes your Jesus a favor for what He did for our servant when he served in Galilee. Therefore, tell me what you want from me today and I shall let this village stand and let your people live because of your Jesus."

Levi looked at the Centurian and said so only the Centurian could hear, "I am under the protection of Jesus. If He can command the wind and the waves and drive the evil from the hearts and minds of demon possessed men and raise the dead to life as I have seen Him do, I cannot and do not fear what you may do to me or the people in this village. God has a plan for us, and His plan will be fulfilled no matter what you intend to do today or tomorrow. Now in the name of Jesus you and your men march out of our village, leave Pradik with us and go. When you realize the power and love of Jesus you and any of your men who want, may return, and you too can be healed of the sickness that resides in your hearts."

When Levi finished speaking the Centurian did exactly as Levi had told him to do and the Roman Centurian and the soldiers left the village. Pradik was still tied and unconscious, but without further damage. Pradik was lying face down in the road where he had fallen. A few minutes after the Romans left the village Levi emerged from the hut and addressed the people who immediately gathered around Levi and also attended to Pradik because Levi and Marium had gone to where Pradik lay and began to help him to his feet.

Someone in the crowd shouted, "Why did they leave so abruptly? What did you tell them and when will they come back?"

"When Jesus was still with us in Galilee the Centurian's father met Jesus and Jesus healed the Centurian's father's servant. It is the providence of God that the Centurian who came to our village today had an experience that caused him to be aware that we as followers of Jesus, the Messiah sent to us from God, can and will protect us as long as we have faith in Him." was Levi's reply.

Almost everyone agreed with Levi, and they all came to him and touched him and expressed their faith in Jesus. Even Pradik wanted to hear more about how Jesus had intervened in the situation with the Romans because Pradik realized that there was something different about the Christians of which he was now a part. When he thought the Christians were different, he thought of how these Christian people seemed to genuinely care for each other and actually cared about him as well. Pradik never heard any of these Christian's shout at each other nor did he detect anything but kindness and expressions of love for each other and for him as well. Pradik had never experienced such kindness and love and he was not only grateful but wanted to stay with these people and find out why they were the way they were.

201

Then the Jewish men from a nearby village showed up and a new problem arose. At first the villagers in the settlement to which Levi belonged, were skeptical of the men from the Orthodox village. The Jewish men that showed up one afternoon were seeking out Levi for a discussion. They wanted to discuss the differences in the beliefs of the two groups. Of course, the people from Levi's village had every reason to be skeptical because of the previous confrontation that had occurred between the two groups in the past. However, the Orthodox Jewish men came bearing gifts of salt and cloth that were always needed by the people.

Yehuda, the leader of the Orthodox Jewish village, spoke to Levi and said for the whole village to hear, "We worship the same Jehovah God. We are looking for the Messiah. You claim to have found the Messiah that we are expecting. We believe that the Messiah will restore the promised land to us and place us in the position that we were in when King David sat on Israel's throne. You believe that Jesus's kingdom is in heaven and that you will join Jesus in heaven when your time on this earth has come to an end. Tell us why we should believe that Jesus is the Messiah and why we are wrong in our expectations of Messiah."

"I will gladly tell you of how Jesus has fulfilled the expectations of the Prophets and how the scripture has been pointing the world to Jesus from the beginning of time." Levi replied.

Levi took the Orthodox men into his hut and pulled out the pages of the book that he was nearly finished writing and laid the paged in front of the Orthodox Jewish men. Levi then said, "I too am a Jew. I went out to see John at the river Jordan when we all heard that he was preaching that the Messiah was soon coming and I wanted to learn as much as possible from such a man as John. Do you remember how all of the scribes and Pharisees also went to see such a man like John? Then one day while I was listening to John, Jesus came to be baptized. When He was baptized the Heavens opened and the Spirit of Jehovah descended on Jesus and the voice of Jehovah was heard saying

'This is my beloved son, in whom I am well pleased.' I knew at that moment that Messiah had come into the world.

"Then one day while I was sitting at the tax collection booth, Jesus walked by and said to me, 'Follow me.'

"I was a tax collector. I was an outcast by my own people and yet Jesus called me. The very same Jesus who God called His Son. I had to follow. I could not resist the Son of God. For three years I followed Jesus. I saw Him perform miracle after miracle. He healed the sick, the blind He gave sight, the deft He opened their ears, He raised the dead, He fed thousands with nothing more than a few fish and a few barley loafs, He commanded the wind and the sea to be calm and it was so, He walked across the water as if it were dry ground, and He called me and was my friend.

"When Jesus spoke, those of us who followed Him hung on every word. Jesus words were clear, and His message was as precious as the finest gold. Jesus gave us the words of life and we believed that He was and is the Son of the Living God and that He came to set those that believe in Him free form the sin that has been in us since we were born so that we can stand before God and be in His kingdom. Jesus spoke with the authority of Jehovah and not as the other teachers of the Hebrew people.

"Jesus gave His life as a perfect sacrifice for the sins of His people.

"The Romans and the Pharisees thought that they were putting Jesus to death. They thought that they were ending our relationship with Jesus by putting Him on the cross. They only succeeded in finally reconciling mankind to God by the sacrificial death and resurrection of Jesus the Son of the living God, the Messiah."

The Orthodox Jewish men stood there speechless for many minutes. One by one they stood and left the hut and then left the village, never to return. Such is the power of the Gospel of Jesus the Messiah, the Son of God, the savior of men and the Christ.

CHAPTER 30

"WHAT GOOD IS IT FOR SOMEONE TO GAIN THE WHOLE WORLD YET FORFEIT THEIR SOUL?"
MARK 8:37

The words of Jesus from His sermon to the crowd of 4000 people that He had feed after Jesus and His disciples had a retreat at Caesarea- Philippi is a question that not only had profound significance at the time that Jesus said these words, but also has profound implications in the face of today's existential generation. In chapter 12 of this book, I mentioned some of the ramifications of the existential philosophy that is prevalent as it relates to the "Prosperity Theology" currently preached in some churches. In chapter 12 I stated that the compact of some Christians has caused them to believe that they can reach a bargain with God in which, if they give to the church, then God will shower them with money. That theology causes men to think that they are on the same level as God. However, God is sovereign, and men are either saved or damned based on the will of God. God created man in God's own image and not the other way around. Genesis 1: 27 and Psalms 100: 3.

Because we are created in the image of God then within every man/woman is a soul that is the seat of a mankind's spiritual nature. The spiritual nature of mankind causes all men/women to ask, "Is there a God and what does God have to do with me?" Mankind also has a non-spiritual self that the Apostle Paul calls the nature of the flesh in men. The spiritual man/woman even after that man/woman is saved is at war with the flesh. In Romans 7:14-25 Paul writes,

"We know that the law is spiritual, but I am unspiritual. Sold as a slave to sin. I do not understand what I do. For what I want to do, I do not do, but what I hate I do. And if I do what I do not want to do, I agree that the law is good. As it is, it is no longer I myself who does it, but it is sin living in me. For I know that good itself does not dwell in me, that is, in my sinful nature. For I have the desire to do what is good, but I cannot carry it out. For I do not do the good I want to do, but the evil I do not want to do- this I keep on doing. Now if I do what I do not want to do, it is no longer I who does it, but the sin living in me that does it.

"So, I find the law at work. Although I want to do good, evil is right there with me. For in my inner being I delight in God's law; But I see another law at work in me, waging war against the law of my mind and making me a prisoner of the law of sin at work within me. What a wretched man that I am! Who will rescue me from this body that is subject to death? Thanks be to God, who delivers me through Jesus Christ our Lord!"

As Paul explains, we all have a sinful nature. The sinful nature is constantly at war with the spiritual nature that we are privileged to receive when we accept the call of Jesus and are saved. So then why are we concerned with the existential philosophy that is prevalent in the world today? Because existentialism disregards God and places self in total control of the way we as human beings view life either in this world or in the world to come.

Jesus said, "What good is it for someone to gain the whole world and forfeit their soul?"

Can anyone actually gain the whole world? When my children were still watching cartoon shows on TV (I would occasionally watch the cartoon shows with them and perhaps paid too much attention to them as I watched) there was a cartoon titled "Pinkie and the Brain" that was about two lab rats in which Pinkie would always ask the Brain at the end of the show, "What shall we do tomorrow?" The Brain would always make the same reply, "Same as always Pinkie, plan on taking over the world." The Brain had a totally narcissistic personality that required him to control everything and everyone with whom he came in contact.

There is a personality defect that has become more recognizable since 2016 and it is diagnosed in the DSM-5 (Diagnostic and Statistical Manual of Mental Disorders, Fifth Edition) as Narcissistic Personality Disorder or NPD. NPD is characterized by; 1) grandiose sense of self-importance, 2) frequent fantasies about having or deserving, 3) belief in superiority of self, 4) need for admiration, 5) entitlement to all that they desire, 6) willingness to exploit others, 7) lack of empathy, and 8) frequent envy. Psychologists and psychiatrists are not certain of the causes of narcissistic personality disorder but are able to make a diagnosis of the disorder from observation.

In a recent article that links narcissistic personality disorder with existential isolation the author Max Karlin, in the <u>Journal of Interactive Psychotherapy and Systemic Analysis,</u> December 20, 2022, "Existential Isolation and Narcissism", writes that "there is an intersect in compelling ways that shed light on the human psyche and our intrinsic need for connection. Existential isolation delves deep into our experiences of loneliness, not just in the physical realm, but on an emotional and cognitive level. It encapsulates a profound sensation of detachment from others, sometimes even amidst seemingly fulfilling relationships...."

"Narcissism, in contrast, presents itself as an overt preoccupation with one's own desires and ambitions.... As outlined by Campbell & Miller (2011), It encompasses an elevated sense of self-worth, entitlement, and palpable lack of empathy. Moreover, individuals with narcissistic tendencies often seek validation and admiration from their peers...." (citations omitted)

"At the heart of existentialism lies the belief that humans inherently crave their own purpose and significance. This autonomy while empowering, also breeds existential angst, demanding choices without any cosmic compass. Herein, narcissism can become a refuge, amplifying self-worth to dodge this existential distress. (Heidegger, 1962; May 1958; Sartre, 2003).

".... In contrast, narcissism impedes authenticity and real understanding of life's purposes."

NPD thus is said to exasperate the sense of loneliness by an unrealistic sense of self-worth by further disabling the individual from meaningful relationships. An individual who is existentialistic and already is viewing life without relying on an external belief system is more likely to suffer NPD. Many view Donald Trump as someone who suffers from the symptoms of NPD.

What then is the remedy for narcissistic/existential angst? As Paul said in Romans 7, "Oh wretched man that I am! Who will rescue me from this body that is subject to death? Thanks be to God, who delivers me through Jesus Christ, our Lord."

If we are made in God's image, we are constantly seeking relationships, because we are not created to live in isolation. We must and do seek relationships throughout our lives. From the time that we are born we want and need others. First our parents (also parents who have children of necessity seek close relationships with their children) then with siblings, then with school mates and friends. These relationships are normal and healthy. By the time we reach adolescence normal individuals seek relationships across gender lines and finally, humans will seek long term relationships with friends and spouses. If we recognize that we have a spiritual nature, we will seek a personal relationship with God.

God also seeks a close personal relationship with the people He has created. The problem is that we have fallen from the perfection that God created us to be. When God made man on the sixth day of creation as expressed in Genesis 1:31, "God saw all that He made, and it was very good."

Then, however sin entered into the equation and that was and is a deal breaker for God. How do I know that sin is a deal breaker between mankind and God, you rightfully ask. Because Jesus has said, "Therefore be perfect, even as your heavenly Father is perfect."

Sin is recognized as a deviation from good moral behavior in every major religion on this planet. However, only Christianity recognizes the concept of original sin, or that sin that is inherent in all human beings from birth. The concept of original sin is rooted in Judaism, but Judaism dose not, of course, recognize that there can be atonement from sin as Christians believe. In Christianity, especially under a Calvinistic point of view, mankind is separated from God because all of mankind is totally depraved and deserves rejection and punishment by God.

The good news of Christianity is that there can be redemption from sin by belief in the death and resurrection of Jesus who substitutes His perfection and pays the price for my/our sin. Further the resurrection of Jesus after His sacrificial death on the cross is evidence that God has fully accepted Jesus's crucifixion and death as a completed payment for the punishment that I/we deserve because of our sin.

Because God demands perfection, the sacrificial death and resurrection of Jesus, the only perfect person to ever walk this earth, brings salvation to believers by becoming the perfect sacrifice and submitting Himself to the punishment for sin that I/we deserve. I/we can become adopted and conformed to the image and likeness of Christ when we repent of our sins and accept Jesus as the only means of attaining a true relationship with God. Jesus said, "I am the way and the truth and the life. No one comes to the Father except through me. If you really know me, you will know my Father as well. From now on you do know Him and have seen Him." John 14:6.

When I accept Jesus into my life, immediately and instantaneously the spirit of God comes into me, and I pass from darkness and death into light and life. Paul puts it like this, "Therefore if anyone is in Christ, the new creation has come. The old has gone. The new is here! All this is from God, who reconciled us to Himself through Christ and gave us the ministry of reconciliation that God was reconciling the world to Himself in Christ, not counting people's sins against them. And He has committed to us the message of reconciliation. We are therefore Christ's ambassadors, as though Christ were making His appeal through us. We implore you on Christ's behalf. Be reconciled to God. God made Him who had no sin to be sin for us, so that in Him we might become the righteousness of God." Corinthians 5:17-21.

Therefore, how does this discussion have anything to do with existentialism and narcissism? Remember the Brain in the cartoon? The Brain was always seeking to take over the world. A narcissistic person (a trait obviously prevalent in authoritarian dictators and want to be authoritarian dictators) will seek to exploit anything and everything that stands in his/her way to the adulation that they seek. Put into the mix an existential belief system that only seeks self-fulfillment, and you have a formula for a person who will try to gain the whole world but who will lose his own soul.

In John 3:17 it is written, "For God did not send His Son into the world to condemn the world, but to save the world through Him. Whoever believes in Him is not condemned, but whoever does not believe stands condemned already because they have not believed in the name of God's one and only Son. This is the verdict: Light has come into the world, but people love darkness instead of light because their deeds were evil. Everyone who does evil hates the light and will not come into the light for fear that their deeds will be exposed, but whoever lives by the truth comes into the light, so that it may be seen plainly that what they have done has been done in the sight of God."

If God demands perfection in order to stand before Him, then how shall we obtain the perfection that God demands of us? The only means available to any of us is to do exactly as Jesus has told us to do. Repent and believe that God sent Jesus to seek and to save the lost sinners of which I am the chief of sinners. When I/we repent, accept Jesus as the only one who can save us from our sinfulness and are baptized, I/we shall be saved. When we are saved, we begin to take on the likeness of Jesus and are on the road to becoming perfect even as our heavenly Father is perfect.

If you are interested in becoming saved by the offer of Jesus to save you from your sinful nature, then I will pray with you and give you further instruction on how to know that you have come into the light and life that Jesus offers to those who accept Him as their savior and friend. I will leave my contact information here and at the end of this book. jeffreysakas@gmail. com or you may write to me through the publishing company listed on the masthead.

It is my prayer that anyone who has a desire to follow Jesus and partake in the joy and fellowship of those who have found the peace and love that God offers will at this very moment surrender themselves to Jesus, my Lord and Savior.

CHAPTER 31
LEVI COMPLETES THE GOSPEL OF MATTHEW AND RETURNS TO ANTIOCH.

After Levi and those who lived in the village by Lake Tuz had been confronted by both Roman soldiers and the Jewish leaders from the neighboring village, Levi finished writing. Levi wrote exactly what he remembered Jesus told His disciples when they were confronted by those who would hate them and cause them to suffer. Jesus said that because of their belief that Jesus had been sent by God; that they would suffer because Jesus suffered.

Levi thought back to when Jesus has sent the disciples out to the Judean villages and had empowered them to heal the sick and to cast out evil spirits. Levi remembered the words of Jesus as he wrote the second discourse that Jesus gave about how His disciples were to only go to the Hebrew people and were to avoid the Gentiles and the Samaritans. The disciples were to announce that the "Kingdom of heaven was coming near, to heal the sick, raise the dead, cleanse those who had leprosy, and drive out demons. Freely you have received; freely give."

"We were sent out like sheep among wolves." Levi remembered. The disciples did as Jesus commanded and when they returned to Jesus there was much rejoicing because the people of Israel wanted to be healed of sickness and they were excited because of the prospect of the coming of the Messiah was very much anticipated and seemed to be happening in their presence.

Jesus told His disciples that even though the world was anticipating a Messiah that the kingdom of heaven was not to have an earthly realm and that eventually even those who welcomed Jesus and His disciples would seek to destroy them because the hearts of men think only of earthly riches and do not store up treasure in heaven. Jesus said, "Anyone who welcomes you

211

welcomes me, and anyone who welcomes me welcomes the one who sent me. Whoever welcomes a prophet as a prophet will receive a prophet's reward, and whoever welcomes a righteous person as a righteous person will receive a righteous person's reward. And if anyone gives even a cup of cold water to one of these little ones, who is my disciples, truly, I tell you, that person will certainly not lose their reward."

Levi remembered the time when the disciples of John the Baptist came to Jesus to ask if He was the one who had been set from God. Jesus replied, "Go back and report to John what you hear and see. The blind received sight, the lame walk, those who have leprosy are cleansed, the deaf hear, the dead are raised, and the good news is proclaimed to the poor. Blessed is anyone who does not stumble on account of me." Jesus knew that John would understand that the prophesy that told of how the Messiah would heal, preach, and conduct His ministry would resonate with John and he would know that Jesus was the one that the world was expecting to come from God.

Levi remembered the parables that Jesus told the crowds that followed Him everywhere He went. Jesus told the stories in illustrations that the people could understand. Jesus spoke of farmers scattering seeds in the fields and how the seeds fell on the different types of ground that did and did not produce a crop.

Jesus told the story of how the enemy of the farmer sowed weeds in the crop to cause confusion. The farmer, Jesus explained, was the Son of Man and the enemy was the evil one. Jesus told the parable of the mustard seed, the story of the hidden treasure and the parable of the fishing net in which the fishermen caught fish that were editable and those that were bad and how they would be separated by the fishermen; implying that the Son of Man was the fisherman who separated saved men from evil men.

Jesus spoke in parables to fulfill the words of the prophet Isaiah who said, "You will be ever hearing but never understanding; you will be ever seeing but never perceiving. For this people's hearts have become calloused; they hardly hear with their own ears, and they have closed their eyes. Otherwise, they might see with their eyes, hear with their ears, understand with their hearts and turn and I would heal them."

Levi was there when Jesus received word that John the Baptist had been beheaded by Herod, and he was there when Jesus had compassion on the crowd that had followed him into a desolate place. Jesus feed them with nothing more than five small barley loafs and two sardines. Levi was in the boat with the other disciples after Jesus dismissed the crowed that He had miraculously feed and had sent the disciples ahead while He took time to be alone and pray. Then, Levi saw Jesus walking on the water and realized that Jesus had amazing powers that could not be explained by anything other than He was the Son of God.

Then Levi heard Jesus tell His disciples that He would be put to death. None of the disciples understood at that time what Jesus meant. It was not until after Jesus was crucified and was raised from the dead and the Holy Spirit came upon them that they, His disciples, began to understand how someone with such power, such goodness, such willingness to take care of even the worst of the people around Him could be put to death.

Jesus took His disciples on a retreat in the region of Cesaria-Philippi. There He asked them, "Who do people say that I am?" At first, the disciples did not know how to answer Jesus. Finally, somebody spoke up and said, "Some say John the Baptist: others say Elijah; and still others, Jeremiah or one of the prophets." Then Jesus asked them, "Who do you say I am?"

Peter who was always quick to jump up and speak said, "You are the Messiah, the son of the living God."

Jesus then replied to Peter and the others there with Him," Blessed are you, Simon, son of Jonah, for this was not revealed to you by flesh and blood, but by my Father in heaven. And I will tell you that you are Peter, and on this rock, I will build my church, and the gates of Hades will not overcome it. I will give you the keys to the Kingdom of heaven. Whatever you bind on earth will be bound in heaven, and whatever you loose on earth will be loosed in heaven."

213

Then Jesus told his disciples that they were not to tell anyone that Jesus was the Messiah.

Levi recalled the day Peter, James and John went on a hike with Jesus and came back but would not say where they were or what happened to them. Later Levi learned from Peter that Jesus had taken those three to a mountain top and there Jesus was transfigured. Jesus was talking to Moses and Elijah. Then a bright cloud covered the mountain top and engulfed them, and God spoke, saying, "This is my Son, whom I love; with whom I am well pleased. Listen to Him."

Jesus for the second time told Levi and the others that He would be delivered into the hands of men and that they would kill Him and that He would be raised on the third day back to life. Levi and the disciples were grief stricken to hear these words but again did not fully understand the meaning.

Jesus continued to teach the disciples about how the kingdom of heaven would be and how they should act with each other and how His followers should act and treat each other. Jesus again resorted to telling parables. Jesus told of the unmerciful servant, who after being forgiven a great amount of money took vengeance on a fellow servant who owed him only a little.

When His disciples tried to prevent small children from approaching Jesus, Jesus said, "Let the little children come to me and do not hinder them, For the Kingdom of heaven belongs to such as these."

Jesus told how it would be difficult for the rich to enter the kingdom of heaven when a rich young man asked Jesus what he must do to receive eternal life. Then Jesus said, "Truly, I tell you at the renewal of all things, when the Son of Man sits on His glorious throne, you who have followed me will also sit on twelve thrones judging the twelve tribes of Israel. And anyone who has left houses or brothers or sisters or father or mother or wife or children or fields, for my sake, will receive 100 times as much and will inherit eternal life. But many who are first will be last and many who are last will be first."

Jesus continued to teach the crowds by telling parables

214

such as the parable of the Workers in the Vineyard in which the owner of the vineyard kept hiring men to work all day and promised the same wages to all. When the men he had hired early in the day protested that they would receive the same pay as those hired last, the owner said, "I am not being unfair to you., friend. Didn't you agree to work for a denarius? Take your pay and go. I want to give the one who was hired last the same as I gave you. Don't I have the right to do what I want with my own money? Or are you envious because I am generous?"

Then Jesus said, "So the last will be first and the first will be last."

Levi finally realized that by telling His followers this parable, Jesus was explaining the sovereignty of God who has the right to treat His creation and those who profess to be Christians and follow Jesus as He chooses. (This scripture is in direct contradiction to the "Prosperity Theology" that relies on the existential angst of people who are suffering from the economic predicament of today's society).

Levi remembered that soon after Jesus had given a series of parables to the multitudes, He for the third time told His disciples that, "We are going up to Jerusalem. And the Son of Man will be delivered over to the chief priests and the teachers of the law. They will condemn Him to death and will hand Him over to the Gentiles to be mocked and flogged and crucified. On the third day, He will be raised to life."

Jesus's statement about His death for the third time again did not register with His disciples. Levi remembered that shortly after Jesus told them about what was going to happen when they went to Jerusalem for the Passover feast, the mother of James and John came to Jesus. She asked that her sons sit on Jesus's right hand and that the other sit on the left when Jesus came into His Kingdom. Jesus told her that she did not know for what she was asking. Then when the other disciples heard about what James and John had put their mother up to, they were indignant. Jesus quickly called a meeting of the disciples and said, "You know that the rulers of the Gentiles Lord it over them, and their high officials exercise authority over them. Not so with you. Instead, whoever wants to become great among you must be your servant. And whoever wants to be first must be your slave-- just as the Son of Man did not come to be served, but to serve, and to give His life as a ransom for many."

Finally, Levi began to write about the last week that he spent with Jesus as Jesus and His disciples came close to Jerusalem. When the group came to Bethphage Jesus sent two of His disciples into Jerusalem to get a donkey for Jesus to ride on when He came into the city. This action fulfilled the prophesy spoken of in Zechariah 9:9, "Rejoice greatly daughter of Zion. Shout, daughter of Jerusalem, 'See your king comes to you, righteous and victorious and riding on a donkey, on a colt the foal of a donkey.'"

Levi could not forget the reception that Jesus received from the throngs that were along the road that Jesus took to arrive in Jerusalem. They shouted, "Hosanna to the Son of David!" All around the city people were asking, "Who is this?" and the reply came back, "This is Jesus, the prophet from Nazareth in Galilee."

Almost as soon as Jesus arrived in Jerusalem, Levi and the other disciples headed to the Temple. Jesus found the Temple courts full of merchants buying and selling. Jesus became indignant and overturned the tables of the money changers and the benches of those selling doves to be sacrificed. Jesus shouted at these merchants, "My house will be called a house of prayer, but you are making it a den of robbers."

Levi remembered how again the sick and the blind and the lame came to Jesus to be healed, but he was also aware that the chief priest and the teachers of the law saw all the wonderful things that Jesus was doing for the people and how the children were shouting, "Hosanna to the Son of David." Levi saw the expressions on the chief priest face and on the Pharisee's faces and realized that they were indignant about what Jesus was doing and Levi realized that those in charge of the Temple hated Jesus.

The next day, after spending the night in Bethny, Jesus

returned to the Temple and those in charge of the Temple came to Jesus and asked by what authority Jesus was teaching the people. Levi realized immediately that the chief priest and the elders who were in charge of the Temple and who wanted to keep their control of the people, were out to get rid of Jesus because the people were listening to Jesus and turning away from the authority of the elders and the chief priest. In other words, they were jealous of Jesus because they could not teach and cause the excitement that Jesus was causing.

Levi recalled how Jesus again told parables to the people who came to listen to Him as He spoke in the Temple courts. The chief priest and the Pharisees realized that the parables that Jesus was telling were directed at them because the parables led to the conclusion that it is not what you say but what you do that is the measure of your righteousness. These stories further infuriated the rulers of the Temple and they even more wanted Jesus arrested. However, because the people who were listening to Jesus believed that He was a prophet the rulers were afraid to have Jesus arrested while He was telling these stories at the Temple.

The Jewish authorities continued to plot ways to cause the people to turn against Jesus. The very next day Jesus again got up early and headed back to the Temple. As He was going, He was hungry and saw a fig tree and went up to it to find figs. There was nothing but leaves and Jesus said, "May you never bear fruit again." Suddenly the fig tree withered. The disciples asked Jesus how the tree withered so quickly, and Jesus replied, "Truly, I tell you, if you have faith and do not doubt, not only can you do what was done to the fig tree, but also you can say to the mountains, 'Go throw yourself into the sea,' and it will be done. If you believe, you will receive whatever you ask for in prayer."

The Pharisees got together and decided that they would test Jesus in such a way that He would be caught in a moral dilemma. They confronted Jesus with a question designed to trap Jesus. They first said so all the people around Jesus could hear that they respected Jesus as a man of integrity, who treated all men fairly. They said this to further make themselves seem as if they too were as happy to hear what Jesus was saying similarly to the crowds that followed Jesus. Then, however, they asked Jesus a question that would cause the people to think that Jesus was against the Jewish authorities who hated the fact that they had to pay taxes to the Roman government. The pharisees asked, "Is it right to pay the imperial tax to Ceaser or not?" The Pharisees thought that if Jesus said that the tax should be paid the people would think that Jesus was in favor of the Roman occupation and if He said no, don't pay the tax, that they could report Jesus to the Roman authorities as a tax evader and a rebellious criminal.

Jesus knew that their intention was evil and said, "You hypocrites, why are you trying to trap me? Show me the coin used for paying the tax." So, they brought Him a Roman coin. Jesus then asked about whose image was on the coin and they replied that the image was that of Ceaser. Jesus then said, "So give back to Ceaser what is Ceaser's, and to God what is God's."

The Pharisees went away scratching their heads because Jesus made the perfect answer. Jesus's answer did not give the Pharisees the ability to tell the Romans that Jesus was a tax evader or that He was rebellious, nor did the answer that Jesus gave cause the people to think that Jesus did not also consider that everyone should consider the obligation that we all owe to God.

Then on that same day the Sadducees, another group who were upset at the popularity of Jesus, came to Him and asked about how married people will get along in heaven. Jesus told them that the question they asked showed that they did not know the Scriptures or the power of God. The Sadducees did not believe in the afterlife. Therefore, their question to Jesus showed that the only reason that the question was asked was for the purpose of showing the absurdity of the parables that Jesus was telling. But the crowds who were there to listen to the words of Jesus realized that Jesus was the greatest of teachers because He spoke to the hearts of the people with the authority of God. Jesus was a great teacher because He knew the hearts and minds of all who listened to Him and spoke directly to each person's needs.

After the conversations between Jesus and the Pharisees and the Sadducees went on for a while, they realized that Jesus was not going be trapped by their questions, so they went away and decided on a different strategy to bring an end to Jesus.

After the Pharisees and Sadducees left, Jesus went into His fourth discourse in which He warned the people of the hypocrisy of the Pharisees. Levi remembered Jesus saying that the people should respect the office of the Jewish teachers of the law but that the people should not do as the Pharisees do. People needed to be careful of what these teachers do because they do not practice what they preach. Jesus pointed out that the Pharisees wanted to make a show out of their piety while in their hearts they only wanted an outward show of religion. Finally, Jesus told the crowd, "The greatest among you will be your servant. For those who exalt themselves well be humbled and those who humble themselves will be exalted."

Levi then remembered how Jesus warned the teachers of the law with seven warnings. Each of the warnings started out with the statement, "Wow to you teachers of the law and Pharisees, hypocrites..." Then Jesus went on to explain that their teachings were incongruous with how God viewed how piety was to actually work in the teachings and actions of those who truly followed God.

Then, Levi remembered the Fifth Discourse of Jesus in which He talked about the destruction of the Temple and the end times when all the earth would be destroyed, and time would come to an end. Jesus said that the time when all this would happen was only for God to know even though the disciples and even Levi wanted to know when the end of time would occur. Jesus gave the people and the disciples broad hents of how the end of the world would happen, but He did not give specific occurrences that would spell out when time would end.

Jesus continued to teach the crowds that came to the Temple to hear His preaching and to be healed of all their sicknesses and to have evil spirits cast out. Finally, Jesus told the crowd that there would come a time when all the world would be judged. Jesus reminded the people and especially the sinners in the crowd that Jesus would ascend His great and glorious thrown and separate the righteous from the sinners as a Shapard separates the sheep from the goats. Jesus said to the righteous that they would enter into heaven because they saw the needs of even the most wretched of the people and treated them with respect and took care of their need, even though the righteous did not realize that was something that would earn a reward. On the other hand, Jesus told the sinners that they would receive eternal punishment because they disrespected the lowliest of the people who God also created.

Levi remembered that after Jesus said these things and had been teaching and telling parables in the Temple courts for several days, that Jesus reminded His disciples that, "As you know, the Passover is 2 days away, and the Son of Man will be handed over to be crucified."

Then the chief priest and the Jewish elders meet at the chief priest palace and hatched a plot of how they could arrest Jesus and kill Him. They decided to wait until the Passover was over because they feared what the people would do if they arrested Jesus while so many people were in Jerusalem for the festival.

Jesus and His men were staying in Bethany when Jesus was not preaching in the Temple. One day while they were at the home of Simon who Jesus had healed of his leprosy, a woman came to Jesus and broke an expensive bottle of perfume over Jesus's head. The whole house was filled with the sweet smell, but Judas who would later betray Jesus said that the perfume was wasted because it could have been sold and the money given to the poor. Judas was in charge of the group's expenses and only said what he did because he wanted the money for himself. Jesus responded and said, "Why are you bothering this woman? She has done a beautiful thing for me. The poor you will always have with you, but you will not always have me. When she poured this perfume on my body, she did it to prepare me for burial. Truly, I tell you whenever this gospel is preached throughout the world, what she has done will also be told in memory of her."

After Jidas had been rebuked by Jesus he went to the Chief Priest and the Pharisees and joined their plot to arrest Jesus.

Levi was with the disciples when they celebrated the last supper that they were to have with Jesus in the upper room that Levi and the other disciples used after Jesus was crucified. It was the very same room in which Levi and Mark met when Levi and Mark discussed the writing of the Gospel that Levi had undertaken to write and was now being publishing with the help of Mark and the scribes in Antioch.

In that same upper room, Jesus told the disciples that one of them would betray Him. Levi recalled that each of the disciples looked in astonishment and disbelief at each other. Jesus was reclining and eating as was the custom at that time when one of the disciples asked Jesus in a whisper who was the one who was a traitor. Jesus said, "The one who has dipped his hand into the bowl with me will betray me. The Son of Man will go just as it is written about Him, but woe to that man who betrays the Son of Man! It would be better for him if he had not been born." As soon as Jesus said this Judas got up from the table and left the room.

Jesus then He took a loaf of bread and broke it and distributed it to the disciples and said, "Take and eat; this is my body." Jesus said this to the disciples to let them know that He would sacrifice His body as a ransom for the sins of those who would follow Him. Then He took a cup of wine, and after He had given thanks, He said, "Drink from it, all of you. This is my blood of the covenant which is poured out for many for the forgiveness of sins. I tell you; I will not drink from this fruit of the vine from now on until that day when I drink it new with you in my Father's Kingdom."

Levi remembered that the group of disciples and Jesus sang

a hymn together and then as was their custom they went to the Mount of Olives. As they were going Jesus said that that very night the disciples were going to fall away from Him and He would be left alone. Levi remembered that Peter spoke up and spoke for the rest of the disciples and said, "Even if all fall away on account of you, I never will."

Jesus, with a very sad expression as Levi recalled said to Peter, "Truly, I tell you, this very night before the rooster crows, you will disown me three times."

Then Peter said, "Even if I have to die with you, I will never disown you." All of the disciples agreed with what Peter said.

Levi remembered very clearly what happened next. The whole group of the eleven disciples (by then Judas was never again to be a part of the fellowship of Jesus's followers) went to the Garden of Gethsemane. They had all been there before because Jesus liked to go there to pray. Jesus then took Peter, James, and John aside and went further into the garden. Jesus then left those three and went further still to be alone to pray. Levi, even though he was further away could hear the agony in Jesus's voice as He prayed. Jesus was very obviously troubled as great drops of sweat poured from His face and body as He agonized about what was about to occur. It was as if His blood was pouring from Jesus as He prayed that God's will would be accomplished and that He would make it through to the finish.

Suddenly the events of that night changed. Levi saw Judas and a squadron of the Temple guards coming into the garden. They were all armed with weapons sufficient to arrest Jesus and to fight off any attempt by the disciples to prevent the Temple guards from taking Jesus into their custody. Very sadly, Levi remembered that Judas betrayed Jesus with a kiss. As Jesus had predicted, the disciples scattered and hid themselves as quickly as they could because they were afraid that they too would be arrested.

As soon as the Temple guards took Jesus away, John went to the Chief Priest palace because John was well known to the Chief Priest and realized that because of that familiarity that

John would be safe as long as he kept his mouth shut. Similarly, Peter also summoned up some courage and went to the Chief Priest palace, but because he was not as well known as John, Peter stood outside the palace until he felt safe enough to go into the courtyard and wait.

Levi was not able to get close to the palace and relied on the description of the events that went on after Jesus was taken to the Chief Priest Palace that was given to the rest of the disciples by John when they all went back to the upper room a day or two later. Levi learned that Jesus was brought before the Sanhedrin. The Sanhedrin was the governing body of the Jewish people. The Sanhedrin also acted as a court of law to try violations of the Jewish law.

While it was generally against established tradition to bring someone before the Sanhedrin in the middle of the night, that is exactly what happened in the case brought against Jesus. The Pharisees and elders brought charges against Jesus in the middle of the night because they did not want the crowd that Jesus had been teaching in the Temple to know what was going on. The trial of Jesus was underway in secret and the deck was stacked against Jesus by the Pharisees and the Sanhedrin and the Chief Priest were accomplices to the decision to bring an end to the life of the only perfect man to ever walk the earth.

In the meantime, Peter was out in the courtyard and a women servant who was standing near Peter said, "Are you not one of the followers of Jesus."

Peter replied, "No mam I do not know what you are talking about, I do not follow anybody."

Then as Peter was warming himself by the fire that had been built in the courtyard someone said, "You look like a person from Galilee because of your clothes, Jesus is from Galilee too. Are you not a part of his followers?"

Peter said, "I am not a follower of this man that is on trial, if that is what you are asking."

A few minutes later, another recognized Peter from being with Jesus while Jesus was teaching in the Temple and said,

"You are one of the followers of the man who is on trial for His life inside the Palace are you not?"

Peter with a snarl and a curse under his breath said, "I am not His follower and I do not know Him, now leave me alone!" Just then a rooster could be heard crowing because the sun was getting ready to break and just then the guards brought Jesus out of the palace and Peter saw Jesus looking at him as Jesus was being taken to the Roman governor's court.

Later, Peter told Levi and the other's when they again gathered in the upper room, when he denied Jesus the third time on the night that Jesus was arrested, he suddenly remembered the words of Jesus about how we would all abandon Him. Peter said that he was so ashamed of himself for not following Jesus to the end that he, Peter, who had been one of the leaders of the group of disciples hid in a dark corner of Jerusalem and wept for many hours.

The remaining disciples kept a low profile, but they somehow heard that Judas had committed suicide by hanging himself. They were later to confirm this when Judas's family came to get Judas's belongings that were still in the upper room. Judas's family also confirmed that after the midnight trial of Jesus before the Sanhedrin at the Chief Priest's palace, Jesus was taken to the Roman governor's courthouse because the Jews had no authority to kill Jesus by crucifixion and that is what the Pharisees wanted to happen. The Pharisees thought that crucifixion would make the people believe that it was the Romans who were out to get Jesus and not the Pharisees.

Levi still had some friends in the Roman government because he had been a tax collector. Levi found out from them that Jesus was then brought before Pilate, the Roman governor. Pilate could not at first figure out why the Sanhedrin had transferred Jesus over to his authority. Pilate questioned Jesus and found that Jesus had not broken any Roman laws. When Pilate found out that Jesus was being charged for the violation of Jewish religious customs, and that the Pharisees were out to get Jesus and blame it on the Romans, Pilate tried to pass Jesus back to the Jewish authorities but that did not work because the Chief Priest and the Elders insisted that Pilate and the Romans deal with Jesus.

While Jesus was in the custody of the Romans, Jesus was abused by the Roman soldiers. The Romans were good at dealing out insults and torture to the Hebrew people because they were cruel and knew that they could get away with cruelty and the Jews were unable to do anything about their cruelty. The soldiers beat Jesus, spit on Him, mocked Him, put a crown of thorns on His head and punched Jesus until His face was almost unrecognizable.

Pilate again tried to pass the case back to the Jewish authorities and offered to release Jesus in a show of friendship to the Jewish people, but by then the Pharisees and their conspirators had whipped up the crowd around the Roman court to demand that Pilate order that Jesus be crucified. In one last gesture to please the mob around the Roman courthouse, Pilate ordered that Jesus be flogged and then be brought out to the front of the courthouse.

When Jesus was brought out to the steps of the courthouse, He was a bloody mess, His back was torn to shreds, His face was so beaten that it was unrecognizable, and He could hardly stand. Even Pilate who was used to seeing the cruelty of the Roman soldiers was taken aback by the sight of Jesus who had stood before him prior to the beatings and floggings. Pilate asked the crowd one last time, "What shall I do then with Jesus who is called Messiah?"

The crowd, the Pharisees, the elders, all shouted back, "Crucify him." Pilate asked again, "What crime has he committed?" The crowd shouted even louder, "Crucify him." Finally, Pilate saw that he could not pass the problem onto someone else, and Pilate gave the order to have Jesus crucified.

Crucifixion was an extremely cruel manner in which to die. In those settings the prisoner was required to carry the cross beam of the instrument of death from the courthouse, the of place of imprisonment, to the place of execution. By the time that the execution of Jesus was ordered, Jesus had been arrested, taken to the Chief Priest palace, ruffed up by the palace guards, taken to the Roman courthouse, beaten, mocked, spit on, punched in the face until His nose was broken, flogged, and humiliated by the crowd and then He was compelled to carry the cross beam to the place of execution.

Jesus was so weak and weary from the torture that as they were going to Golgotha, the place of execution, Jesus stumbled, and a man named Simon from Cyrene was compelled by the soldiers to carry Jesus's cross.

When the procession finally arrived at Golgotha, Jesus was stripped naked, was laid on the ground and His hands were nailed to the cross beam. The cross beam was then pulled up to a precut notch in the vertical pole that formed the platform on which Jesus's body would hang until the weight of His own body would eventually suffocate Him. After the cross beam was pulled into place, Jesus's feet were nailed to the vertical pole so that He would suffer more and so that He could not thrash around while He died. Above His head Pilate ordered that a sign be affixed to the cross that Jesus was nailed to, saying, "THIS IS JESUS, THE KING OF THE JEWS."

The soldiers soaked a sponge with sour wine and mixed it with bitter gall and stuck it on a pole and put it up to Jesus's face, but after tasting it Jesus refused the drink.

Two other prisoners were also crucified at the same time. One on Jesus's right and the other on His left. People came by the place where the crucifixion was taking place and they mocked Jesus by saying, "He was going to destroy the Temple and raise it up in three days, let Him save Himself." The Chief Priest and Elders passed by and said, "He saved others, let Him save Himself. He is the king of Israel! Let Him come down from the cross and we will believe Him. He trusts in God. Let God save Him. He said He was the son of God." In the same way the other two prisoners who were also being crucified mocked Him.

Later the eleven remaining disciples heard that Jesus stayed on the cross from noon until about three in the afternoon. It was reported to the disciples the Jesus shouted out in His agony, "My God, my God why have you forsaken me." Some of the witnesses to the execution thought that Jesus was calling on Elijah to rescue Him and they told the others to wait and see if Elijah would respond.

Then at three in the afternoon Jesus shouted with a strong voice, "IT IS FINISHED!" Jesus gave up His spirit and died. A soldier standing close to the cross took his spear and pierced Jesus's body with a spear near where His heart would be located, and water and blood came out of His body.

A report was made to Pilate that the prisoner, Jesus, had died. Pilate was surprised that Jesus had died so quickly.

A man named Joseph from Arimathea who was a follower of Jesus, went to Pilate and asked to be allowed to take Jesus's body from the cross and to bury Him. Pilate agreed. Joseph had Jesus's body wrapped in clean linen cloth and took the body to a tomb that also belonged to the same man. Joseph's tomb was cut into the rocks and formed a small cave. Joseph had a large rock rolled in front of the opening to the tomb to seal the tomb after Jesus body was placed in the tomb.

Mary Magdaline and some of the other women who followed Jesus watched where Jesus's body was taken and reported what they had seen and heard to Levi and the other disciples. The disciples by then had all secretly returned to the upper room where they had eaten the Passover meal with Jesus.

Levi was with the other disciples, and they all were very depressed because of the events that led to Jesus's death. They also felt ashamed of themselves for having run away from Jesus as He was going through His agony. They feared the trial, and the torture of the Roman and Temple soldiers. The disciples feared the rejection of the crowd who Jesus taught at the Temple as recently as the day before. Even though many in the crowd who called for Jesus's crucifixion, had been healed of sickness or who had evil spirits cast out of them by Jesus, became willing conspirators with the Pharisees. In other words, the disciples felt sorry for themselves, and they were afraid that the Jewish mob who had yelled "crucify him" might come for them as well.

By Levi's calculations Jesus was crucified and died on Friday around 3:00 in the afternoon. Joseph had laid His body in the tomb as the dusk was settling on Jerusalem and the call to prayer was heard from the Temple as the Sabath was beginning that Friday evening. None of the disciples or the women who were with the disciples went out from the upper room for fear of the Jews and the Romans.

It was reported to the disciples that Pilate ordered a guard to be placed at the tomb where Jesus's body was buried. Pilate did this at the insistence of the Jewish leaders because they did not want anybody to claim that Jesus was still alive. The report said that there were 3 Roman soldiers at Jesus's tomb.

Despite all the fear and depression of the group of disciples and the women in the group, on early Sunday morning Mary Magdaline and some of the other women decided to go to the tomb and perform the customary rituals on Jesus's body. The women got up as Levi was awakened by their movement in the room and as they headed for the tomb which was not more than a mile away from the upper room.

Later Mary gave the disciples a breathless account of what happened at the tomb when they arrived. Not knowing how they would be able to get the stone that blocked the tomb's entrance rolled away, the women went in faith that they could perform the customary anointments for the body of Jesus.

The women described that when they arrived at the tomb the soldiers were lying on the ground, not asleep but more pet-rified by what they had witnessed. An angel was sitting on the stone that had been rolled away from the entrance to the tomb. The angel was dressed in dazzling white and said, "Do not be afraid. I know that you are looking for Jesus's body. He has aris-en. Come and see where He was lying. Then go to His disciples and tell them that He is risen from the dead and that He will meet them again in Galilee."

Mary looked into the tomb and Jesus's body was not there. As the women were heading back to the upper room they were greeted by Jesus. Jesus told the women to tell "His Brothers" to meet Him in Galilee."

That report prompted John and Peter to jump up and run to the tomb. John, who was younger than Peter arrived at the tomb first and looked around to see if the tomb was actually empty. Peter made it to the tomb moments later, but he did not linger outside. Peter rushed into the tomb and found that Jesus's body was not where it had been laid. Instead, Peter saw the burial clothes neatly folded and an angel inside the tomb telling him that Jesus was alive and that they would see Jesus soon.

Later, Levi found out that the Roman soldiers reported the events at the tomb concerning the resurrection of Jesus to the Chief Priest. The Chief priest gave the guards a bribe to tell anyone who asked, that Jesus's disciples came and were grave robbers and took the body away. The soldiers took the money and kept their mouths shut.

Levi and the other disciples took the women's report to heart and traveled to Galilee. They went to the place that they often gathered with each other and with Jesus. They met on a mountain top. As promised, Jesus appeared to the eleven and said," All authority in heaven and on earth has been given to me. Therefore, go and make disciples of all nations, baptizing them in the name of the Father, and of the Son, and of the Holy Spirit, and teaching them to obey everything I have commanded you. And surely, I am with you always, To the very end of the age."

Just as Levi remembered all of the events that he witnessed and as the Holy Spirit gave him the ability to remember and write what he saw, heard and experienced, Levi wrote the book that he and Mark had discussed. When Levi finished writing the last pages of the Gospel story, he thought about what should come next in his life and his commitment to the commands of Jesus.

Levi had been living with the group of Christians near the shores of Lake Tuz for a few years while he wrote and evange-lized those who came to the village. Levi continued to disciple Pradik and many others, telling them of the love of Jesus and how He had taught the crowds in Galilee, Judea and lastly in Jerusalem to live Godly and meaningful lives. Levi was now an old man. His life had been so mundane before he was called one day at his tax collector's bench to follow Jesus. Since Jesus called his name and said, "Follow me," Levi's life was one adventure after another.

Now Levi felt the calling of the Holy Spirit to travel again to Antioch and to meet again with Mark. Levi's plan was to discuss the publication of the Gospel account of the life, death and resurrection of Jesus and how the Gospel according to Levi that was also being called the Gospel of Matthew, could be best used to proclaim the life and teachings of Jesus.

The distance from Lake Tuz to Antioch was far and difficult for a man now as advanced in age as Levi, but suitable arrangements were made for the journey. As soon as the weather permitted in the Spring of the year 87 AD, Levi along with Marium who had become Levi's helper, Levi said his goodbyes to the loving friends at the village and started the long walk from Galatia to the coast and the city of Antioch.

Chapter 32
The possibility of perfection.

My parents were a blessing to me. I was well taken care of and loved as I progressed from birth to being a toddler, to interacting with other children and then going to school. When I was born my father was in the Navy. His parents immigrated to the United States from Hungary just before World War I. My parents grew up during the Great Depression of the 1930's. My father joined the Navy as soon as he graduated from high school and his first tour of duty sent him to Pearl Harbor. He was there when the Japanese attacked on December 7, 1941.

Both of my parents were, in my estimation, extremely smart people. My mother grew up in very rural North Carolina and graduated from formal education after completing the eleventh grade. The lack of formal education did not reduce my mother's intelligence, but it did cause her to feel a slight bit of inferiority especially when my father returned to college after retiring from the Navy and obtained his doctorate degree from Vanderbilt University.

Because my parents were smart, they insisted that me and my sister were also as smart are they were and therefore insisted that we excel in school. My father would always want to know why I did not make the highest grade on every school assignment that I was required to complete. In other words, my father demanded perfection from me in my schoolwork. I think that the demand for perfection drove my sister away from the family before she was actually ready to be on her own.

When Jesus commanded that His disciples and all those who would become His followers throughout the centuries that followed His death and resurrection to, "Therefore be perfect as your heavenly Father is perfect," was He making an impossible demand for which His followers to comply?

In the 2nd Chapter of this book, I related the story of the seminar I attended at Peachtree Baptist Church during the late autumn of 2016 in which Dr. Peter Rhea Jones lead a study of the Sermon on the Mount. Matthew 5-7. I recall Dr. Jones asking the class at the end of the first session if anyone had any questions about their reading of the Sermon on the Mourn that they would like to bring up for discussion. I asked about the meaning of Matthew 5:48. I wanted to know if Jesus actually demanded perfection from all Christians.

I recall the consensus of the group that was gathered there that evening. Even the thought of Dr. Jones was that it is impossible for anyone but Jesus to be prefect. That got me to thinking and prompted me to write this book. I ask myself over and over again what did Jesus mean when he said these words?

I assume that it is possible that the Bible that I read has an error and Jesus did not really say those words. It could be that there is a misinterpretation of the Aramaic words that Jesus spoke when His words were translated into English. It could be that the writer of Matthew 5:48 misunderstood what Jesus was saying or that somehow Jesus did not really mean to say that we humans needed to find a means of becoming prefect.

On the other hand, what if Jesus actually said we need to become as perfect as God. What if the writer of Matthew 5:48 was standing close enough to Jesus to hear His exact words and the words He spoke are accurately recorded? Is it reasonable to demand perfection from the people that the creator created? These questions and many more similar questions about the demand for perfection have rolled around in my mind ever since that autumn night in 2016.

I have always heard that there are no perfect humans. I have been told that we are all imperfect creatures and that we must recognize that everyone is flawed and that we should not get our expectations up too high when we deal with others. We should never insist that anybody with whom we deal will meet the standard of perfection in any dealing that we may have with another human being. The command of Jesus as recorded in

Matthew 5:48, however seems to be very clear and unambiguous. Jesus demands perfection clearly and simply.

Are we doomed? Will none of us ever get to stand before God and avoid the punishment for our sinfulness? Are we all going to hell? Remember God is righteous and according to the Old Testament only God is righteous.

As for humans Paul quotes the scriptures to claim that "None are righteous not even one, there is no one who is righteous: there is no one who seeks God." Romans 3:10-11. As Christians we are taught that, "All have sinned and have fallen short of the glory of God." Romans 3:23.

My mother put Bible verses on my bedside table when I was a child. The one that I remember most vividly is, "For the wages of sin is death, but the gift of God is eternal life in Jesus Christ our Lord." Romans 6:23. As a child I knew instinctively that I was a sinner, and if we all were honest with ourselves, we too would understand that we are born with a sinful nature. From the earliest we are prone to tell lies, take other children's toys, break things just for meanness's sake and do stuff to each other that we know is wrong. In Christian terms this is referred to as original sin. I have discussed the doctrine of original sin in Chapter 30 of this book, and from personal observation I agree that from birth that we are all sinners.

Recently, I have had many conversations with people who claim to be atheist. Most of the people are younger and most of those that I have had conversations with are from Asia. In my conversations with these I always state that I am a Christian and then ask, "Do you believe in God?" At first, I was surprised by the response that was given. The response was, "No, I am an atheist, I do not believe in God. While I respect other's beliefs it is a waste of my time to believe in any religion."

It is my belief that to deny that God is the creator of the universe and all that is within the universe, is a sin. I do not know if it is because the governments of China, Vietnam, and North Korea, officially discourage belief in anything but the ruling government, that those I have talked to have decided that God does not exist. While the young people that I have had these discussions with are mainly from Asia I am also aware that the churches that I have attended are more likely than not to have ageing populations and therefore younger people even in America have turned away from church attendance. Whether that turning away from formal religion means that the younger generations have denied the existence of God, remains to be determined.

All of the above leads me to wonder if my belief in God and my Christianity has put me in a distinct minority. Certainly, the Christian Church is not the same Christian Church that I have been a part of for most of my life. However, I emphatically believe that God is the same God that He has always been. "Jesus Christ is the same yesterday, today and forever." Hebrews 13:8. Even further back in history, the Prophet Jeremiah declared to Israel that God, "[Has] loved you with everlasting love; [God has] drawn you with everlasting kindness." Jeremiah 31:3.

God and His only begotten Son are the same as they have forever been. God has loved His elect to such an extent that He is willing to allow Jesus to take on human life, as a perfect human, and to suffer and die a cruel death so that we (the human species of this planet) can by belief in Him escape the punishments that we deserve because of our sinful nature.

Because Jesus shed His perfect blood as a substitute for the punishment that I/we deserve, then why should I/we not gladly accept Jesus's sacrificial death and resurrection. The initial cost for this acceptance is just to believe that there is a God and that God loved us so much that He sent His only begotten Son. (Of course, the moment I/we accept Jesus; that is totally and without reservation accept Jesus, life as I/we knew it before our commitment will have changed forever.)

Earlier I asked that all true Christian pray for revival. It is essential that we make the love of Jesus Christ known to the lost and dying world that more and more denies the existence of God. In the Old Testament, the history of the Jewish people is rife with times when they called on God to rescue them from Egyptian enslavement, from the harassment of the other populations surrounding the land that they were promised, from foreign invasion, from captivity in Babylon and from the occupation of their land by the Greeks and then the Romans.

God heard the prayers of His people and brought them out of Egyptian bondage. God sent judges (soldiers) to fight off the Philistines and other groups of people in Cannan that sought to destroy the Jewish people. God brought back a remanent from Babylonian captivity and allowed the Jews to prosper until their sins could not sustain their part in the covenant relationship between the Hebrews and God. God then sent His only begotten Son to rescue the world from the underlying cause of the predicament that pledged the Jews and mankind in general. Jesus came to rescue God's people from the depravity and imperfection of sin.

If there was no sin in our lives, we too would be perfect, but because we are born into sin and cannot keep ourselves from sinning, we need a savior. Therefore, when we repent of our sinfulness, ask Jesus to wash us with His blood, and fully commit ourselves to the saving grace that God pours out on those who are His elect, we take on the perfection of Jesus because He lives within us.

Then the answer to the question that is posed by the commandment of Jesus to, "Therefore be perfect, as your heavenly Father is perfect," is yes, it is possible for us as those who profess that Jesus is our savior to become perfect. It is not only possible to be perfect it is a demand and a commandment for every Christian to keep. Jesus has paid the price for the debt that I owed. Romans 8:29 states, "For those God foreknew, he also predestined to be conformed to the image of His Son, that He might be the first born among many brothers and sisters. And those He predestined, He also called. Those He called, He also justified. Those He justified, He also glorified." We are becoming conformed to the image of Jesus. We are becoming perfect. Thanks be to God!

Jesus's resurrection is proof that God is fully satisfied that the sacrifice that Jesus made covers my sin and I can stand before God as a part of His family. I can stand because I am becoming the exact image of Jesus. God shouted out His love for Jesus when Jesus submitted to baptism and again when Jesus was transfigured. Matthew 3;17 and Matthew 17:5. The love that God has for Jesus, that irresistible grace that God provides to His elect, will cause salvation to reign mercy and perfection on those who fully accept Jesus as savior and follow Him.

You may be asking yourself what ever happened to James and Jim the two men in my Sunday school class that were battling over the finances of Peachtree Baptist Church. Honestly, I do not know what the final outcome of the struggles that went on at Peachtree after I left Atlanta and moved to Texas. I know that Dr. Vestel retired and that he was replaced by Paul Capps. I have heard the Paul Capps after a short time as the Senior Pastor of Peachtree resigned and took a job at Emory University. From time to time, I received emails regarding events at Peachtree Baptist and I continue to pray for the church and the fellowship there.

It is my prayer that the will of God will be manifest not only at Peachtree Baptist Church but also within the Universal Christian Church so that the calling of Jesue for His disciples to seek and to save the lost will be accomplished. In the powerful name of Jesus, Amen.

Afterword

While the story of Levi as I have written is mostly based on my imagination, there are historical facts presented that assisted me in the story. The fact that the Romans occupied all of Palestine before Jesus started His ministry in Galilee and Judea is a historical certainty. The fire that consumed Rome in 60 AD is undisputed as is the cruel reign of Nero as emperor of the Roman empire and the persecution of Christians by Nero is well known. The facts surrounding the destruction of Jerusalen and the quick succession of Roman emperors is a historical reality.

On the other hand, the character identified as Mark in my story is purely fictional, as is the Levi character portrayed herein. While the book of Mark in the New Testament was probably written by someone known as Mark, and the author of Mark most likely relied on the first-hand account of the life, ministry, death and resurrection of Jesus given to him by one of the apostles (probably Peter) it is unknown who the author actually was.

Similarly, the author of the book of Matthew is unknown although in the early years of Christianity, historians attributed the book of Matthew to the apostle who was referred to as both Levi and Matthew. Compare Luke 5:27 and Matthew 9:9. Scholars contend that the Greek language used to write the book of Matthew was too perfect for a Galilean tax collector who more likely than not spoke and wrote in Aramaic.

There is also controversy concerning the life and death of the apostle Matthew. The Catholic Encyclopedia states that the apostle Matthew, after leaving Palestine traveled to the southern shores of the Caspian Sea. Further the Catholic Encyclopedia states that St. Matthew engaged in evangelism in the province of Ethiopia (not the African country of the same name, but a province south of the Caspian Sea) and was martyred when he spoke out against the King of the region for sexual assault on a young woman. The story states that when St. Matthew confronted the King about assaulting a much younger woman, the King had Matthew killed by his guards on the spot. The Renaissance artist Caravaggio painted a depiction of the death of St. Matthew in 1599-1560. The painting is located at San Luigi die Frances in Rome.

Other sources concerning Matthew do not list him as being among the martyrs. Foxe's Book of Martyrs, complied by the noted theologian, clergyman and historian, does not list Matthew as a martyr. Other sources contend that Matthew lived to an old age and died of naturel causes. I will not speculate on the life or end to which Matthew may have come.

It is my intent to write what may have occurred in the lives of the two authors of the Gospels of Matthew and Mark. It is my belief that the accounts of the life, teachings, miracles, death and resurrection of Jesus as given to us in the Holy Scriptures are profitable for understanding the events described in the Gospel accounts in the New Testament and those accounts should be studied and relied on to come to a knowledge of the love that God displayed to us through His only begotten Son, Jesus Christ, my Savior and Lord.

In this book I have tried to stay close to the account of Jesus teachings. In the 23rd chapter of Matthew, Jesus states His fifth discourse (also called the Olivet Discourse) with an admonishment of the Pharisees and gives 7 wows in which He calls the Pharisees hypocrites and also warns the people He was teaching that they should listen to what the Pharisees were teaching but to not do as they were doing because their actions did not follow what they were teaching. I do not intend my words concerning the Jewish people of the times that I have depicted in this book to be taken as in any way to be anti-sematic. I have a long and loving relationship with many Jewish friends. I went to a high school that sat in the middle of a large Jewish neighborhood in Nashville, Tennessee. One of my dear friends and study partner in law school is Jerry Wasserman. My first employer after graduating from law school was Israel Katts, and one of my law partners was Mike Froman, each of whom is Jewish. I have great admiration for my Jewish friends and consider any anti-sematic sentiment in this time to be against the teaching of Jesus.

ACKNOWLEDGEMENTS

I want to acknowledge the people who have contributed to the writing of this book. I have had the joy of studying the life and ministry of Jesus Christ since I was a child. There have been numerous Sunday school teachers and pastors who have encouraged me to accept Jesus into my life and to follow Him earnestly and completely. My mother was a great influence in my relationship with Jesus. She always prayed for me, as did my father, and encouraged me in my walk with Christ. I thank my loving parents for their lifelong love and support.

I also want to thank my children who have put up with my desire to write and to teach the stories of the Bible. My son, Nick, has also read and given me helpful advice about the pages that I have written. My daughter is a great source of encouragement in all that I do.

My thanks also go out the Dr. Peter Rhea Jones, Pastor Emeritus of the First Baptist Church of Decatur, Georgia for his teaching the seminar that got me interested in the subject of Jesus commandment in Matthew 5:48.

Thanks to Renae Murphy for her help in reading and editing the pages that I have regularly sent to her for comment. Renae has been invaluable to me in the writing of this book.

I also thank my publisher, Mauldin Pond Press, for their assistance in putting this book together and seeing it to final publication.

June 27, 2024.

Jeffrey L. Sakas
jeffreysakas@gmail.com

www.ingramcontent.com/pod-product-compliance
Lightning Source LLC
Chambersburg PA
CBHW071721120626
46550CB00001B/333